IMAGES
of America

BOTETOURT COUNTY REVISITED

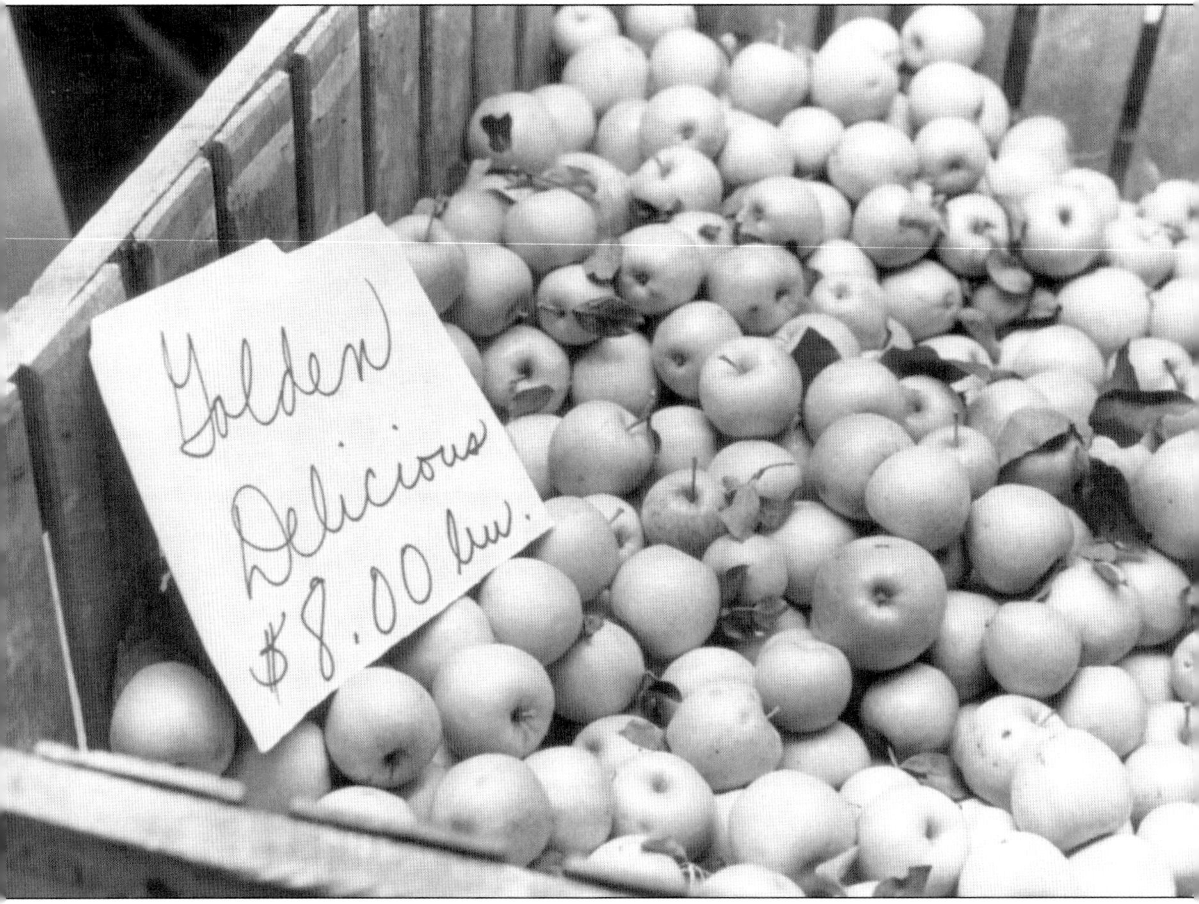

By 1814, Thomas Jefferson had planted four varieties of apple trees at Monticello. Jefferson brought renown to the Albemarle Pippin, which he exported to England, thus expanding the fame of Virginia apples. In 1924, there were nearly 125 commercial orchards in Botetourt, mostly located in the southern section of the county. The Golden Delicious variety is often eaten fresh, but is also an excellent baking apple. (Courtesy of the *Fincastle Herald*.)

On the Cover: These youngsters are caught relaxing on the "beach" beside the Town Branch swimming hole in Fincastle around 1910. The Ammen Woolen Mill is visible in the background. Although their names were not recorded, they seem to be a typical group of country kids enjoying a summer's day. (Courtesy of Botetourt County Historical Museum.)

IMAGES
of America

BOTETOURT COUNTY REVISITED

Debra Alderson McClane

ARCADIA
PUBLISHING

ISBN 978-1-4671-2135-4

Published by Arcadia Publishing
Charleston, South Carolina

Printed in the United States of America

Library of Congress Control Number: 2013947902

For all general information, please contact Arcadia Publishing:
Telephone 843-853-2070
Fax 843-853-0044
E-mail sales@arcadiapublishing.com
For customer service and orders:
Toll-Free 1-888-313-2665

Visit us on the Internet at www.arcadiapublishing.com

This book is dedicated to the people who call beautiful Botetourt County home and who appreciate its past, present, and future.

Contents

ACKNOWLEDGMENTS

A book like this can be successful only with the support of generous institutions and individuals. I have been assisted by both. I would like to thank Jason Bond, Virginia Department of Transportation; Jamison Davis, Virginia Historical Society; Beth Harris, Special Collections, Wyndham Robertson Library, Hollins University; Dyron Knick, Roanoke Public Library; Cara Lundgren, Special Collections at James Madison University; Weldon Martin and Patty King, Botetourt County Historical Society; Lisa McCown, Special Collections, Leyburn Library, Washington & Lee University; Dale Neighbors, the Library of Virginia; David Puckett, Frontier Culture Museum of Virginia; Jane Wills, Digital Library and Archives, Virginia Tech; and my friends at the Virginia Department of Historic Resources archives.

Individuals who generously shared photographs and memories include Benton Bolton, Edna Brogan Bolton, Anna Noel Damerel, Judy Deel, Paul Garber, Phyllis Garst, Howard Revercomb Hammond, Joseph Obenshain, Betty Jeter Painter, John W. "Jack" Rader Sr., Lewis Sifford, Sarah Spencer, Judy Tweel, and Sybil Young.

I have also gleaned from numerous articles in the county's weekly newspaper, the *Fincastle Herald*. Over the years, Edwin McCoy and contributing writers Cathy Benson and Anita Firebaugh have profiled many of Botetourt's historic communities and places. These articles have proven very helpful in my research. Mike Lee of Pico also shared several postcards from his business, Mike's Postcards, which helped illustrate the early-20th-century motels and businesses along Botetourt's roadways.

Thanks to my two editors at Arcadia, Lissie Cain and Julia Simpson, for their encouragement and support.

Every member of my family also contributed to this work. My parents, John and Doris Alderson, helped to gather images and provided contacts, information, and courier services. My brothers, John Mark and Curtis, also helped with photographs and suggestions for content. Thanks again to my husband, Patrick, whose patience seems unending.

Several photographic courtesies have been abbreviated in the text as follows: Botetourt County Historical Museum (BCHM); Norfolk and Western Historical Photograph Collection, Norfolk Southern Archives, Norfolk, Virginia, courtesy of the Digital Library and Archives, Special Collections, Virginia Tech, Blacksburg, Virginia (NWHP, DLA, VT); Virginia Department of Historic Resources (VDHR); and William Garber Photographic Collection (P0002), Special Collections, Carrier Library, James Madison University, Harrisonburg, Virginia (JMU).

INTRODUCTION

This book is the second volume on Botetourt County, Virginia, in Arcadia's *Images of America* series. Like the first book, completed about seven years ago, this volume presents images from Botetourt's past but also ties the past to the present. There are certain themes that consistently run through our history: farming, industry, close-knit communities, and local businesses. The natural beauty of the county is also a constant.

In my first book, I tried to represent as many of the county's localities as possible. In this volume, I revisit some of those areas but focus on the people who built, owned, operated, and worked in these places. Many generous individuals have made this possible by sharing their family photographs, histories, and stories with me. Most of the families presented here are examples of the hardworking people who continue to live in Botetourt and who make our county a special place. Many have been successful in their undertakings and have provided valuable service to our communities.

I have conducted primary research for many of the captions contained in this volume, and I have also relied on historical information gathered by historians before me. Robert Douthat Stoner's *A Seed-Bed of the Republic* continues to be the most comprehensive county history. In recent years, several historical volumes that focus on specific communities in the county—including Trinity, Lithia, Mill Creek, Troutville, Fincastle, and Buchanan—have supplemented Stoner's work. A bibliography of these sources is included at the end of this book. Every effort has been made to confirm dates, places, and names in the images shown.

For those just learning about the county, and as a refresher for others, the following is an abbreviated history of Botetourt. In 1770, the Virginia General Assembly created Botetourt County from lands formerly in Augusta County. Later, portions of Rockbridge County were added. Named for Norborne Berkeley, Baron de Botetourt, a popular Colonial governor of Virginia, the original boundaries of the county stretched west to the Mississippi River and encompassed land that would become Kentucky and portions of Ohio, Indiana, Illinois, and West Virginia. During the Colonial period, the county served as the gateway to western lands due to its location at the intersection of the Great Wagon Road and the Wilderness Road. The county's buildings and culture reflect the varied traditions brought by German, English, and Scots-Irish settlers.

The first half of the 19th century was a prosperous one for the county. With an economy based on agriculture, associated industries soon developed, including blacksmiths, wheelwrights, tanneries, and, most importantly, mills. Significant crops included hemp, wheat, corn, and tobacco. The county's soil and geography were well suited to raising livestock and to producing grains and hay. Iron furnaces began to thrive off of the county's rich deposits of brown and red hematite ores. Limestone and marble mining soon followed. With increased industry and new and improved transportation routes, including turnpike roads and the arrival of the James River and Kanawha Canal in 1851, county residents fashioned a good living in the surrounding valleys and hills.

Such prosperity, however, was halted with the start of the Civil War in 1861. A total of 12 military companies were mustered from the county for service in the Confederate army, and a home guard was also established. The county's black population during this time included a number of free blacks, as well as enslaved people. Like many rural counties, Botetourt appears to have been lax in enforcing laws that required free blacks (including freed slaves) to register annually, and population records are therefore sporadic. African American merchants, tradesmen, preachers, and farmers contributed to the county's diverse population.

Economic recovery was slow in the late 19th century, but new industries, including mineral mining, were aided by the arrival of the railroad, which superseded the canal. Farms diversified and dairying and orchards became common in the county. Mineral springs resorts also developed during this time. In the 20th century, agricultural-related industries thrived in Botetourt's towns, including Buchanan, Troutville, and Fincastle. Daleville became the site of a four-year college. Company towns developed at the sites of mineral operations, many of which were served by the railroad.

The 20th century and the first decade of the 21st century have been a time of rapid change and advancement for Botetourt County. The interstate highway system and Virginia's secondary road system have brought increased traffic and development to the county, and tourism that draws heavily on the county's natural resources continues to contribute significantly to county revenues.

While I was working on this book, I heard an interview with Jeff Rosenheim, the curator of photographs at the Metropolitan Museum of Art in New York. He was speaking about an exhibit of Civil War–era photographs and how those photographs changed the way that we view war. He said, "I think that we are, as a nation, only as good as our memory and the facts of these photographs, their tradition, gives us something that we cannot forget. What we really have is the beginning of an archive . . . of who we are, or at least who we were. That is the treasury that we build our history from."

I hope that some of the images in this book will help us to remember who we were and what our county was built on. You probably have similar photographs in your own home, and I would encourage you to date them, label them, and pass them on.

One

Farms, Families, and Homes

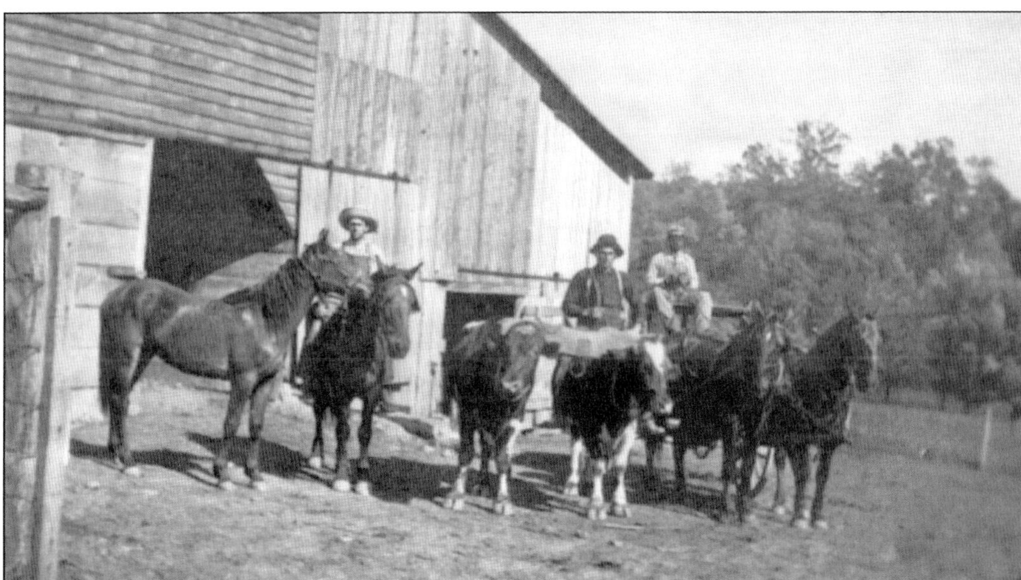

This photograph was taken around 1911 at the farm owned by Chester L. Sifford near the corner of Route 11 and Brughs Mill Road in Nace. Pictured are, from left to right, Henry Obenshain, Chester Sifford, and Henry Robertson. Sifford, seated on yoked oxen, purchased his farmland from Alice Brugh and Boyce Obenshain. Sifford (born 1885) married Halley J. Stevens (born 1889) in 1909. (Courtesy of Sarah Spencer.)

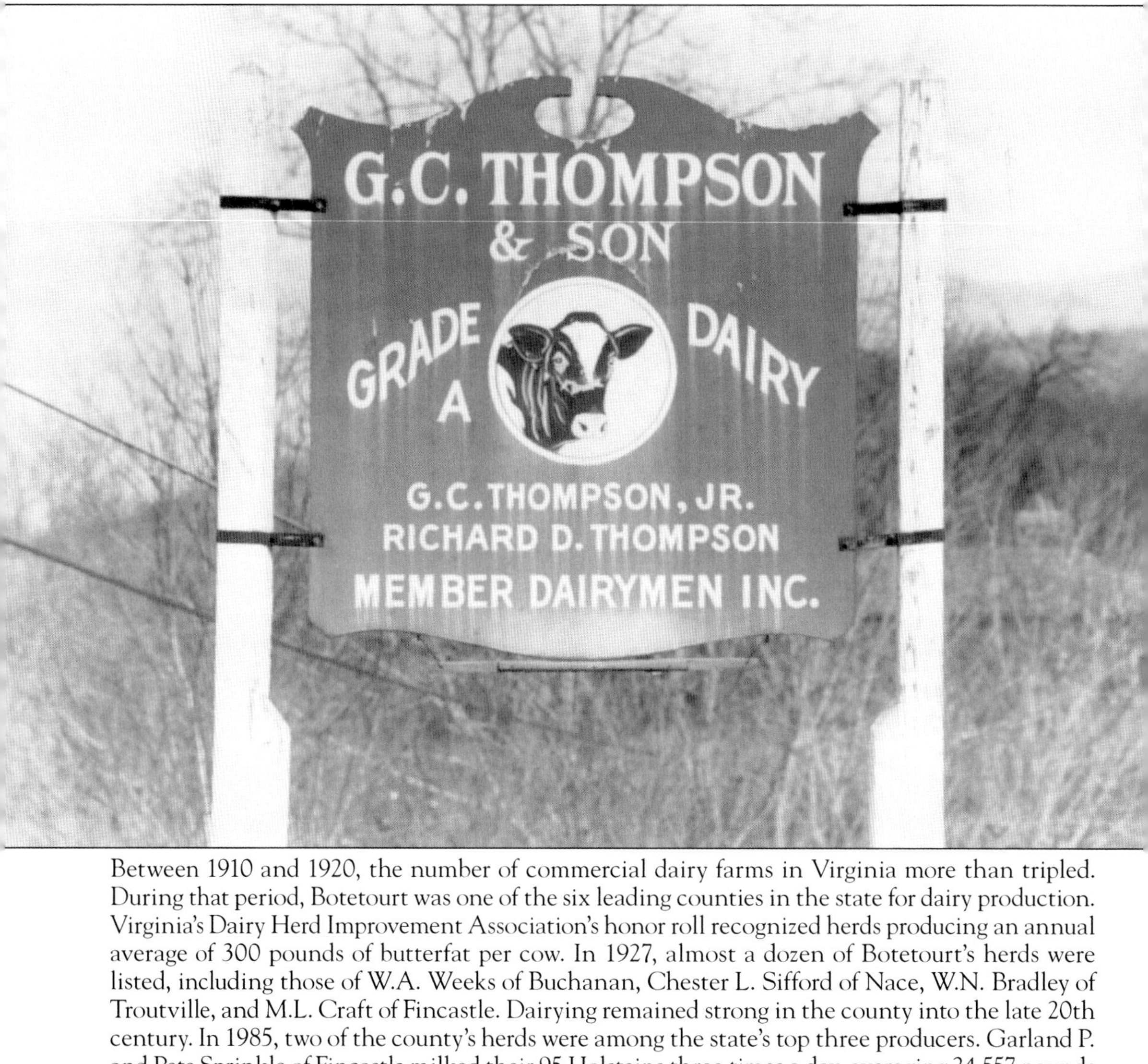

Between 1910 and 1920, the number of commercial dairy farms in Virginia more than tripled. During that period, Botetourt was one of the six leading counties in the state for dairy production. Virginia's Dairy Herd Improvement Association's honor roll recognized herds producing an annual average of 300 pounds of butterfat per cow. In 1927, almost a dozen of Botetourt's herds were listed, including those of W.A. Weeks of Buchanan, Chester L. Sifford of Nace, W.N. Bradley of Troutville, and M.L. Craft of Fincastle. Dairying remained strong in the county into the late 20th century. In 1985, two of the county's herds were among the state's top three producers. Garland P. and Pete Sprinkle of Fincastle milked their 95 Holsteins three times a day, averaging 24,557 pounds of milk and 839 pounds of butterfat per cow. Their top cow, No. 197, produced 29,736 pounds of milk and 1,165 pounds of butterfat that year. Grover C. and Richard Thompson of Gala, whose dairy sign is seen here, milked their 115 Holsteins twice a day and averaged 19,446 pounds of milk and 729 pounds of butterfat per cow. (Courtesy of the *Fincastle Herald*.)

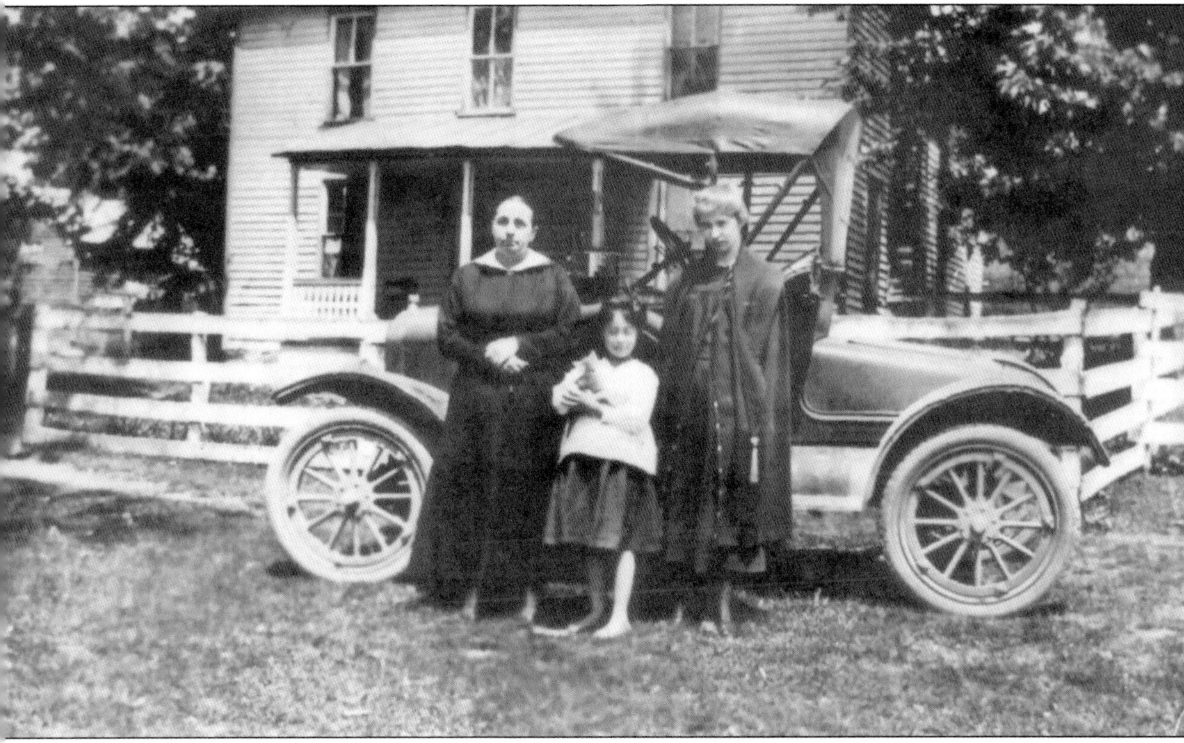

In 1883, James Edward Stevens married Lucy Beale Obenshain, the daughter of "Hotel Sam" and Lucy Halley Obenshain. Soon after their marriage, James built a house along Beckner Branch just west of the Obenshain home in Mill Creek. The Stevenses had nine children and attended Mill Creek Baptist Church. James worked in various mills in the area and operated his own farm and cannery. This 1918 photograph shows, from left to right, Lucy Stevens; her youngest daughter, Manie, with kitten; and her daughter-in-law Helen Lemon Stevens, the wife of her son Frank, in front of the Stevens house. In addition to the farmhouse, other buildings on the farm included a granary, a corncrib, a barn, and livestock pens. The springhouse is seen here behind the house to the left. In the late 1960s, Interstate 81 was built through the middle of the farm. The buildings are still standing but have deteriorated. (Courtesy of Judy Deel.)

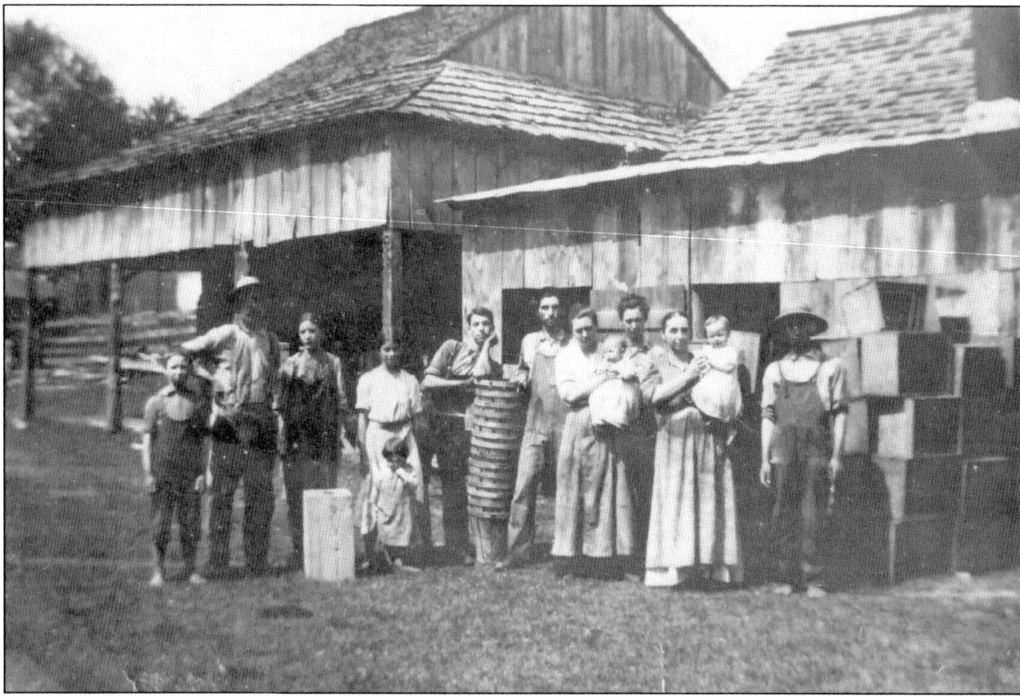

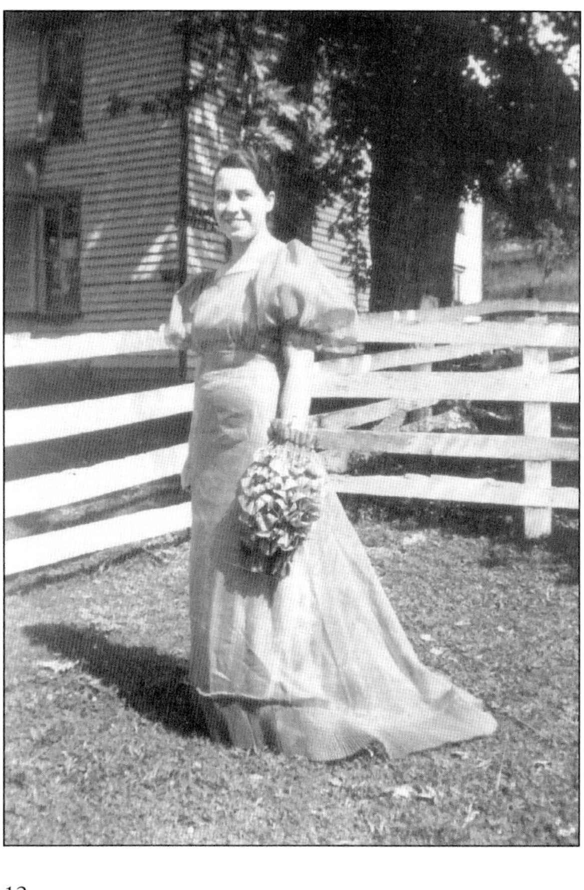

Like many Botetourt farmers, James Stevens operated a cannery on his Beckner Branch farm. Above, family members pose in front of the farm buildings that comprised the cannery. James stands second from the left, and brothers Lyle (left) and Tilghman (right) stand near the center with a stack of five-eighths-bushel baskets. These baskets tapered to the bottom and were the standard container for collecting vegetables for market. (Courtesy of Judy Deel.)

Manie Loucile Stevens was the youngest child of James and Lucy Stevens. Her passion for education took her to Hollins College, where she earned a teaching degree. She taught in elementary, middle, and high schools in Botetourt, Roanoke City, and Roanoke County for 40 years. In 1936, she married Ira Watson Sifford. She is pictured here in her wedding dress. (Courtesy of Judy Deel.)

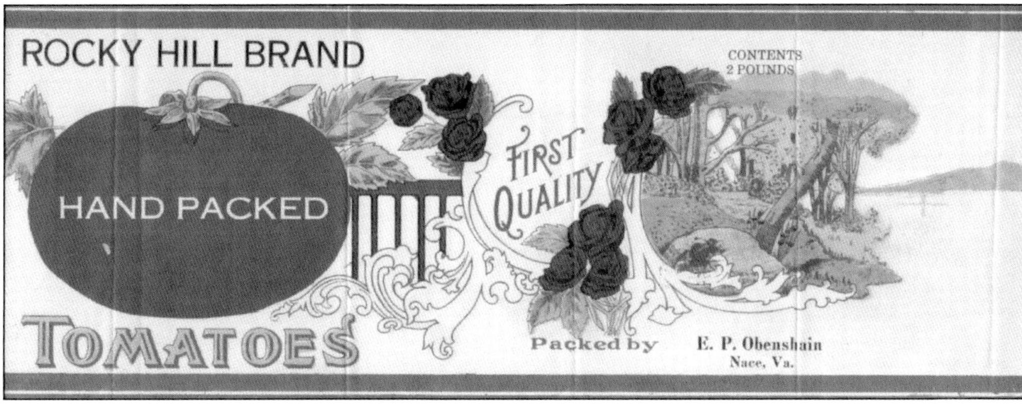

Around 1906, Elmer Peyton "E.P." Obenshain began canning vegetables at his farm on the Blue Ridge Turnpike near Mill Creek. He canned beans, corn, apples, sweet potatoes, and tomatoes. Obenshain also purchased tomatoes from area farmers for canning. This label shows Obenshain's Rocky Hill Brand tomatoes. The cannery remained in operation until after World War II. (Courtesy of Judy Deel.)

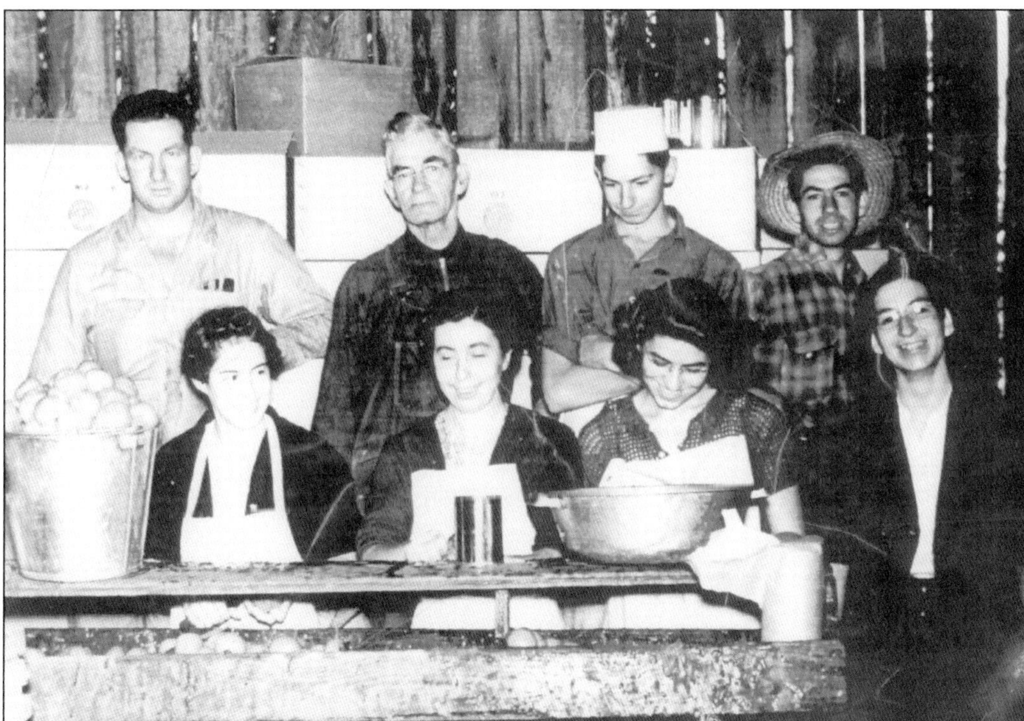

Neighbors and family members worked at the Obenshain cannery peeling, labeling, and hauling. This photograph, taken around 1940, shows members of the extended Obenshain family taking a break from work at the cannery. They are, from left to right, (first row) Audrey Simpson Kelley, Myra Stevens, Grace Obenshain Austin, and Mary Lucy Obenshain Deel; (second row) Lee Obenshain, Elmer Peyton "E.P" Obenshain, Dewey Obenshain, and Elmer Peyton Obenshain Jr. (Courtesy of Judy Deel.)

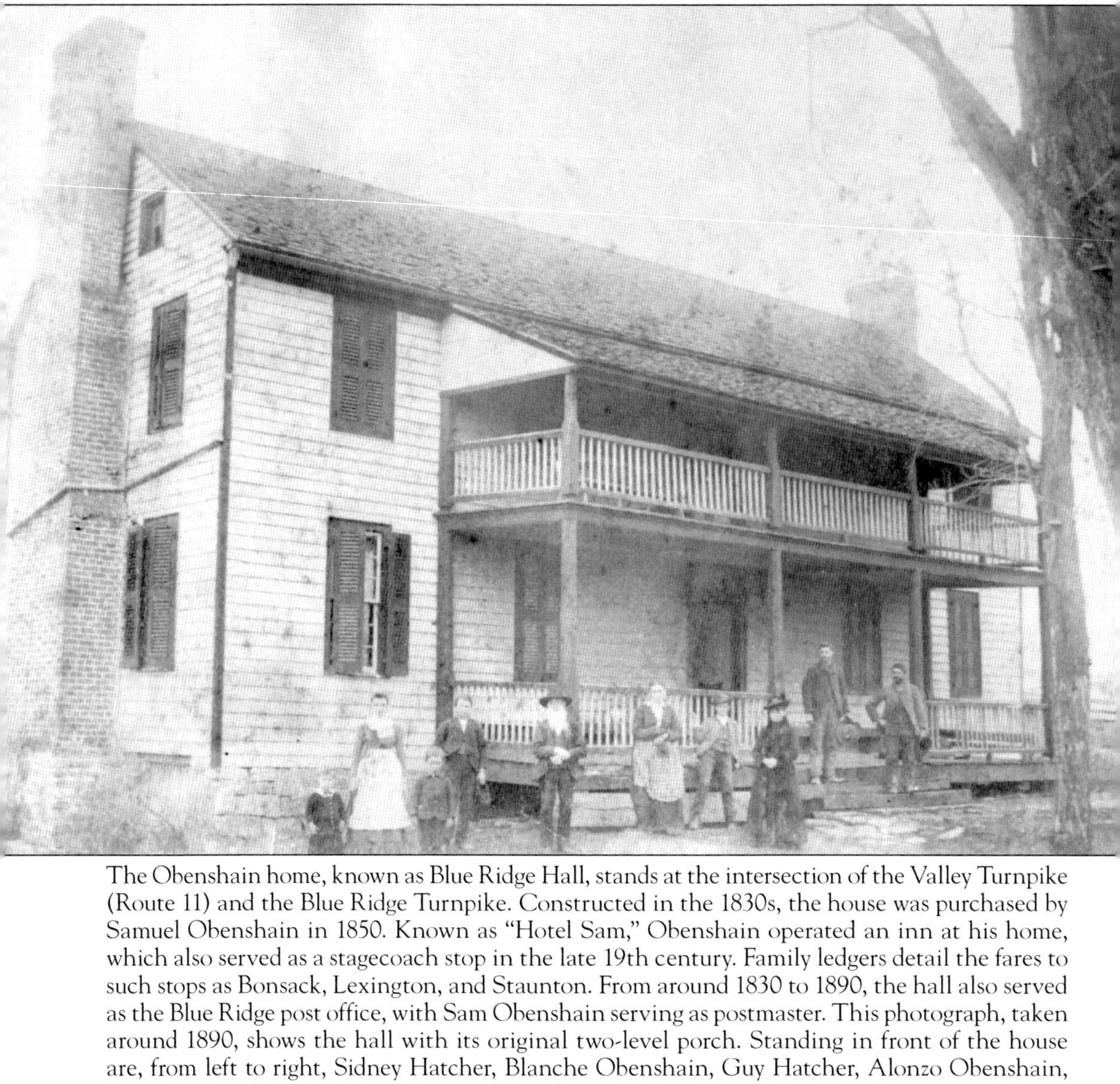

The Obenshain home, known as Blue Ridge Hall, stands at the intersection of the Valley Turnpike (Route 11) and the Blue Ridge Turnpike. Constructed in the 1830s, the house was purchased by Samuel Obenshain in 1850. Known as "Hotel Sam," Obenshain operated an inn at his home, which also served as a stagecoach stop in the late 19th century. Family ledgers detail the fares to such stops as Bonsack, Lexington, and Staunton. From around 1830 to 1890, the hall also served as the Blue Ridge post office, with Sam Obenshain serving as postmaster. This photograph, taken around 1890, shows the hall with its original two-level porch. Standing in front of the house are, from left to right, Sidney Hatcher, Blanche Obenshain, Guy Hatcher, Alonzo Obenshain, Samuel Obenshain (with beard), Lucy Obenshain, Halley Obenshain, Cora Hatcher, and Boyce and Jim Stevens (on the front steps). (Courtesy of Joseph Obenshain.)

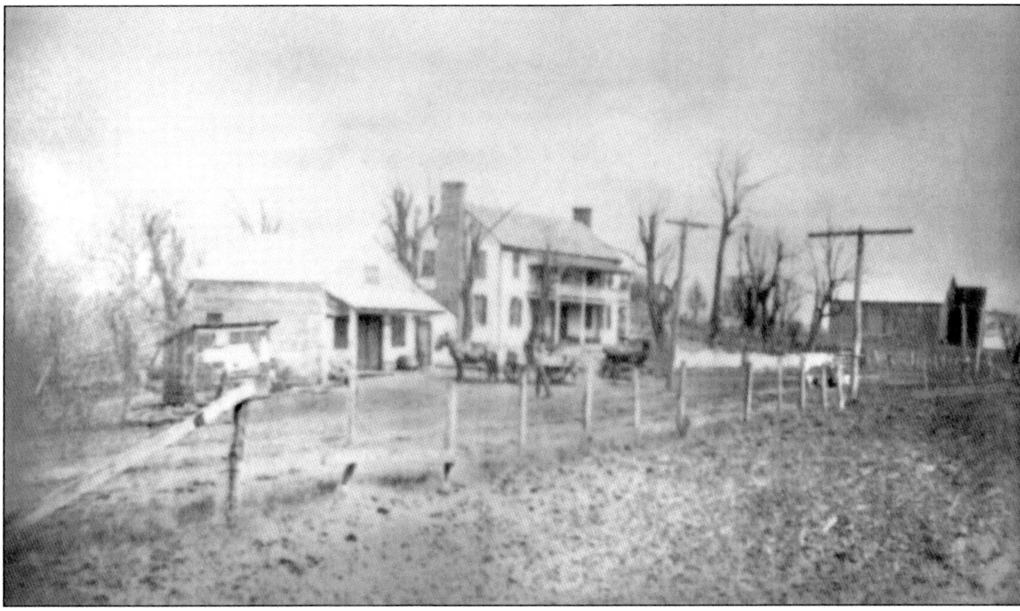

This view of Blue Ridge Hall shows the house around 1910. Route 11, still unpaved, runs along the front of the house. The post office/store building and the chicken house to the left of the house, as well as the barn on the right, are no longer standing. Little Sam Obenshain, about 10 years old, can be seen crossing the road on the right. (Courtesy of Joseph Obenshain.)

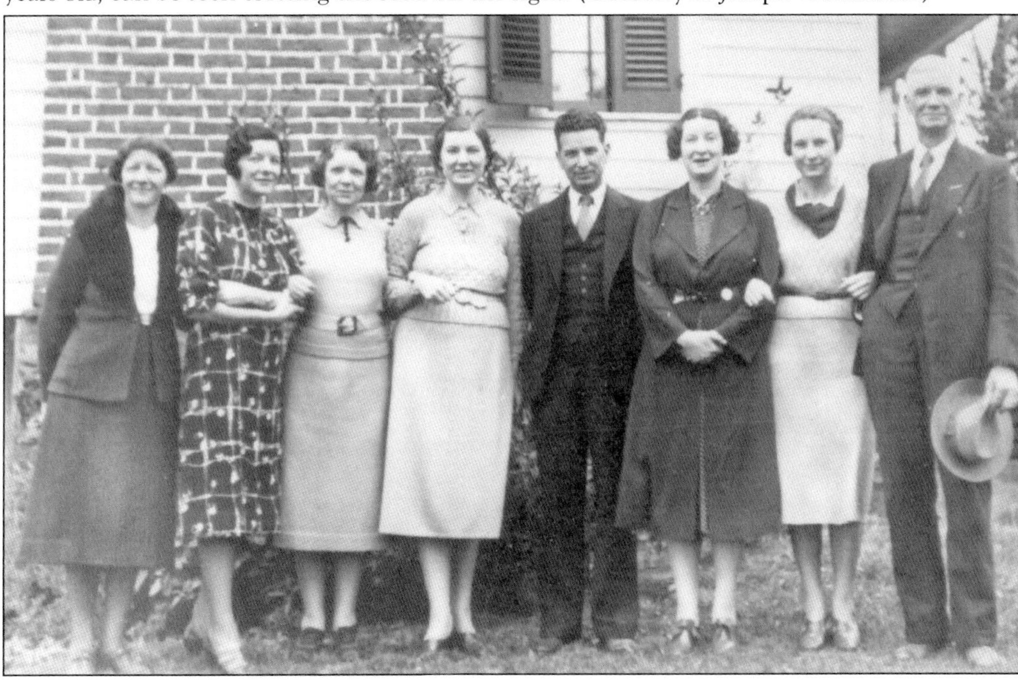

The Obenshain family is seen here beside Blue Ridge Hall around 1940. Boyce Putney Obenshain (far right) was the son of Hotel Sam. Boyce's wife, Ida (née Shockley), died in 1909. His children stand to his right (from right to left): Blanche Garland, Ann, Samuel S., Clarice Clark, Mildred Smith, and twins Elizabeth and Lucy. Four of the Obenshain daughters were teachers. Sam was a professor of agronomy at Virginia Tech. (Courtesy of Joseph Obenshain.)

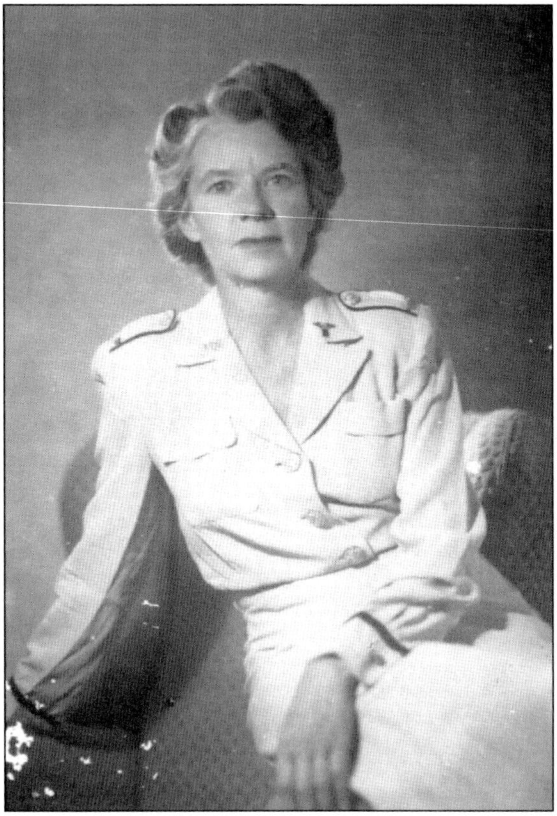

By 1930, Mildred Obenshain Smith was widowed. When World War II began, having graduated from nursing school at the Lewis-Gale Medical Center, she enlisted with the 8th Evacuation Hospital, which was formed at the University of Virginia's medical school. She rose to the rank of first lieutenant in the Army Nurse Corps. The nurses of the unit arrived in Casablanca, French Morocco, in March 1943 following the Allied assault. In July 1943, the unit was sent to Sicily and mainland Italy. Smith is shown at left in her Army uniform and below about to shake hands with English prime minister Winston Churchill. The latter image was taken in August 1944 when Churchill visited Italy. Pictured are, from left to right, Capt. Helen Wharton, Lt. Gen. Mark Clark (5th US Army), Churchill, Lt. Sue Hornbarger, and Smith. (Both courtesy of Joseph Obenshain.)

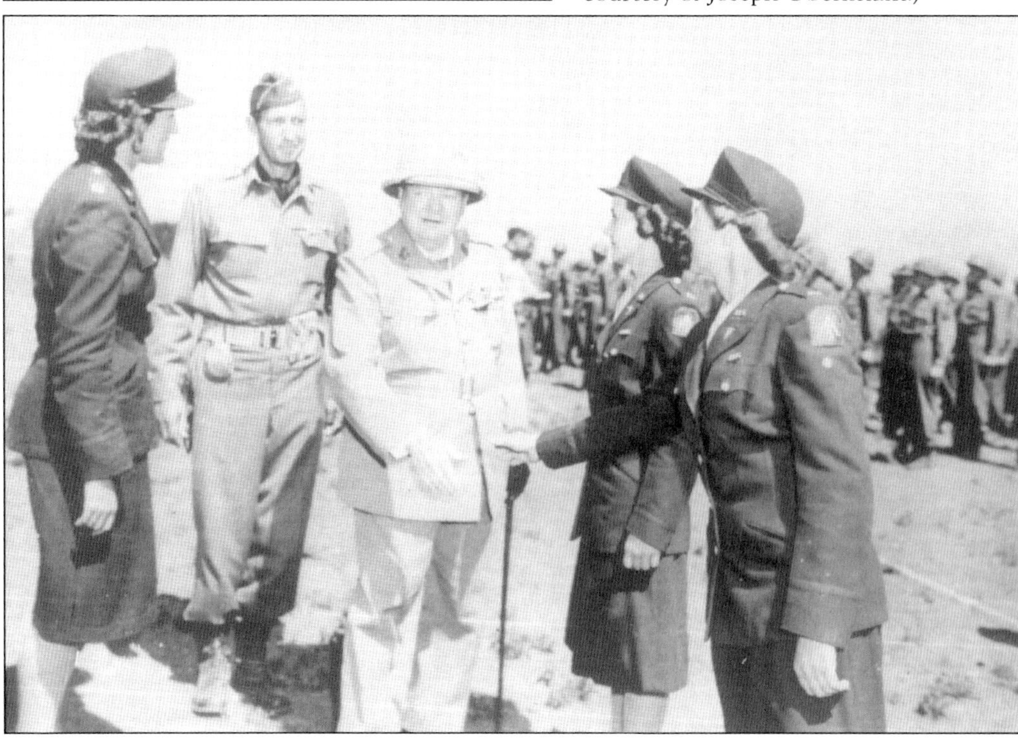

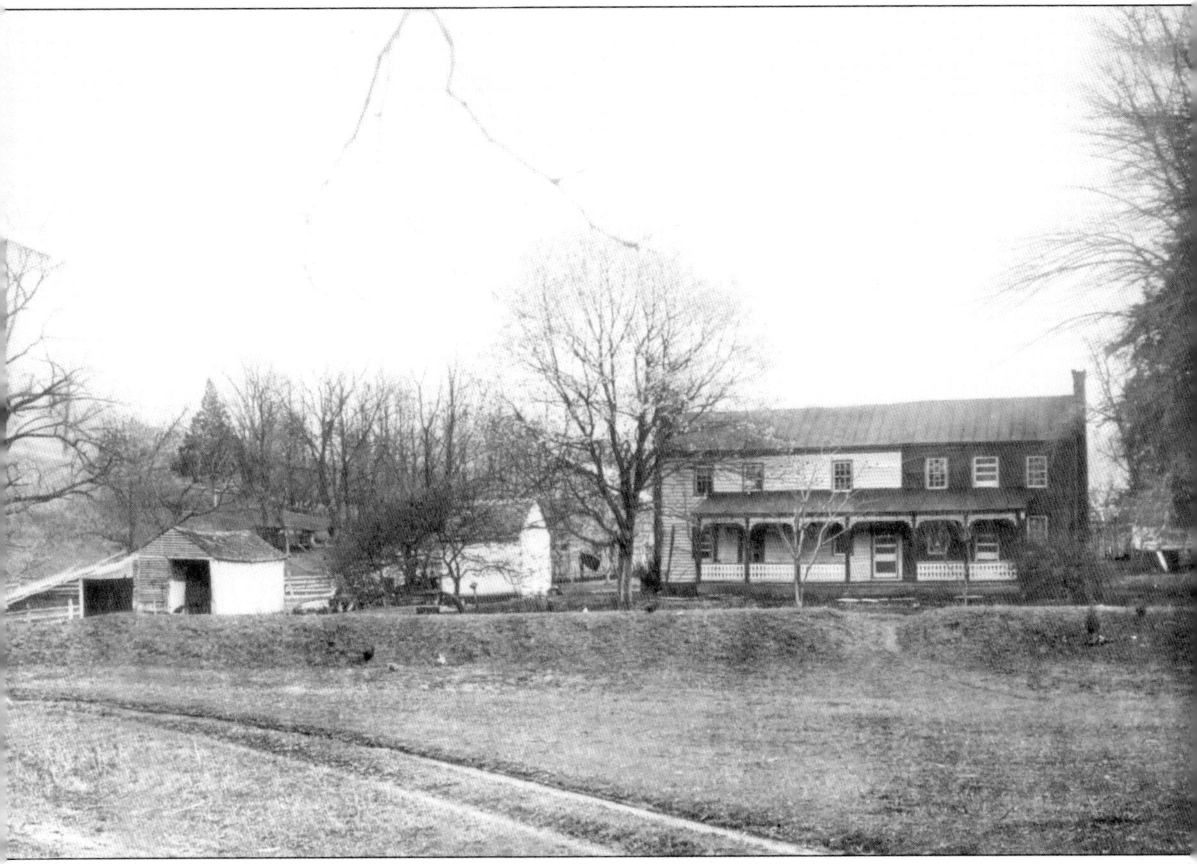

George Washington Rader of Nace was very active in the Lutheran Church and was among the first group of trustees of Roanoke College when it moved from Staunton to Salem in 1842. The Rader home, seen here, began around 1800 as a one-room hewn-log structure (left). In the 1830s, the brick section (right) was built and a frame hyphen connected the two sections. George's brother Samuel, a brick maker and builder, is credited with building the first Mill Creek Baptist Church and likely built the brick part of George's home. The brickwork on the house is very fine, is laid in a Flemish bond pattern, and features penciling on the joints. The interior features faux-marbled and grained woodwork. This c. 1890 photograph shows some of the farm buildings, including, from right to left, the smokehouse, the corncrib, the root cellar, and the harness repair shop. The 1850s post-and-beam bank barn, visible through the trees behind the house, is set on a stone foundation. The former bed for the Shenandoah Valley Railroad is also visible in front of the house. (Courtesy of John W. Rader.)

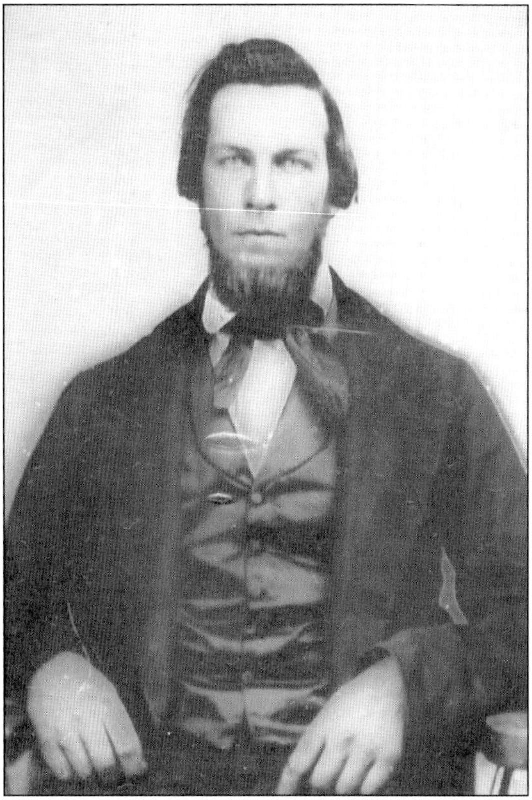

As a child, Adam Rader, born in 1761, immigrated to America from Germany with his family. Around 1802, he moved to Botetourt and established his leather shop near present-day Troutville. In 1819, his son George Washington Rader (left) married Susanna Kessler and purchased a farm from her father. Located in Nace and known as Cave Spring Farm, the land remains in the Rader family today. (Courtesy of John W. Rader.)

George Washington and Susanna Rader had seven children: Elizabeth, John K., W. Rowland, Cassandra, Mary Ann, Eliza Jane, and Susan. In 1921, Rowland's grandson Karl Rader married Lucille Landers and purchased the George Washington Rader farm. Karl (below) died in 1989, and Lucille died in 2006, just before her 104th birthday. Their son John W. Rader Sr. and grandson David continue the farm operations today. (Courtesy of John W. Rader.)

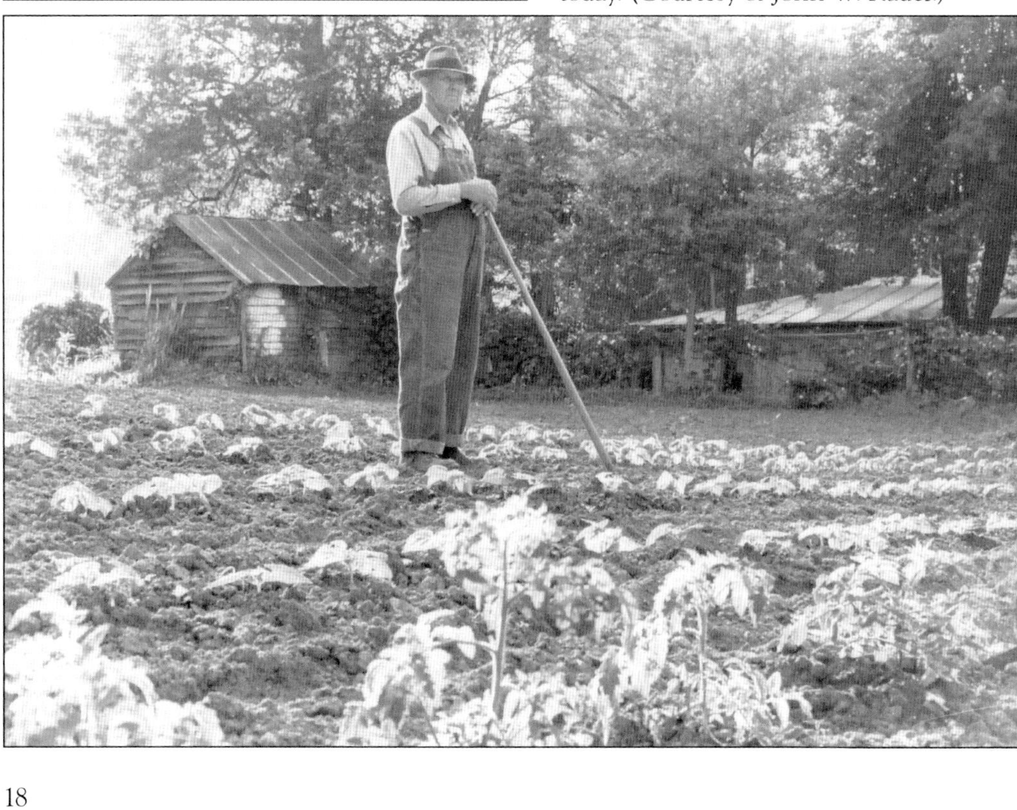

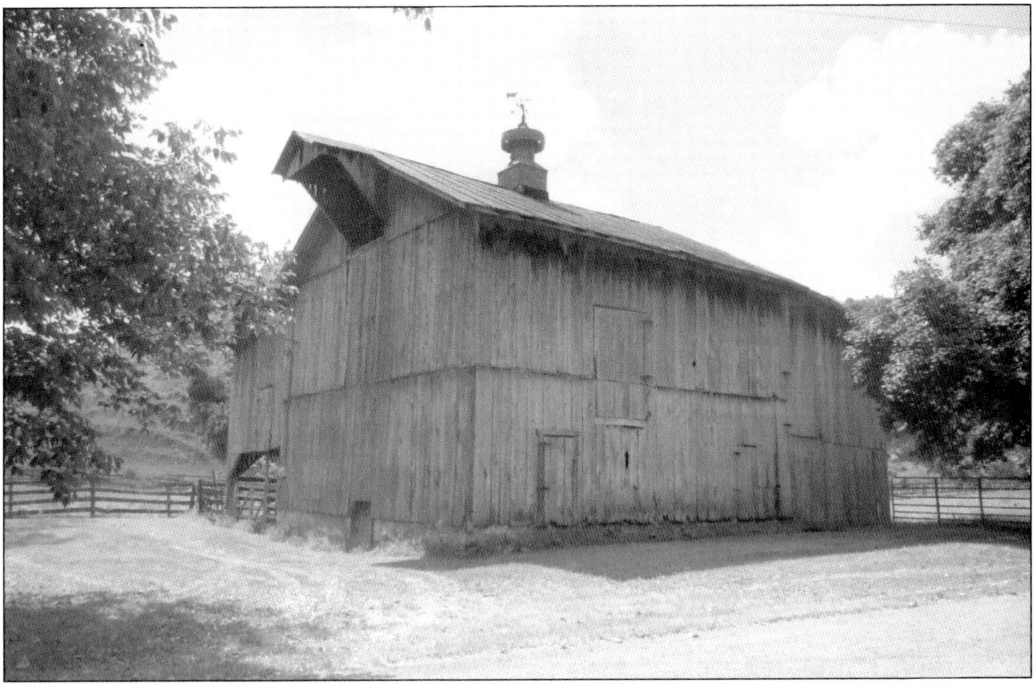

In 1806, Daniel Brugh built a gristmill on the Great Wagon Road along Looney's Mill Creek. The millrace was an engineering feat running from a stone dam, around a hill, and into a sluice to the waterwheel. The mill continued operations until 1925, when it was converted for use as a barn. Much of the original building material is intact. (Courtesy of John W. Rader.)

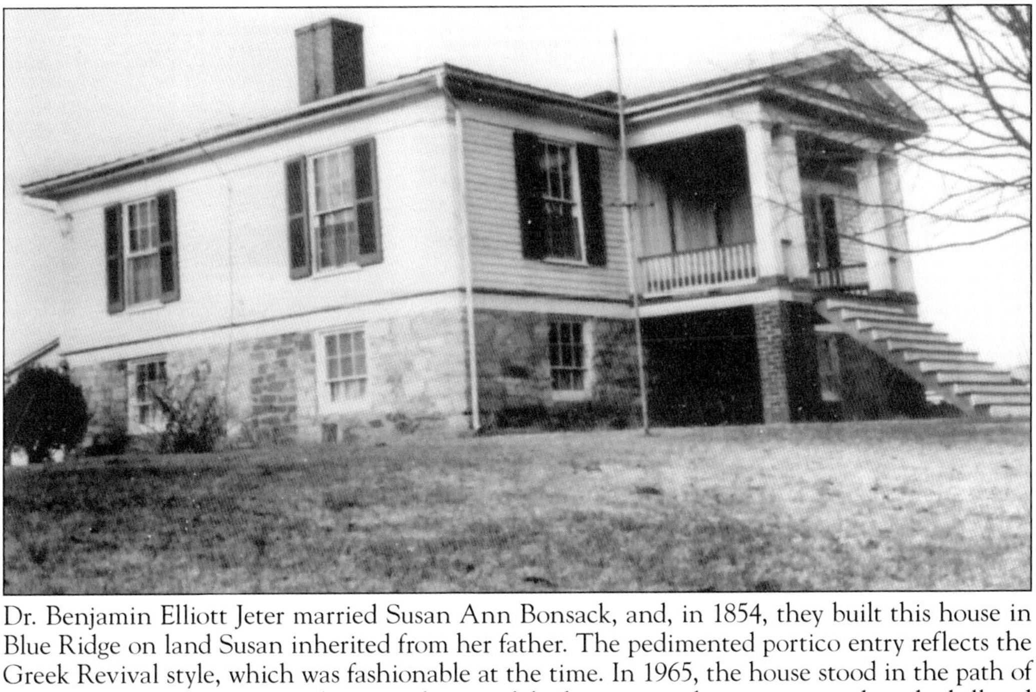

Dr. Benjamin Elliott Jeter married Susan Ann Bonsack, and, in 1854, they built this house in Blue Ridge on land Susan inherited from her father. The pedimented portico entry reflects the Greek Revival style, which was fashionable at the time. In 1965, the house stood in the path of the widening of Route 460. The second story of the house, seen here, was carted up the hill and set on a new stone foundation. (Courtesy of Betty Jeter Painter.)

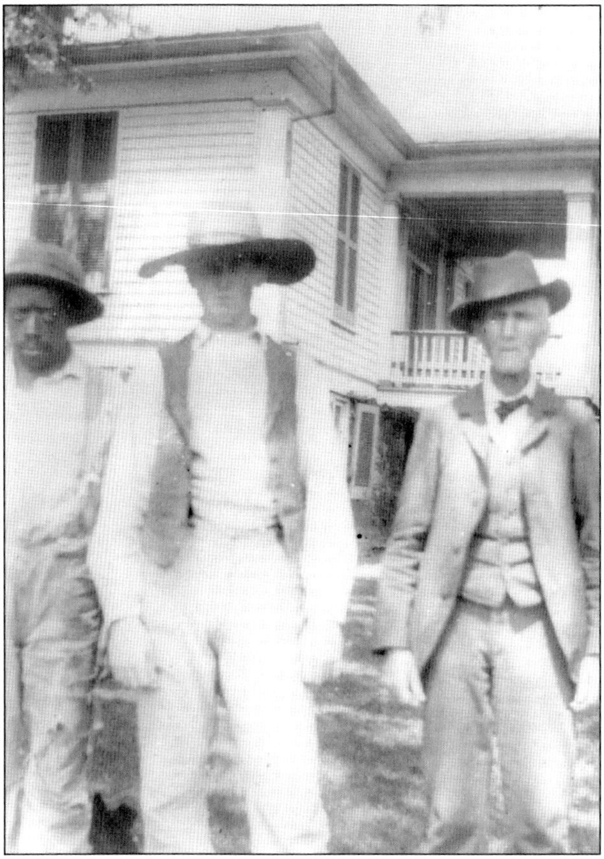

This photograph, taken around 1900, shows Dr. Benjamin Elliott Jeter (right) and his son Jacob in front of the old Jeter home place. The gentleman on the left is Charlie Mills, a former slave who worked on the Jeter farm. Dr. Jeter received his medical degree from the University of Pennsylvania and practiced medicine in Bonsack from 1850 until his death in 1903. The family retains Dr. Jeter's medical saddlebag and his journal of patient visits. (Courtesy of Betty Jeter Painter.)

Jacob Bonsack Jeter's son Richard inherited the farm from his father. Richard (right) is seen below with Chamler Horne, who built the corncrib seen on the left. The Jeter barn, erected in 1871, is visible in the background. Richard farmed the Jeter place until his death in 2007. Richard's son Ned and Ned's sons (fourth and fifth generations) now operate the farm, raising livestock and numerous truck crops. (Courtesy of Betty Jeter Painter.)

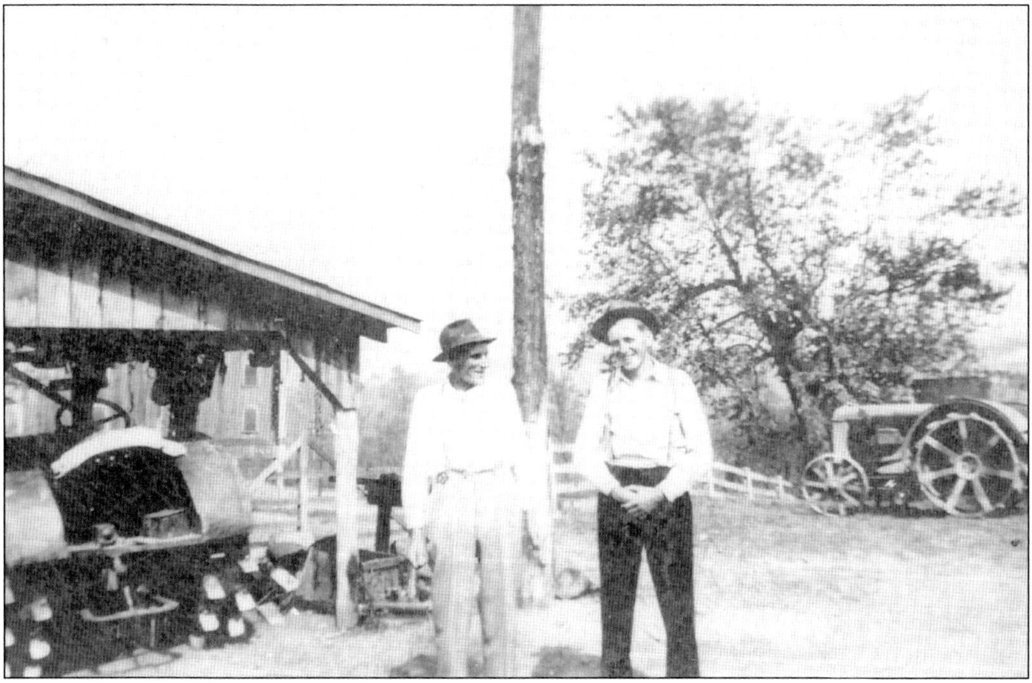

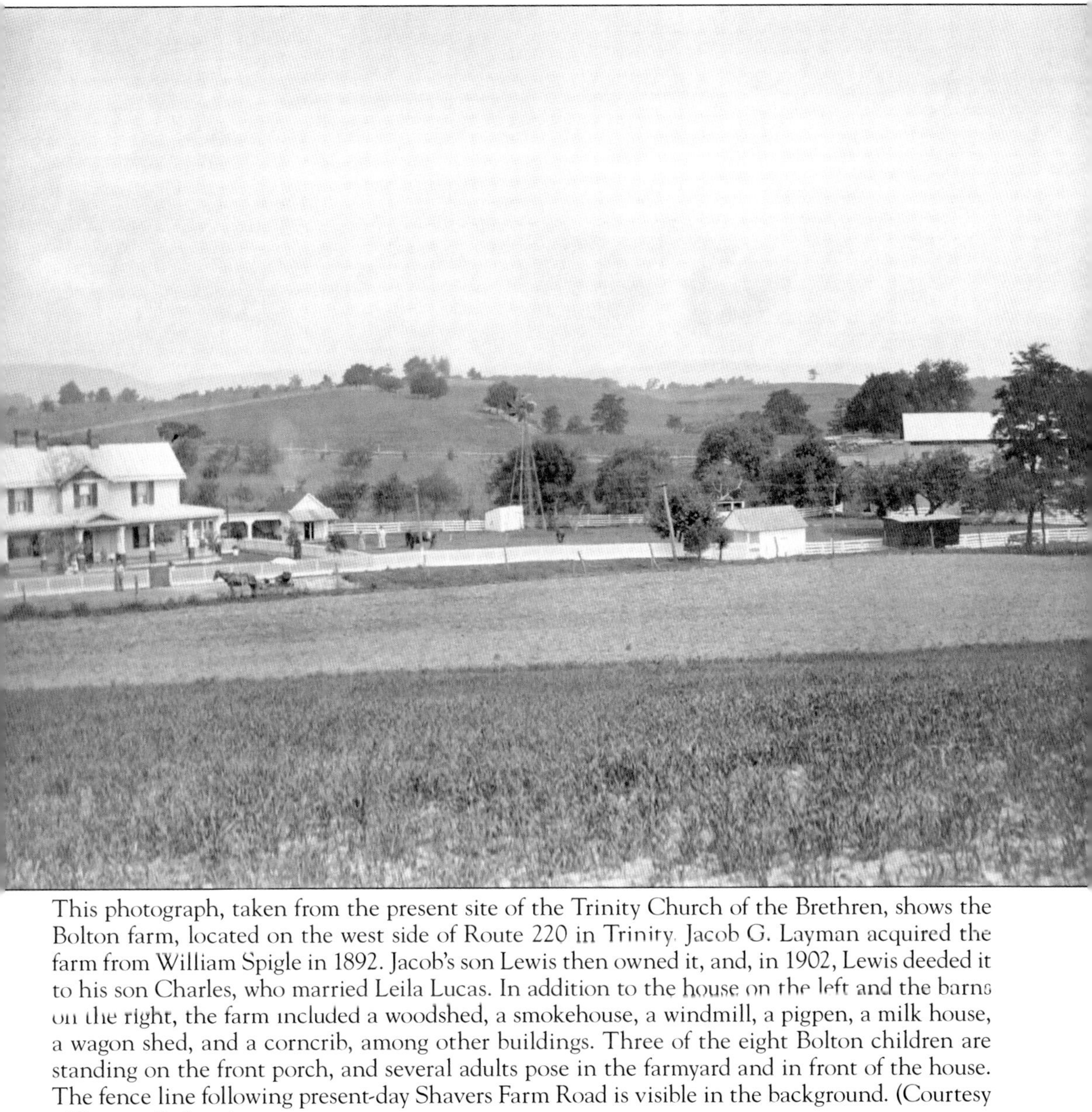

This photograph, taken from the present site of the Trinity Church of the Brethren, shows the Bolton farm, located on the west side of Route 220 in Trinity. Jacob G. Layman acquired the farm from William Spigle in 1892. Jacob's son Lewis then owned it, and, in 1902, Lewis deeded it to his son Charles, who married Leila Lucas. In addition to the house on the left and the barns on the right, the farm included a woodshed, a smokehouse, a windmill, a pigpen, a milk house, a wagon shed, and a corncrib, among other buildings. Three of the eight Bolton children are standing on the front porch, and several adults pose in the farmyard and in front of the house. The fence line following present-day Shavers Farm Road is visible in the background. (Courtesy of Benton Bolton.)

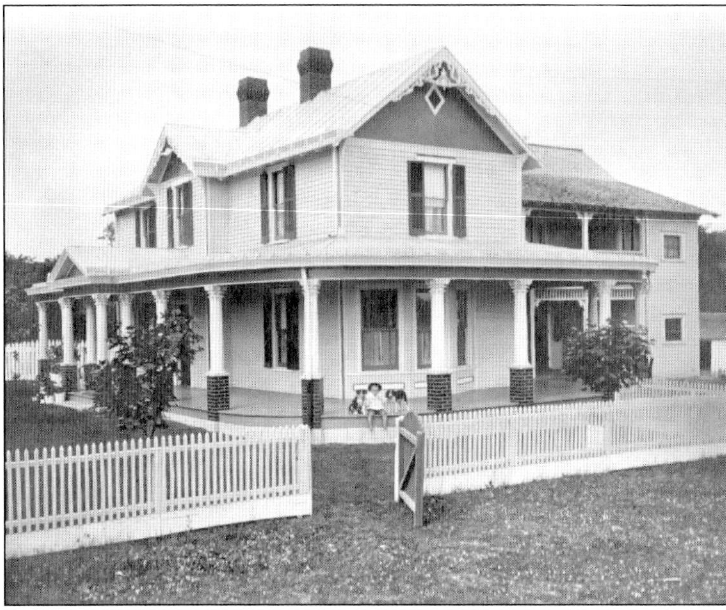

The Bolton house was demolished when Route 220 was widened to four lanes in the 1970s. Although a common farmhouse form, with the earliest section dating to around 1800, this house was elaborately embellished with brackets and gingerbread sawn work in the eaves. The house also featured a wraparound, columned porch and a rear two-story ell. Here, one of the Bolton children poses with two pets. (Courtesy of Benton Bolton.)

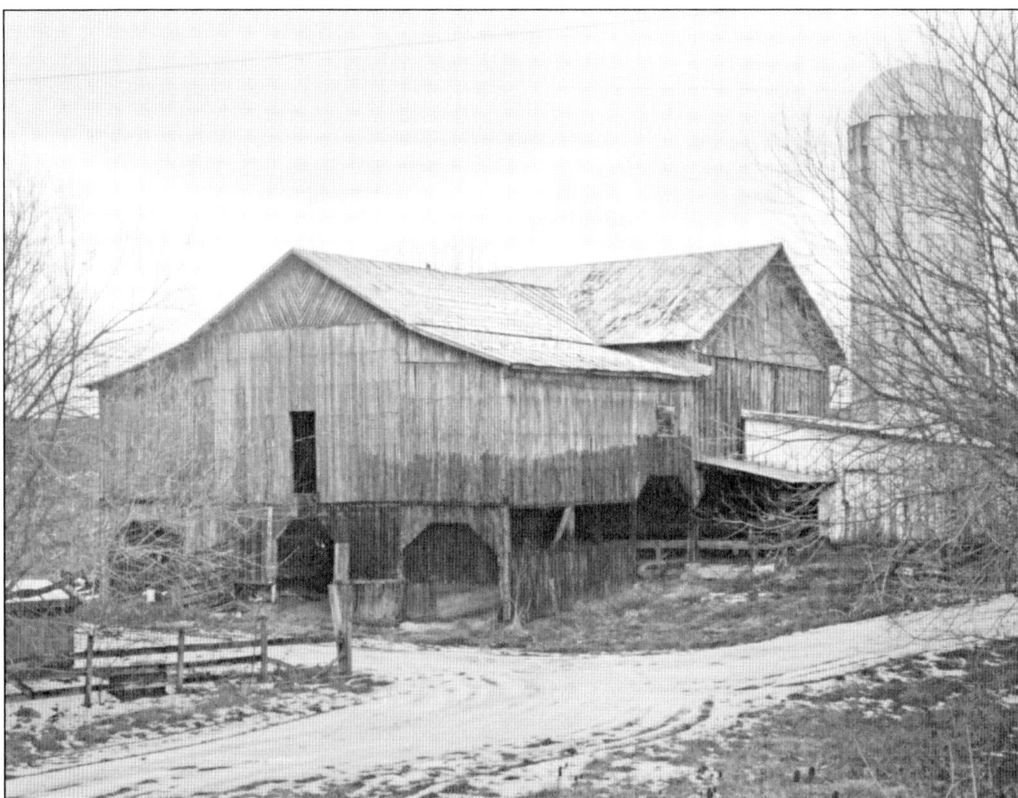

This photograph shows the Bolton barns, at the southwest corner of Shavers Farm Road and Route 220, after the farm had ceased operations. The large barn is banked into the hill at the rear, where a concrete silo is located. A separate concrete-block milk room is located to the left, outside of this view. These buildings are still standing. (Courtesy of Benton Bolton.)

On June 5, 1945, Woodrow "Woody" and Edna Brogan Bolton posed for this wedding photograph at Edna's mother's house in Fincastle. Woody, who was serving at Fort Story, is wearing his Army uniform. After a honeymoon to Natural Bridge, Woody deployed to the Pacific Theater with Company B, 306th Infantry Regiment. Upon his return, he and Edna operated the Bolton dairy farm in the Trinity area. (Courtesy of Edna Brogan Bolton.)

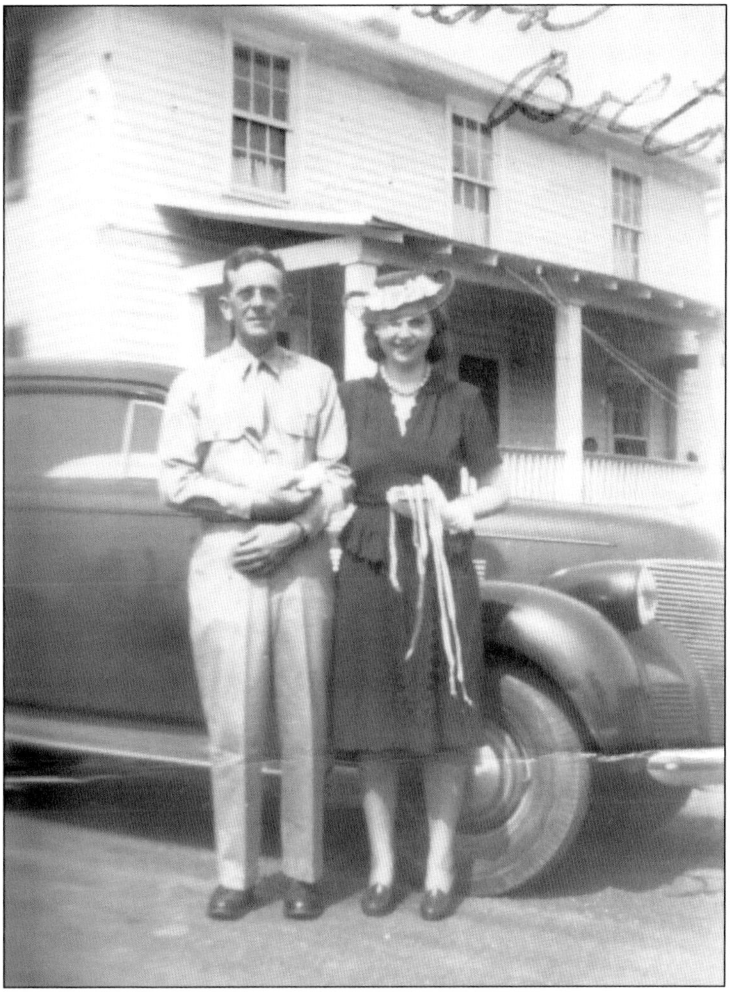

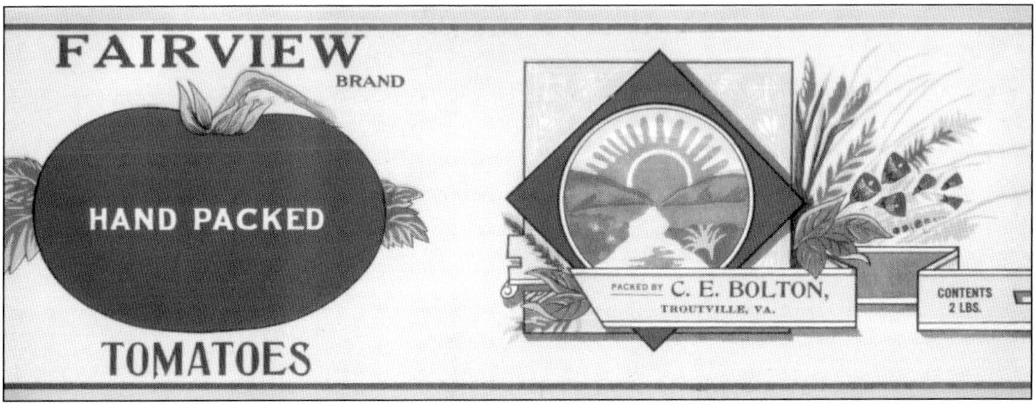

In the early 20th century, Botetourt was the second-largest canning county in the United States. Nearly every farm in the county had a cannery. In the 1920s and 1930s, large canneries took over operations, with individual farmers continuing to supply the fruits and vegetables. This label is from the Charles E. Bolton cannery on Route 220. It was one of the largest in the Trinity area. (Courtesy of Benton Bolton.)

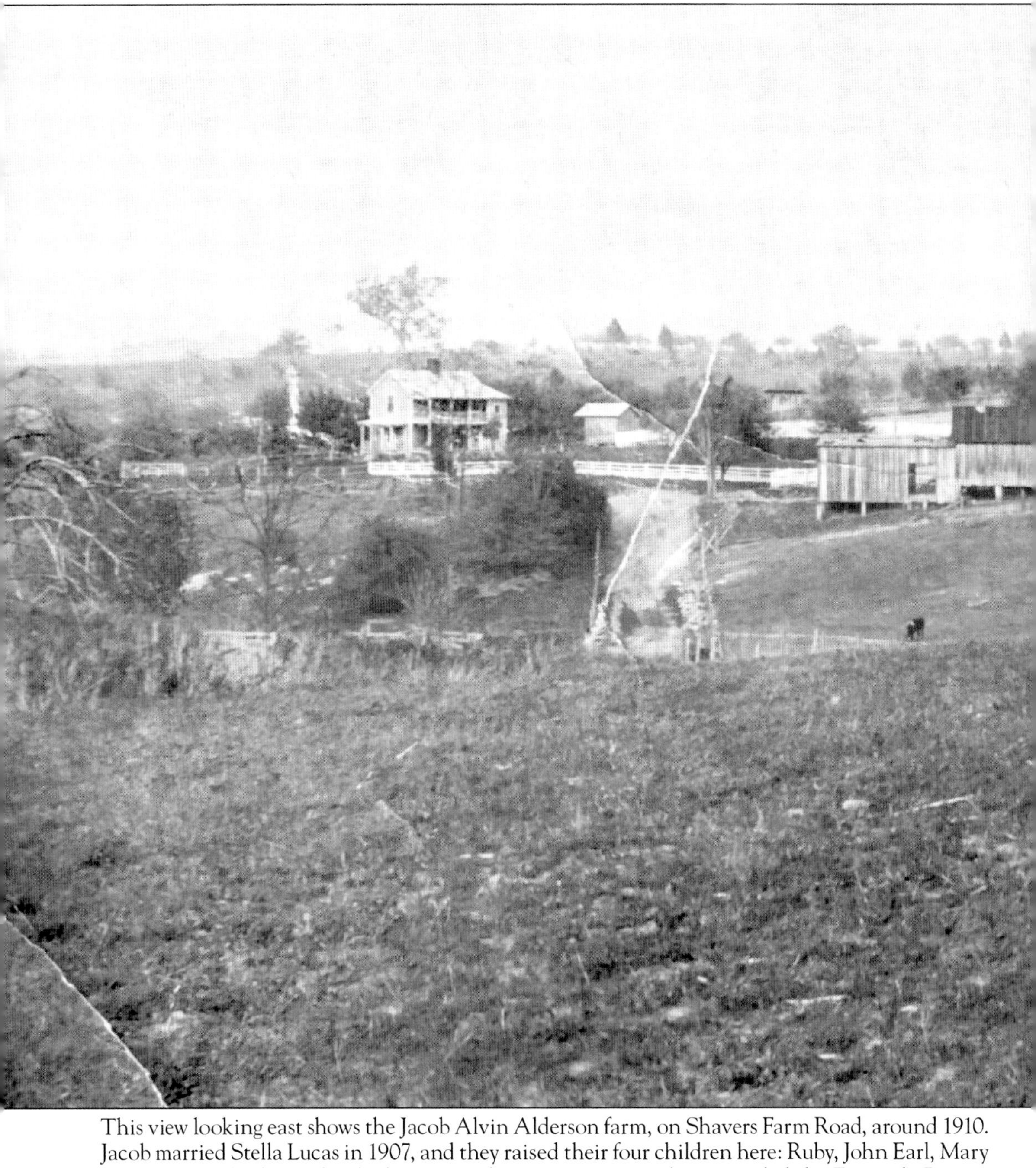

This view looking east shows the Jacob Alvin Alderson farm, on Shavers Farm Road, around 1910. Jacob married Stella Lucas in 1907, and they raised their four children here: Ruby, John Earl, Mary Hazeltine, and Alma, who died at age 16 from pneumonia. They attended the Fincastle Baptist Church, and their children attended Trinity School. In addition to the farmhouse, which was

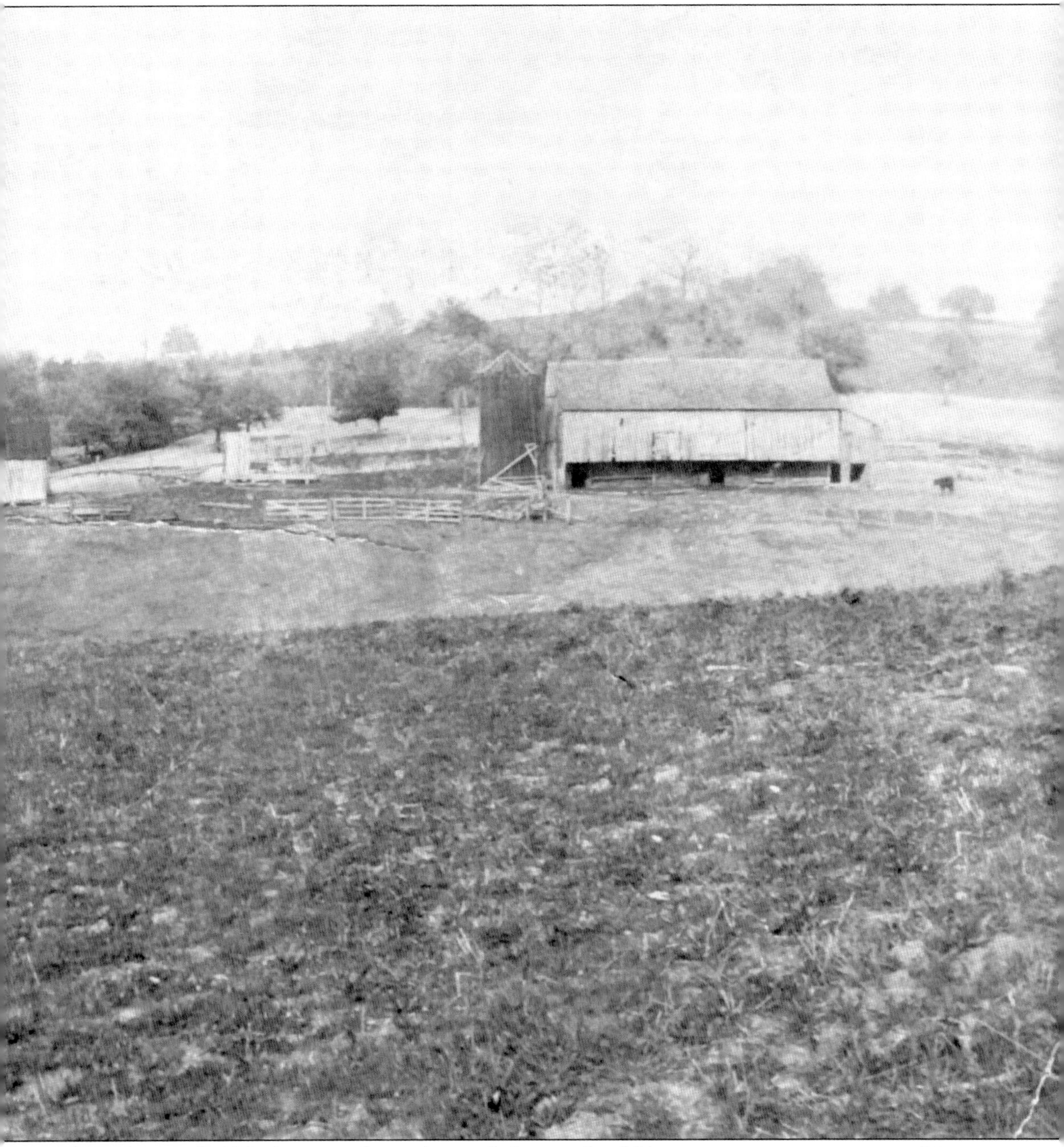

enlarged around 1950, this view shows the smokehouse, the Alderson tomato cannery, a machine shed, the corncrib (under construction), and the bank barn and wooden silo. Third-, fourth-, and fifth-generation Aldersons now live on the farm. (Courtesy of John E. Alderson Jr.)

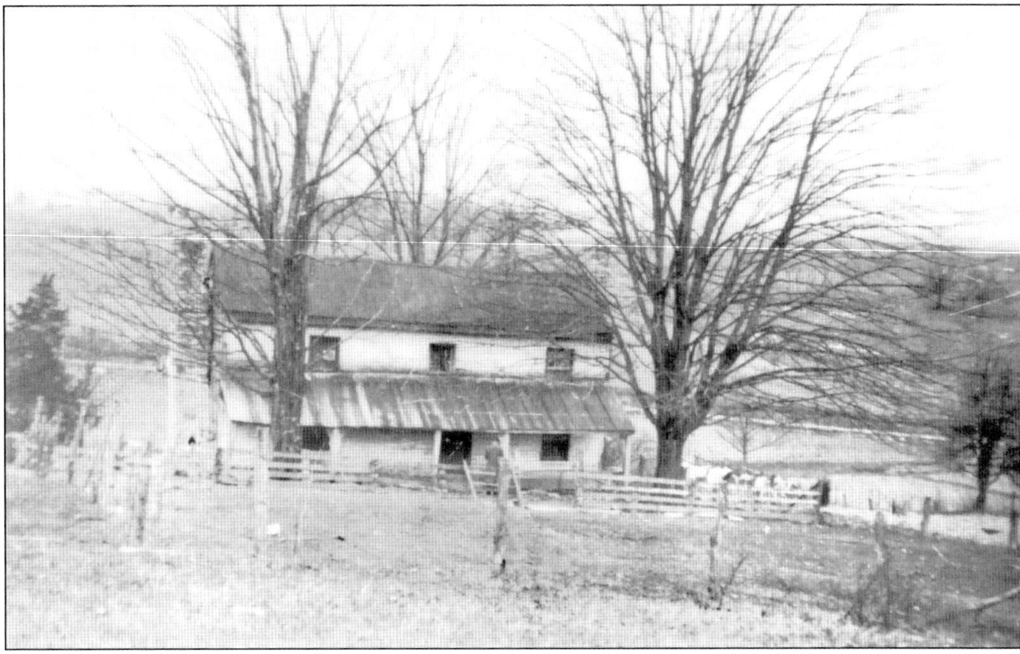

The Thomas Alderson house, located between Trinity and Blacksburg Road, was built around 1800. It was constructed out of logs with large stone chimneys on both ends. This photograph was taken in 1938 as part of the Virginia Historical Inventory survey. Only a portion of the north chimney remains at the site today. Present-day Shavers Farm Road is visible in the background. (Courtesy of the Library of Virginia.)

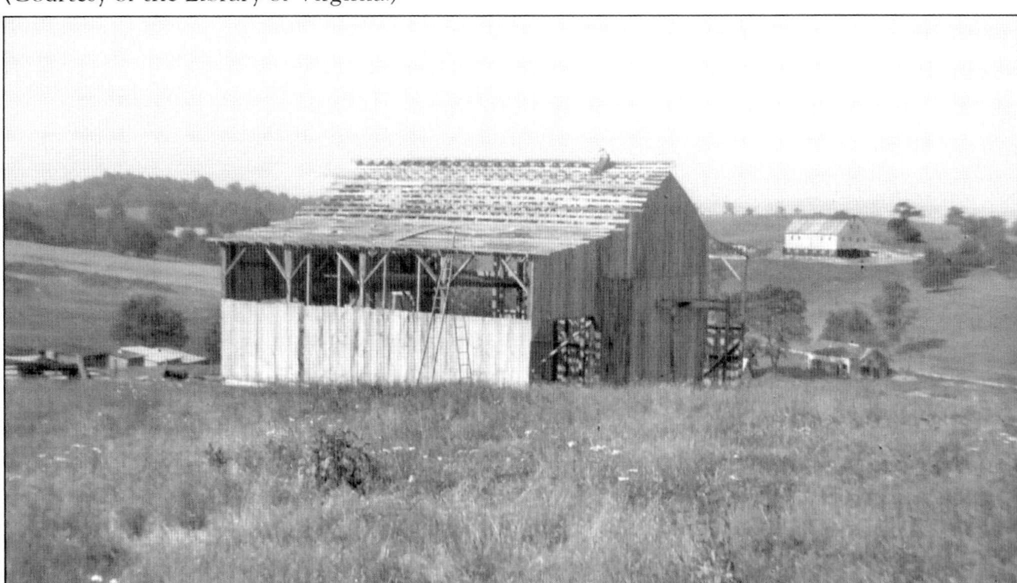

Earl Alderson's barn was under construction in this 1951 photograph. This large hay barn still stands on Shavers Farm Road. Earl's chicken houses are visible on the left. The barn in the background was built by the Bolton family. In 1929, Edward H. Stevens Sr. purchased the farm, which remains in his family today. The Bolton cannery, no longer standing, is in the middle right background. (Courtesy of John E. Alderson Jr.)

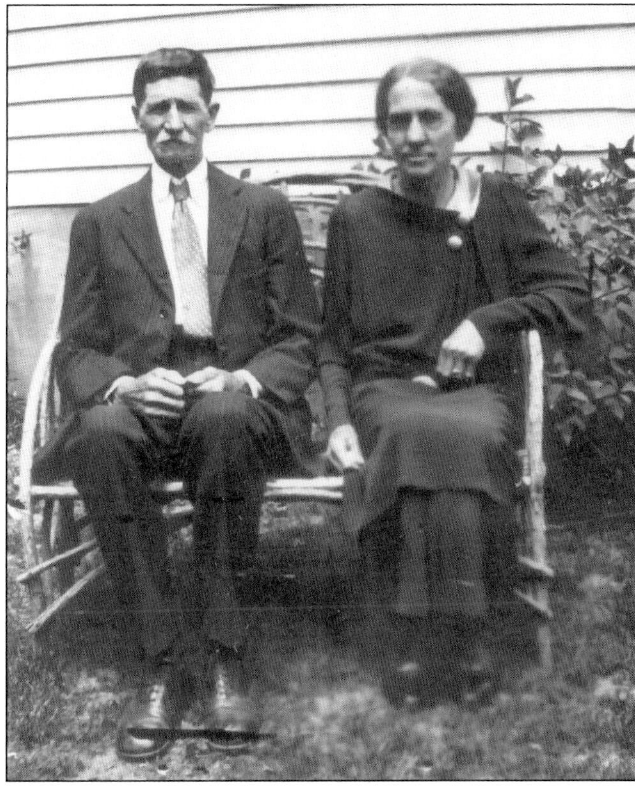

Stuart Franklin Noel and his wife, Jennie Entsminger, sit outside of their home on their 30-acre farm in the Forest Grove area. They married in 1890, and this photograph was taken around 1910. Stuart was a farmer and also worked at the Eagle Rock Lime Quarry for over 20 years. (Courtesy of Anna Noel Damerel.)

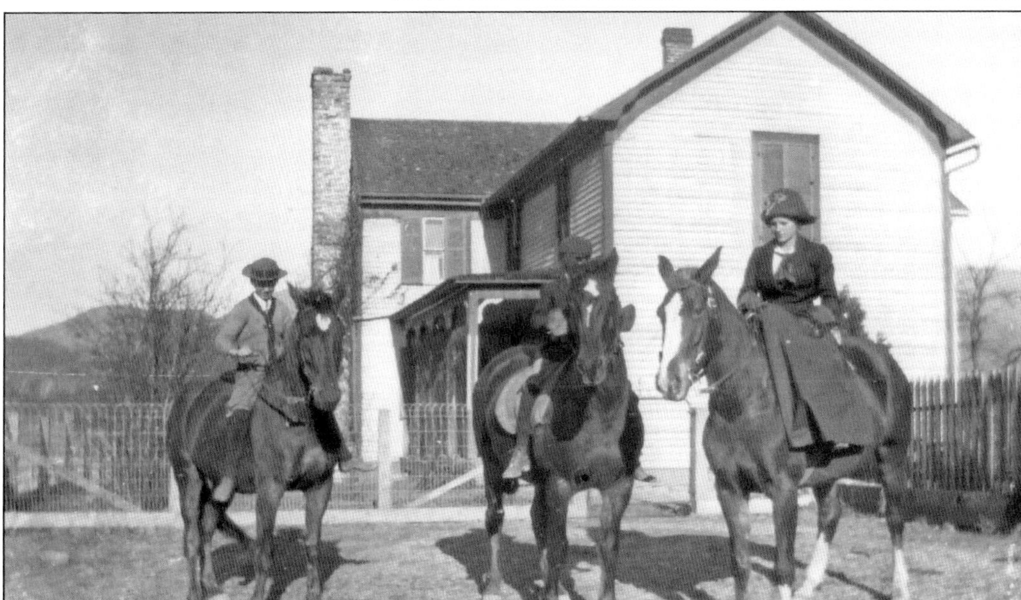

Charlotte Persinger (right) and probably her two younger brothers, Maxheimer and Orth, are pictured here around 1908 at their father Joseph's house on Salt Petre Cave Road. The Persingers owned the house from 1890 to 1975, when the Noel family purchased it. Charlotte attended the State Teachers College in Farmville, Maxheimer moved to Michigan and worked at General Motors, and Orth worked as a railroad clerk. (Courtesy of Anna Noel Damerel.)

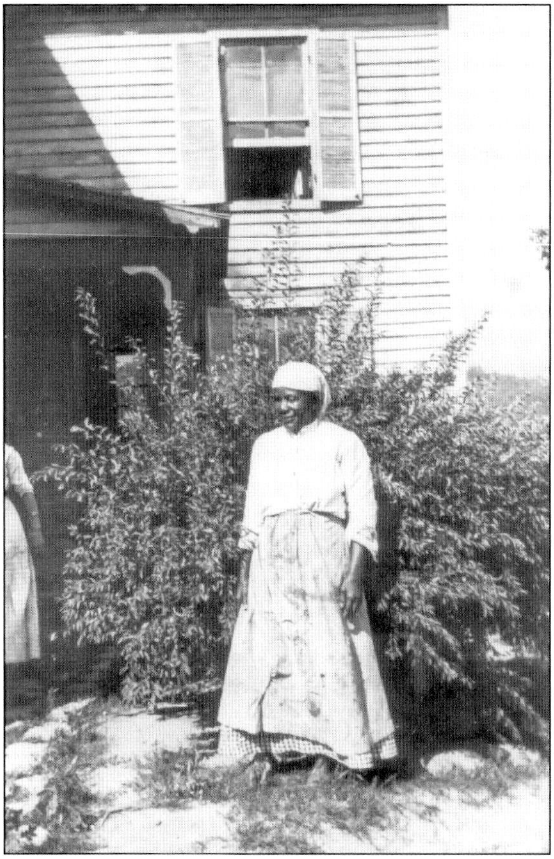

This unidentified woman stands in front of the home of Joseph Persinger in Salt Petre Cave around 1907. Judging from her apron and head cover, she appears to be a cook for the family. One of the Persinger daughters can be partially seen on the left. (Courtesy of Anna Noel Damerel.)

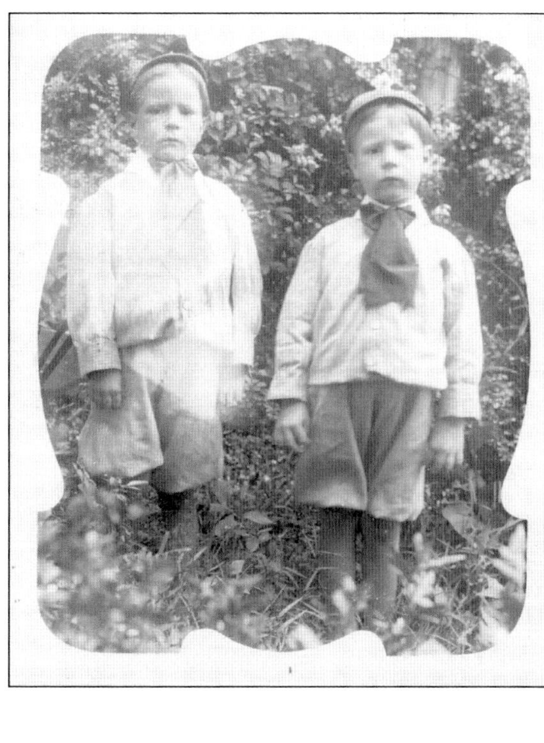

In 1905, these adorable twin boys, Curtis and Cletus, were born to James and Mary Elizabeth Zell Wilhelm. Curtis married Myrtel Newcomb, and they lived on the old Burger farm on Lapsley's Run. In 1926, Cletus married Callie Armentrout, and they lived near Midway School. Both brothers later moved to Roanoke; Curtis worked at a mill, and Cletus worked at the Viscose silk mill. (Courtesy of Anna Noel Damerel.)

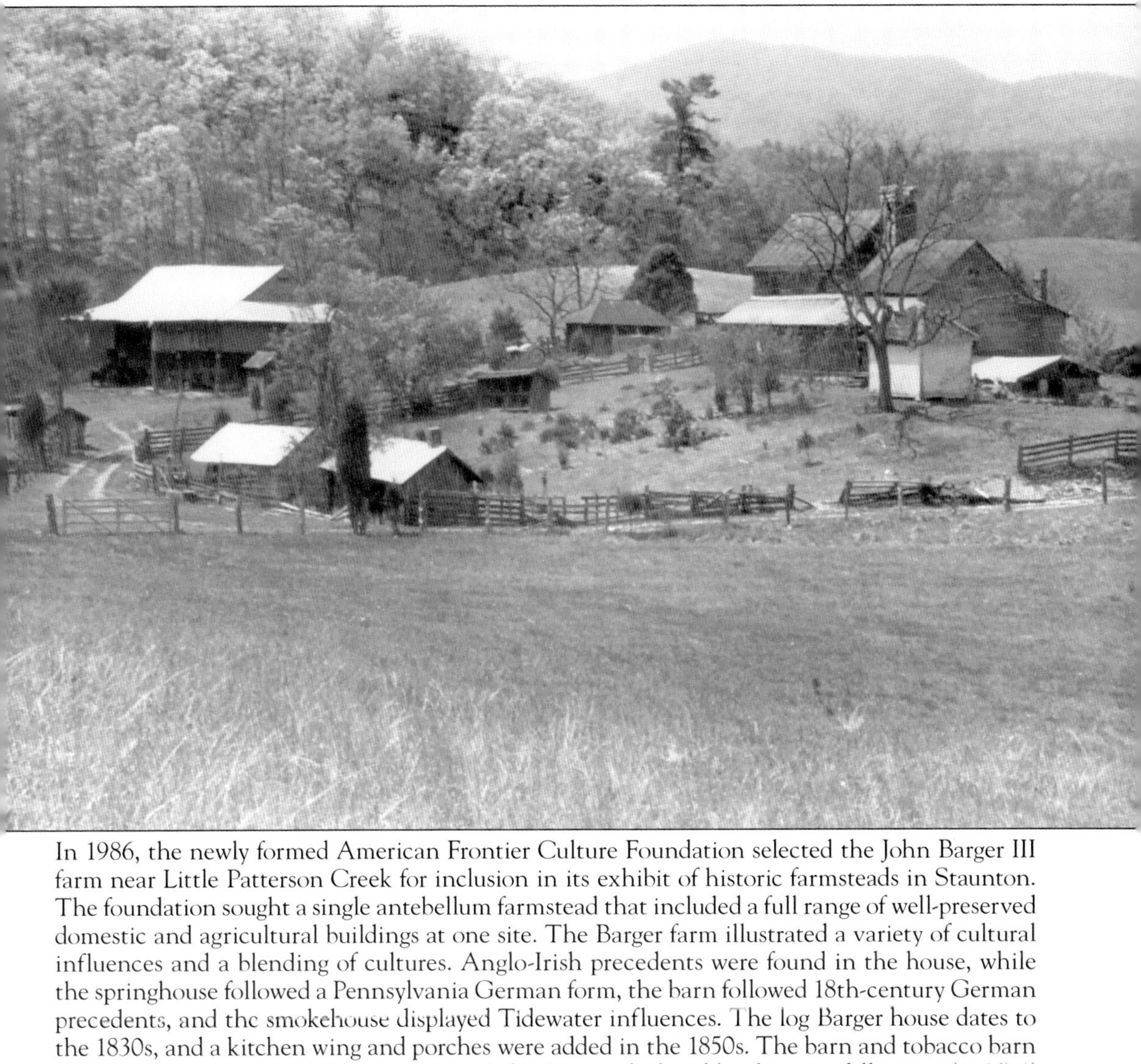

In 1986, the newly formed American Frontier Culture Foundation selected the John Barger III farm near Little Patterson Creek for inclusion in its exhibit of historic farmsteads in Staunton. The foundation sought a single antebellum farmstead that included a full range of well-preserved domestic and agricultural buildings at one site. The Barger farm illustrated a variety of cultural influences and a blending of cultures. Anglo-Irish precedents were found in the house, while the springhouse followed a Pennsylvania German form, the barn followed 18th-century German precedents, and the smokehouse displayed Tidewater influences. The log Barger house dates to the 1830s, and a kitchen wing and porches were added in the 1850s. The barn and tobacco barn were constructed around that same time. John Barger declared bankruptcy following the Civil War, and the farm went through several owners before Lucian and Catherine Riddlebarger, the nephew and niece of John Barger, purchased it in 1884. They continued to farm the land actively into the 1940s and owned the property at the time the museum acquired it. (Courtesy of the Frontier Culture Museum of Virginia.)

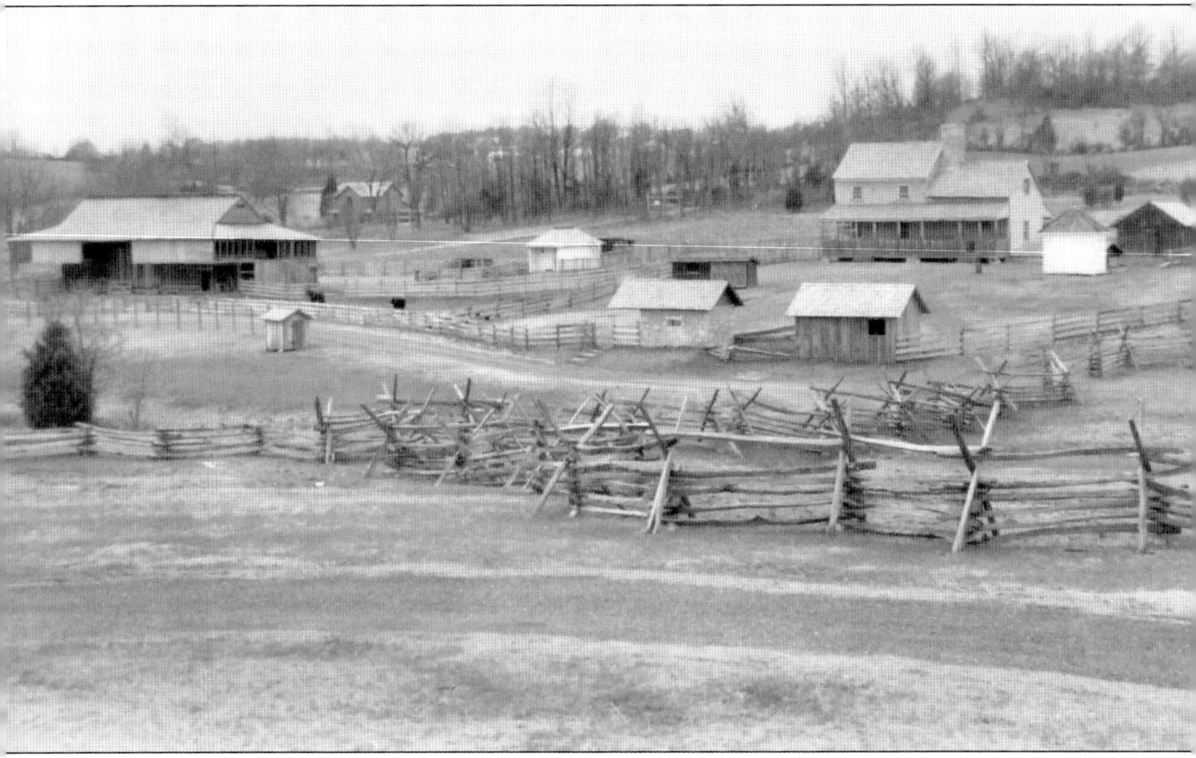

In 1791, the Barger farm was part of a 100-acre land grant from Gov. Beverley Randolph to William Maxwell. The land passed through several owners until 1832, when John Barger III purchased it. Barger, who had descended from German immigrants, added acreage to the farm and built his home, barns, and outbuildings in the next few decades. In 1872, following the devastating economic effects of the Civil War, Barger was forced to sell the farm at auction. In 1986, after a yearlong search, the Frontier Cultural Museum Foundation selected the Barger farm for its new outdoor history museum, which commemorates the contributions that 18th- and 19th-century pioneers made to the development of America. The museum buildings depict the ways in which settlers blended various cultural influences into their own traditions. The Barger farm, an example of an 1850s American farm, is contrasted against English, Scots-Irish, and German examples. This photograph shows the Barger farm relocated and reassembled on the museum property. Its setting and orientation closely mimic its original surroundings. (Courtesy of the Frontier Culture Museum of Virginia.)

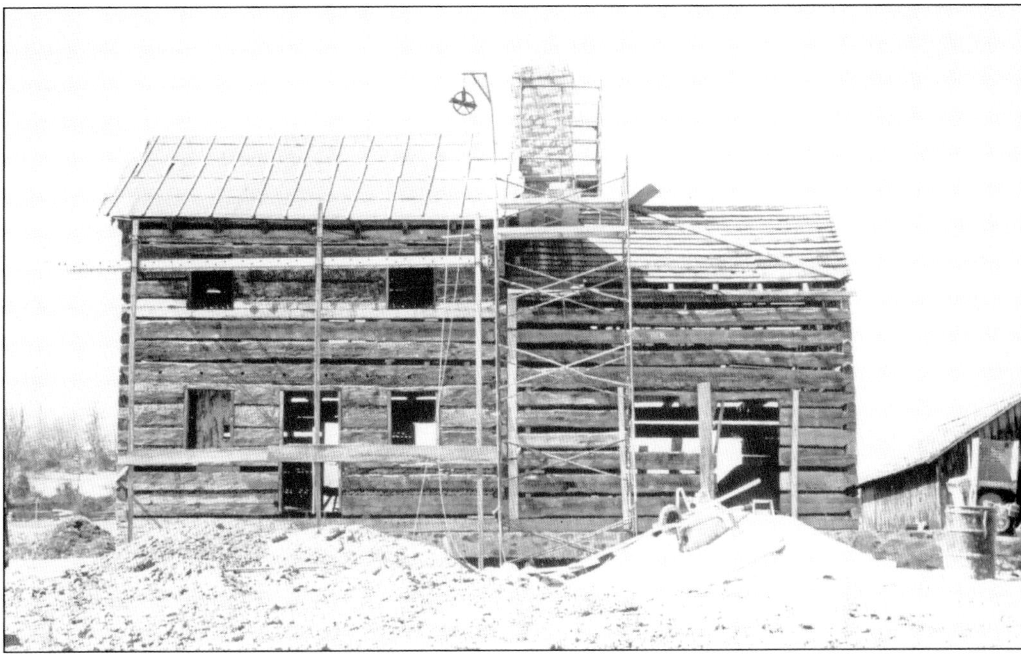

The reconstruction of the Barger farm involved a painstaking process of preparing measured drawings and numbering each log, stone, and timber in the buildings. The buildings were then dismantled, transported to Staunton, and reassembled. The house was the first building reconstructed. Above, it is shown in progress. The large logs of the building are connected with V-notches. Below, builders reconstruct the house's stone chimney. Numbers on each stone indicated its location. The restoration of the buildings removed much of the 20th-century fabric and restored some of the historic elements of the house. (Both courtesy of the Frontier Culture Museum of Virginia.)

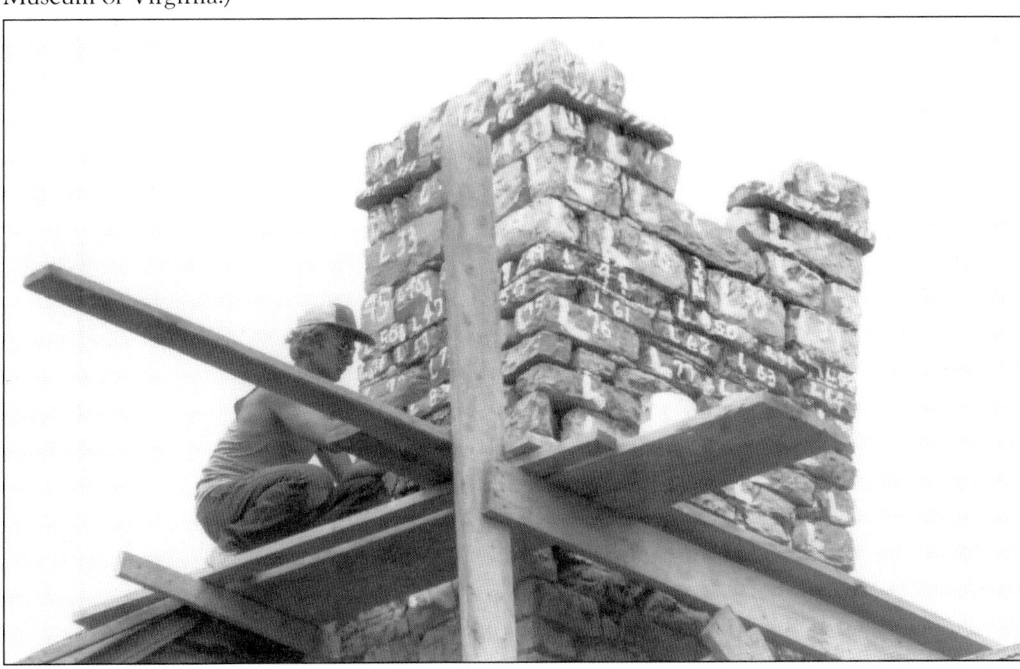

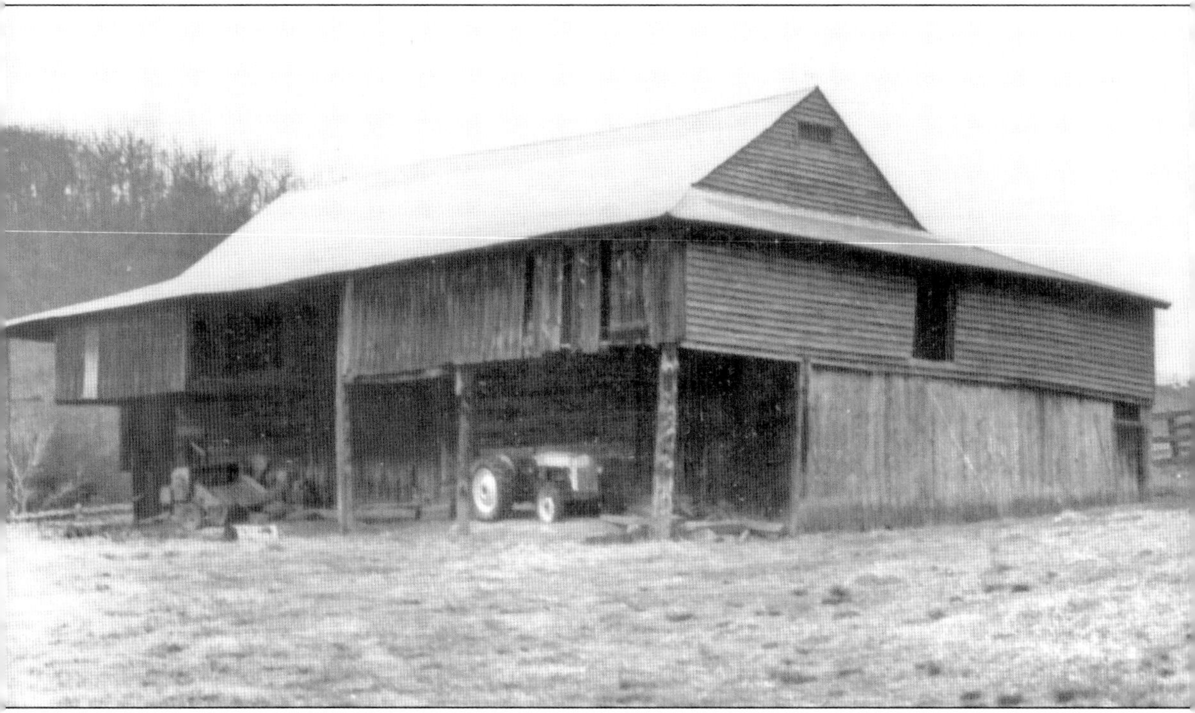

John Barger built this two-story, double-pen log barn in 1855. The unusual barn features a central threshing floor with a granary and animal pens to either side. The second floor holds cantilevered bays that extend out 10 feet on three sides of the barn. The cantilevers greatly expanded the enclosed area for hay and straw storage. The design is said to reflect Swiss and German precedents. Museum literature indicates that this type of barn emerged in America only after the Revolutionary War, and other examples were found in Pennsylvania, western Maryland, and Virginia. The barn is seen here at its original site in Botetourt. Pre–Civil War records lead historians to believe that John Barger III was not a slave owner. The 1860 census named two men in the Barger household who were likely free blacks working on the farm. The impact of the war and the Reconstruction period on the economy of the South, as well as accrued debts, resulted in Barger's filing for bankruptcy in 1869 and then selling the farm at auction in 1872. (Courtesy of the Frontier Culture Museum of Virginia.)

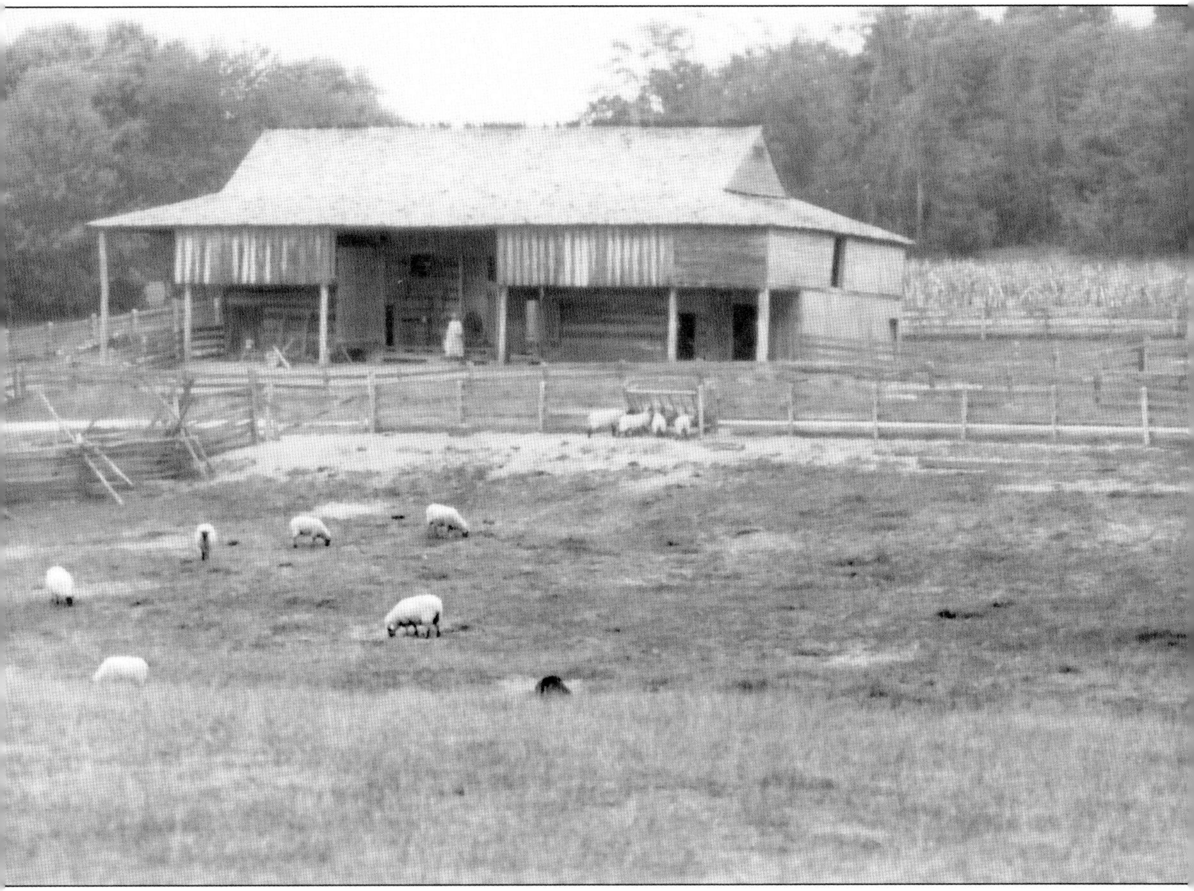

The 1855 construction date of the Barger barn is carved into one of the logs on the front of the barn. Dendrochronological testing of the wood confirmed this date. During the restoration of the barn at the museum, the modern (post-1910) siding and barn doors were replaced with more appropriate 19th-century replicas. The barn is a central element to the museum's interpretation of mid-19th-century farm life, and it is actively used for hay and equipment storage and livestock shelter. This image shows the reconstructed barn at the museum site in Staunton. The farms at the Frontier Culture Museum represent "reconstituted rural spaces." Rather than a static collection of buildings, the working farms provide visitors with an opportunity to witness actual household and farm activities carried out with tools and furnishings typical of the region and period represented. In recent years, West African and Native American settlements have been included in the museum exhibits. (Courtesy of the Frontier Culture Museum of Virginia.)

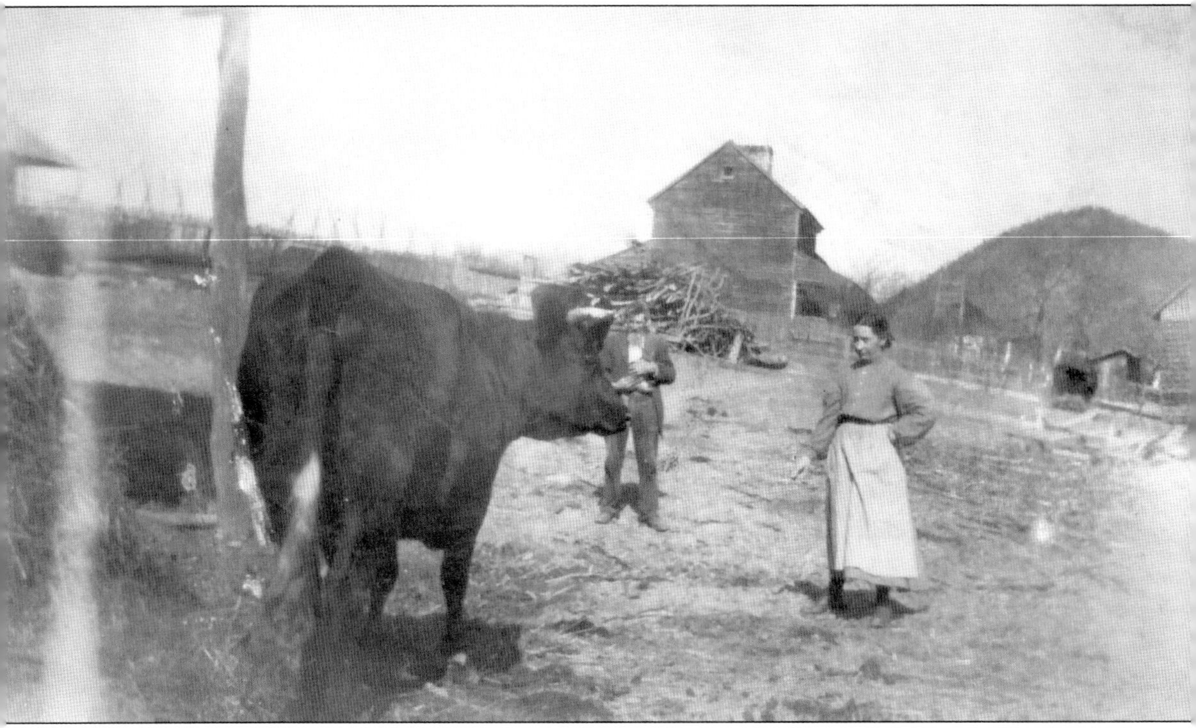

In 1875, Lucian Riddlebarger married Catharine Switzer, and, in 1884, they purchased their uncle John Barger's farm. The highly productive Riddlebarger farm was one of the last Botetourt County farms to grow tobacco. In addition, the family harvested wheat, oats, and hay and raised cattle, horses, and hogs. The Riddlebargers were animal lovers and took especially good care of their horses and cattle. In this photograph, Lucian and his daughter Belle stand in the barnyard around 1900. Belle also loved her pet dogs, and when her beloved terrier Billy died, she asked that it be buried in the family plot at Mount Moriah Church. Instead, he was buried at the farm in what became the pet cemetery, located behind the smokehouse. After their parents died, Belle and her two brothers remained on the farm. In 1968, Benjamine, the last family member to live on the farm, deeded it to his nephew James Riddlebarger and his wife, Phyllis. (Courtesy of the Frontier Culture Museum of Virginia.)

During the Civil War, Martin Van Buren Hickok (1836–1913) served in Company D, 11th Virginia Infantry (the Fincastle Rifles). Hickok, who rose to the rank of lieutenant, served as the unit's color bearer and sustained seven wounds during the war. He returned home and married Martha Hammond, the widow of Robert J. Thrasher. Martin and Martha are seen here with two of their grandchildren around 1910. (Courtesy of Howard Revercomb Hammond.)

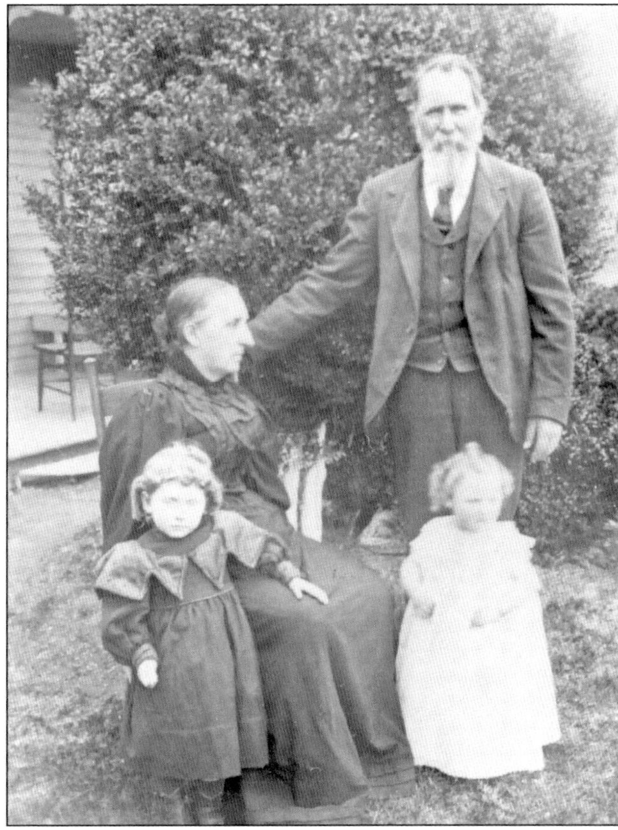

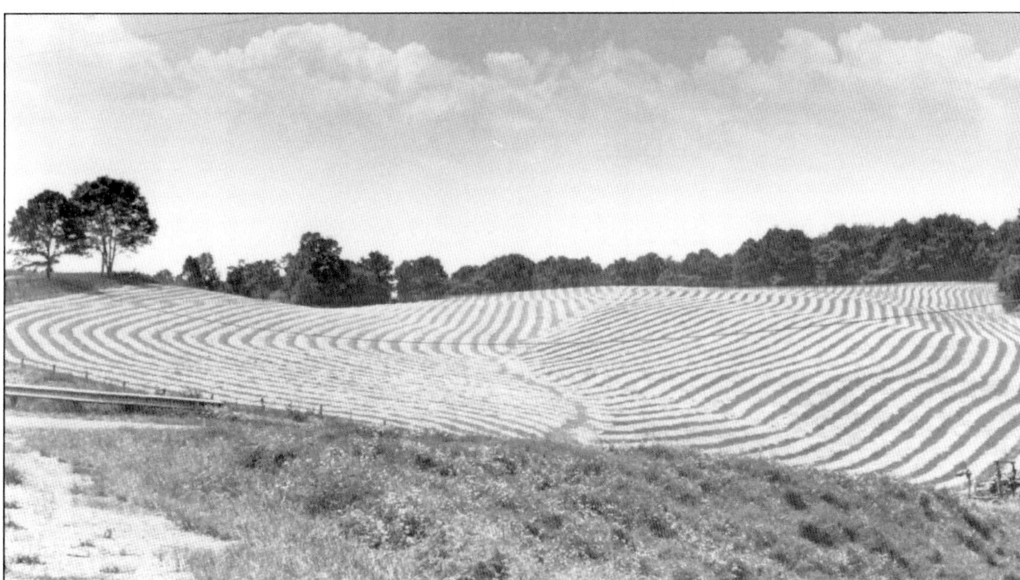

In this summer image, mown hay is raked into windrows, making for an artistic pattern following the topography of the hill. The smell of freshly cut hay is one that residents relish. Hay is grown on over 18,000 acres in Botetourt and on approximately 1.2 million acres in Virginia. County farmers produce both round and square bales for their own livestock. (Courtesy of the *Fincastle Herald*.)

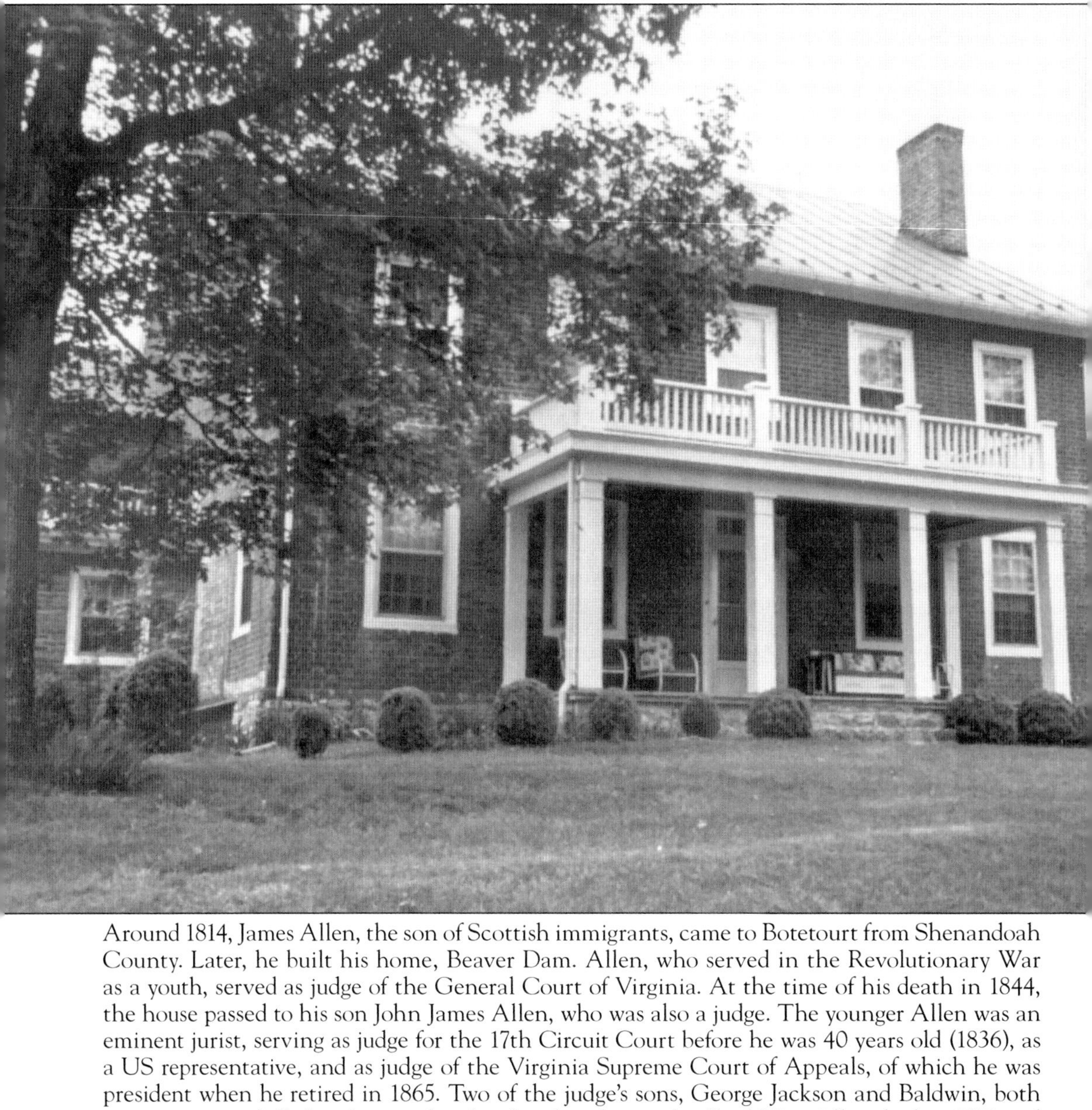

Around 1814, James Allen, the son of Scottish immigrants, came to Botetourt from Shenandoah County. Later, he built his home, Beaver Dam. Allen, who served in the Revolutionary War as a youth, served as judge of the General Court of Virginia. At the time of his death in 1844, the house passed to his son John James Allen, who was also a judge. The younger Allen was an eminent jurist, serving as judge for the 17th Circuit Court before he was 40 years old (1836), as a US representative, and as judge of the Virginia Supreme Court of Appeals, of which he was president when he retired in 1865. Two of the judge's sons, George Jackson and Baldwin, both teenagers, were killed within weeks of each other during the Civil War. Allen died in 1871 and left Beaver Dam to his son John J. Allen II, who was also a judge. Since 1900, the Wickline family has owned Beaver Dam, operating one of the county's remaining dairy farms there. (Courtesy of VDHR.)

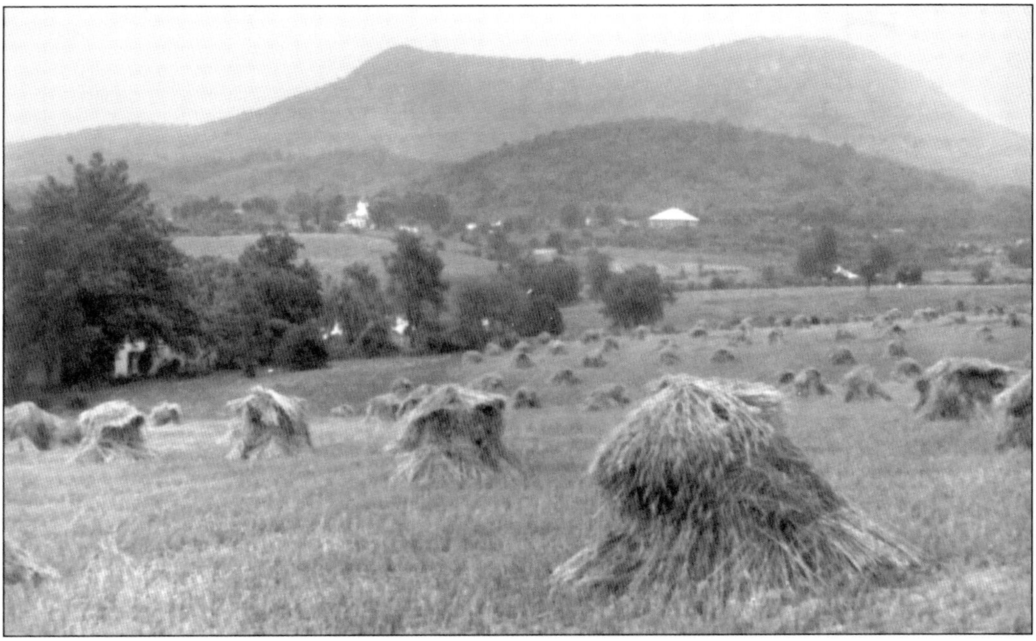

The Goodman family moved to the Roanoke Valley in 1867 and built their home, East View, near the present Hollins exit on Interstate 81. According to Helen Prillaman's history, Edward Carvin owned the farm in the early 1900s and then sold it to Christian Nininger. This view shows a field of shocked wheat on the Goodman farm looking north toward Tinker Mountain. (Courtesy of Hollins University, Wyndham Robertson Library Special Collections.)

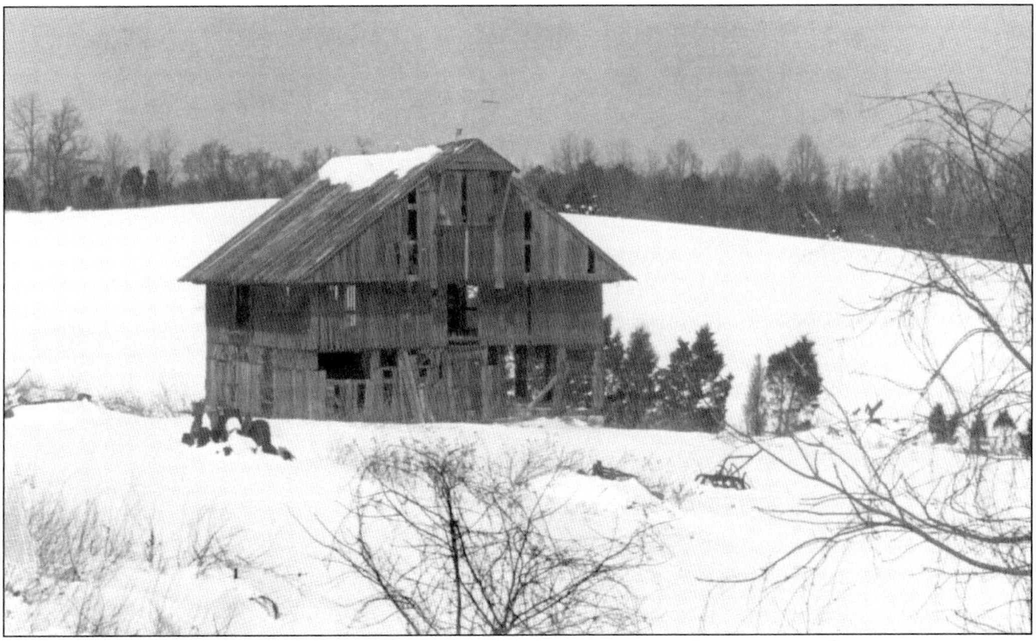

Like many of the state's rural counties, Botetourt is dotted with numerous barns. Most retain their historical use and have been enlarged or modernized, and some have been modified for other uses. Others have fallen out of use but remain as reminders of the agricultural heritage of the area. (Courtesy of the *Fincastle Herald*.)

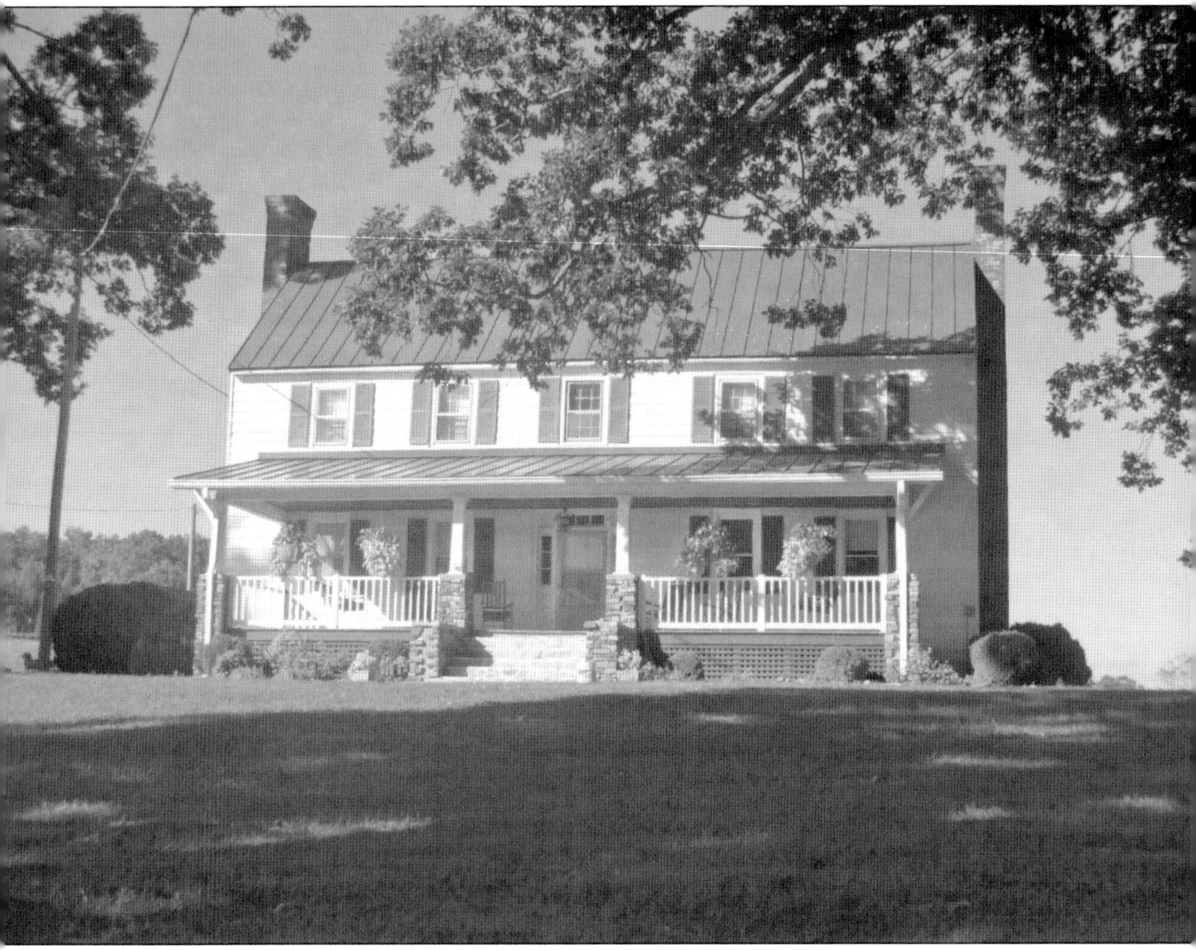

Collins and Jean Craft own Highland Grove Farm, located on Brughs Mill Road. It is registered as a Virginia Century Farm with the Virginia Department of Agriculture. A Century Farm is one that has been in the same family's ownership for 100 years or more. At present, Botetourt has 10 Century Farms, although many more likely also qualify for the honor. (Courtesy of the author's collection.)

Two

Artisans, Craftsmen, and Businesses

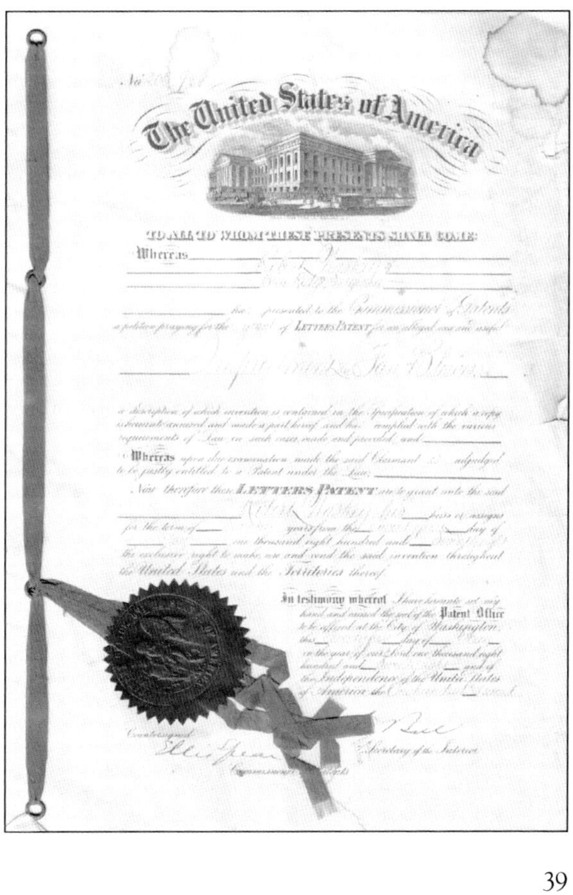

Brothers Robert and George Washington Waskey and Sam Obenshain operated the Waskey & Obenshain Mill in Springwood and the Arch Mill near Mill Creek. On May 21, 1878, Robert Waskey received federal patent No. 203,966 for his invention to increase the capacity and efficiency of industrial fan blowers. (Courtesy of BCHM.)

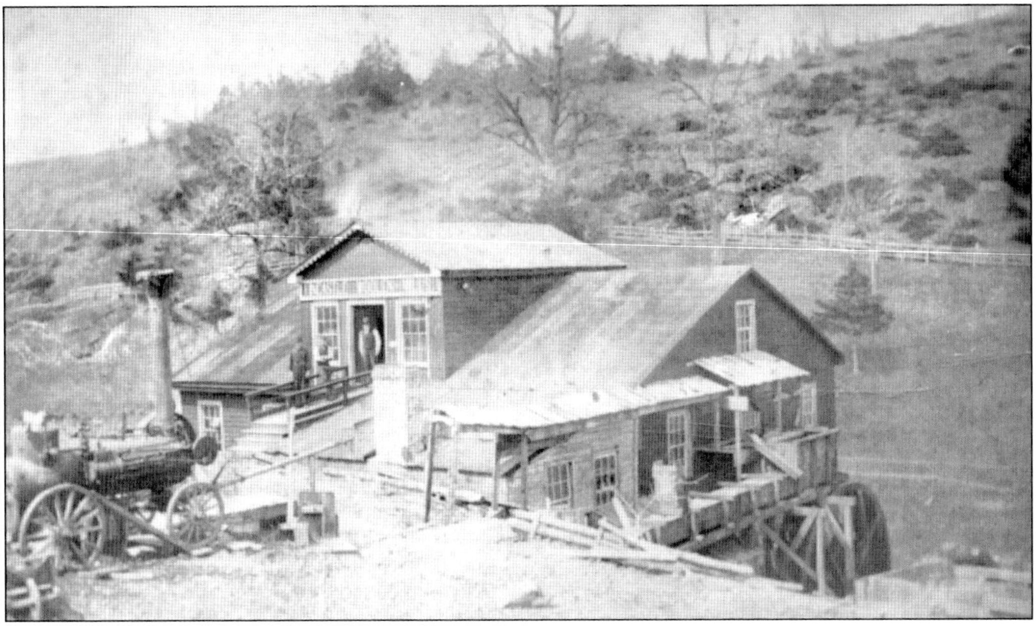

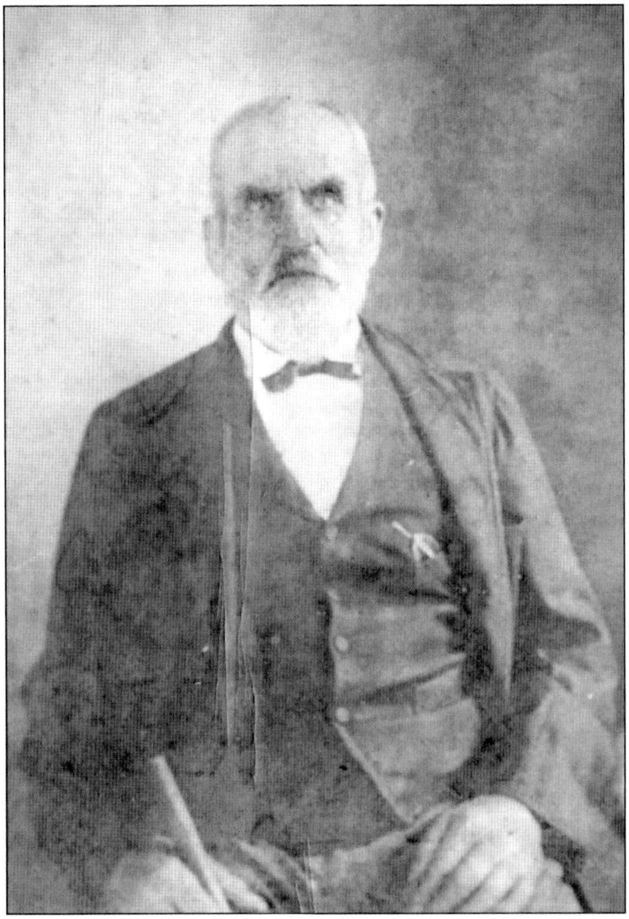

In 1749, Durst Ammen emigrated from Switzerland to Pennsylvania. Around 1784, he purchased a farm on Looney's Mill Creek. In 1826, Ammen's great-grandson Benjamin purchased Cross Mill from his father-in-law, Thomas Cross. This may have been the original Miller's Mill that predated the founding of Fincastle. At this site, he operated a gristmill, a sawmill, and a woolen mill (above). The Ammen Mill became famous for its Fincastle blanket patterns. At the time of Benjamin's death in 1867, his son Michael (left) operated the mill. The Botetourt County Historical Museum has an Ammen wool blanket on display. Benjamin and his wife, Naomi, are buried in the Fincastle Presbyterian Cemetery. Michael died in 1903 and is buried in Godwin Cemetery. Reports claimed that a fire in the mill resulted in the paralysis (possibly a stroke) that caused his death. (Both courtesy of BCHM.)

The local craftsmen in the community of Amsterdam, located along the Great Wagon Road, were well known for their carriages and furniture. The census lists William Keeling and his son Charles W. (pictured here) as coopers and furniture makers. Their split-bottom chairs were used in area homes and churches. Charles made the pews and choir chairs for the Amsterdam Methodist Church in the early 1930s. (Courtesy of BCHM.)

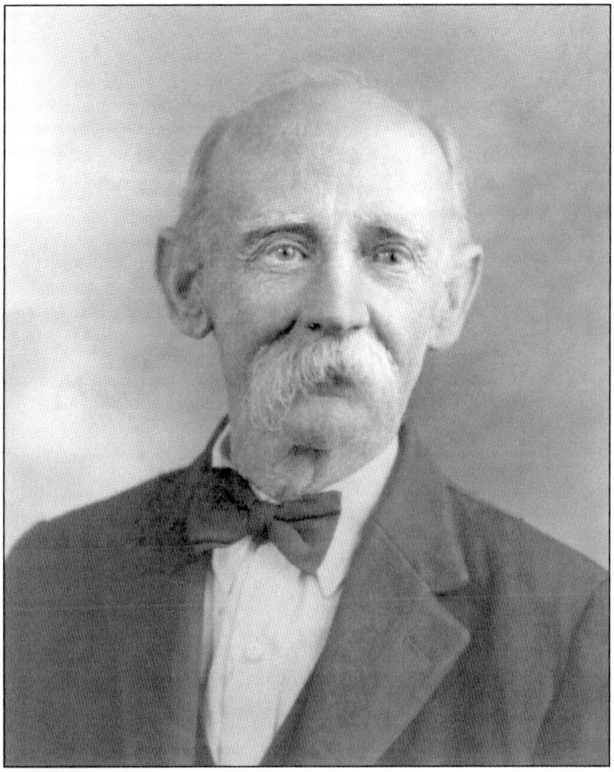

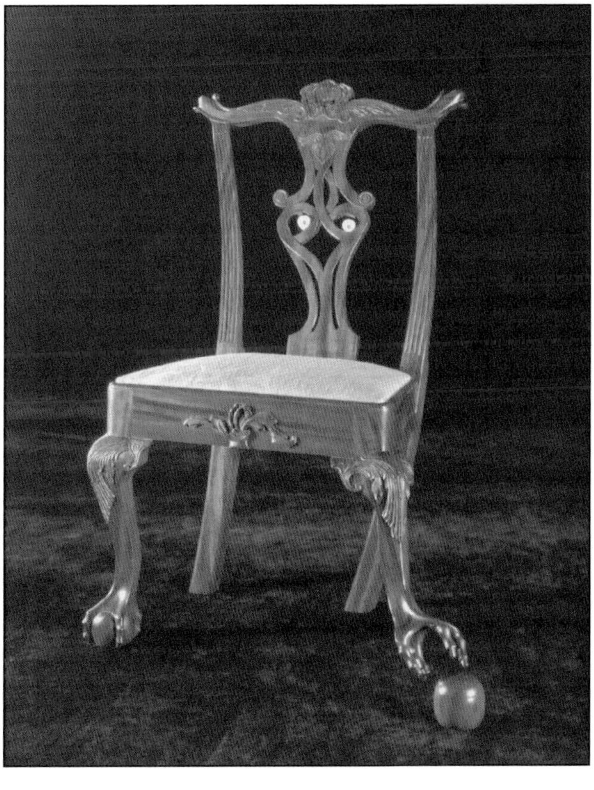

This mahogany chair, titled *Oops*, was hand-carved by Fincastle-based furniture maker Jacob Cress. The piece was part of the Renwick Gallery's 2004 exhibit Right at Home: American Studio Furniture, in Washington, DC. The show highlighted the originality, craftsmanship, and personalities of studio furniture artists. Cress calls these pieces "animated," but he also makes "normal" furniture in many styles. (Courtesy of Smithsonian American Art Museum, gift of the artist, ©1997, Jacob Cress.)

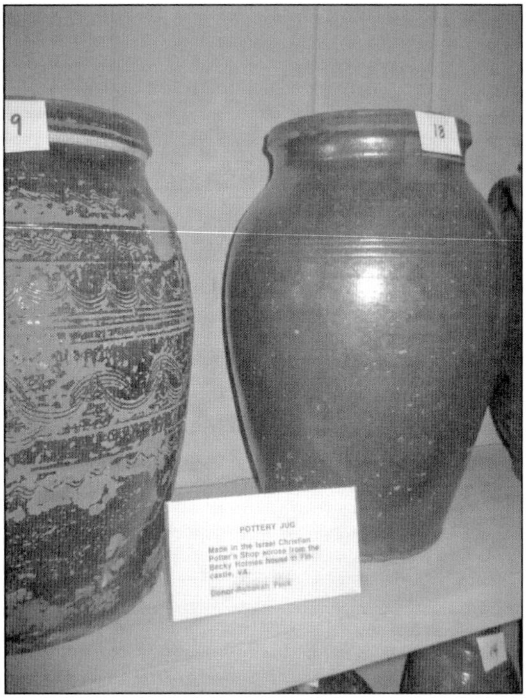

In the late 1800s, Botetourt was a significant pottery center for the region. At least 11 potters worked in the county during this period. They produced earthenware vessels from local clays that were then given a lead glaze to make them impermeable. Few of the vessels were signed, making identification difficult. The vessels shown at left were created by Israel Christian of Fincastle and exhibit freehand incised decoration. (Courtesy of BCHM.)

O.M. Bowyer's foundry and machine shop was located in Fincastle along the Town Branch, where the former Fincastle Mart stands (now a restaurant). Bowyer advertised that he was "prepared to do all kinds of repairing of machines engines, etc. . . . and to make any and all kinds of castings." The 1910 advertisement below was aimed particularly at the local farmers and canneries. (Courtesy of John E. Alderson Jr.)

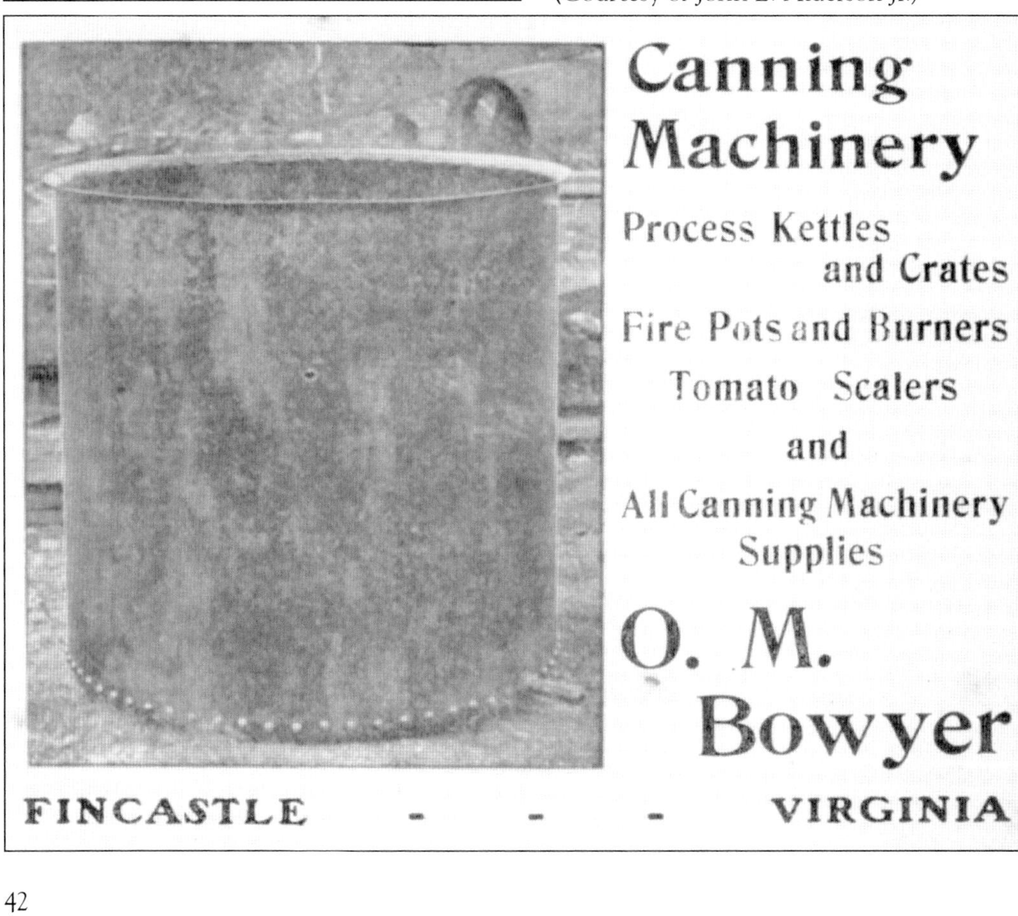

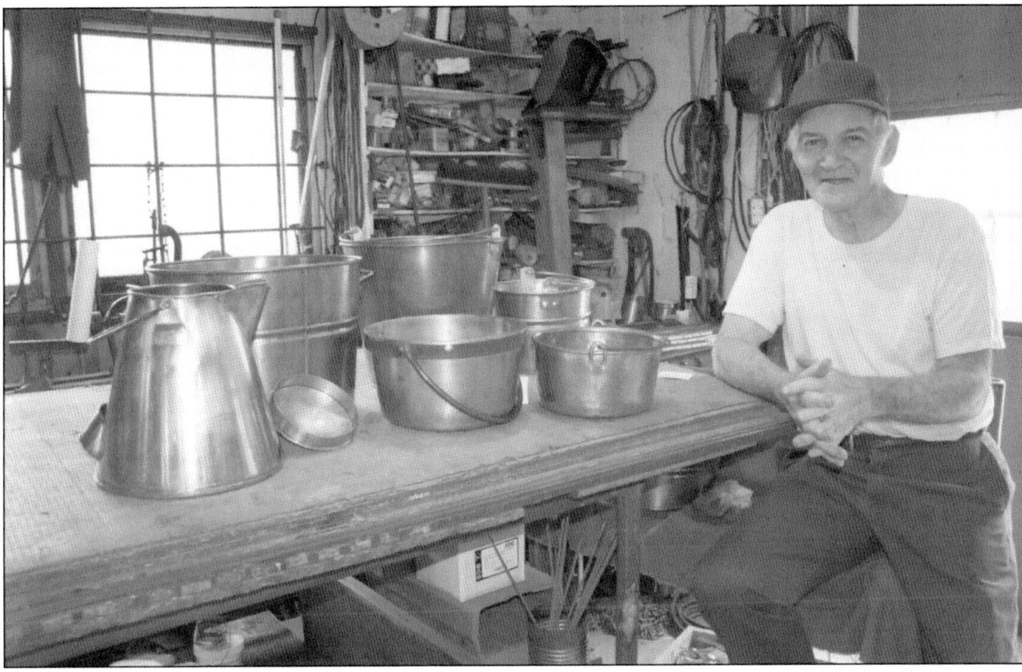

For over 30 years, self-taught coppersmith Porter Caldwell has operated Caldwell Mountain Copper in Fincastle. Caldwell and Faye, his wife of over 50 years, produce handmade copper kettles, buckets, and vessels. Caldwell hammers and shapes flat copper sheets into forms that are then hand-polished. The Caldwells design their own patterns but also produce vessels based on 18th-century patterns. Porter is seen above in his workshop with some of his finished products. The couple also takes their trade into schools for demonstrations. Below, the Caldwells display their vessels and describe the process to some county schoolchildren who are wearing period dress for the occasion. (Above, courtesy of Faye Caldwell; below, courtesy of the *Fincastle Herald*.)

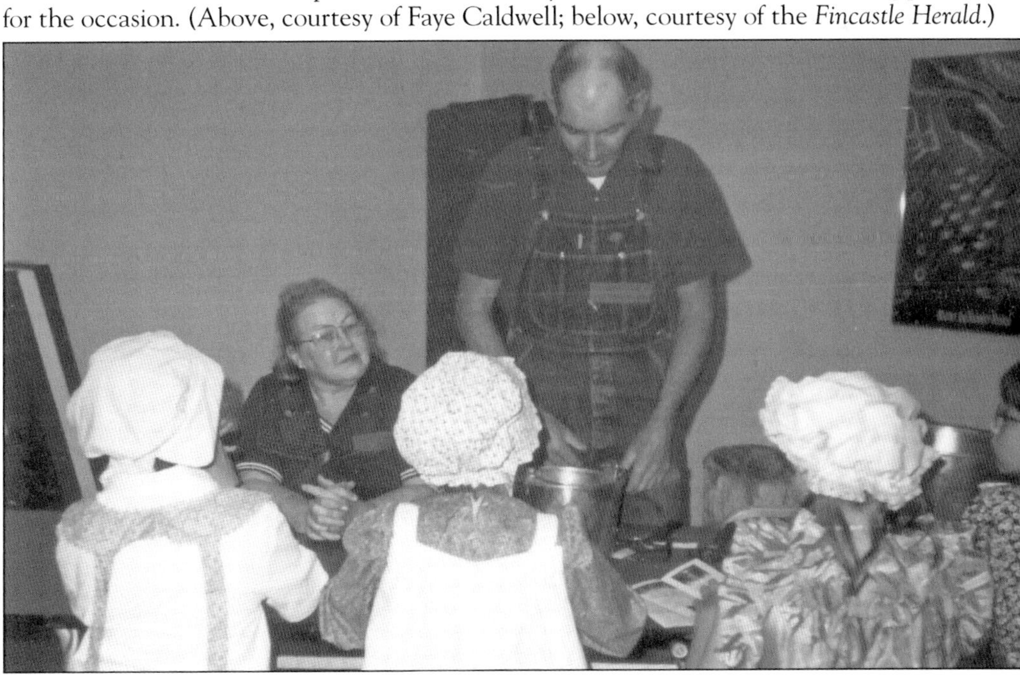

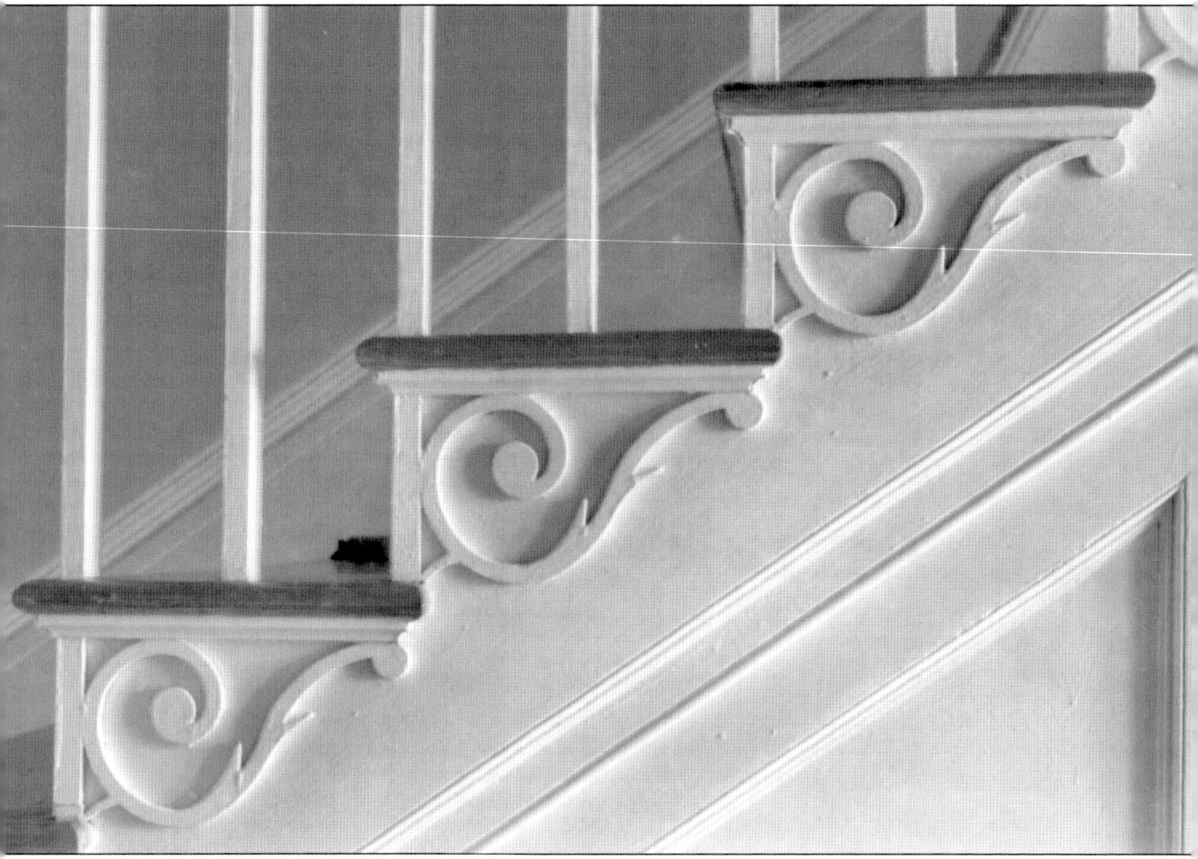

Many of Botetourt's early houses exhibit the craftsmanship of local carpenters and builders. These skilled workers created details in woodwork that reflected typical architectural styles, but some details also sprang from the carver's imagination. In 1824, Robert Harvey built his new home, Hawthorne Hall, north of Fincastle. The house reflects a refined design that illustrates many of the architectural trends adopted in the early 19th century by local builders for well-to-do property owners. Federal-style motifs are used throughout the house, including the decorative scroll brackets that embellish these stair treads. According to F.B. Kegley, Harvey established an ironworks in about 1787 and also owned grist and powder mills. He was also a county commissioner and a colonel in the local militia. He served two terms as a delegate to the Virginia General Assembly. The fashionable style of Hawthorne Hall would have reflected Harvey's prominence in the community. In the 1970s, George E. Holt Jr. and his wife, Elizabeth "Betsy" Stoner Holt, restored Hawthorne Hall and listed it in the National Register of Historic Places. (Photograph by Leslie A. Giles; courtesy of VDHR.)

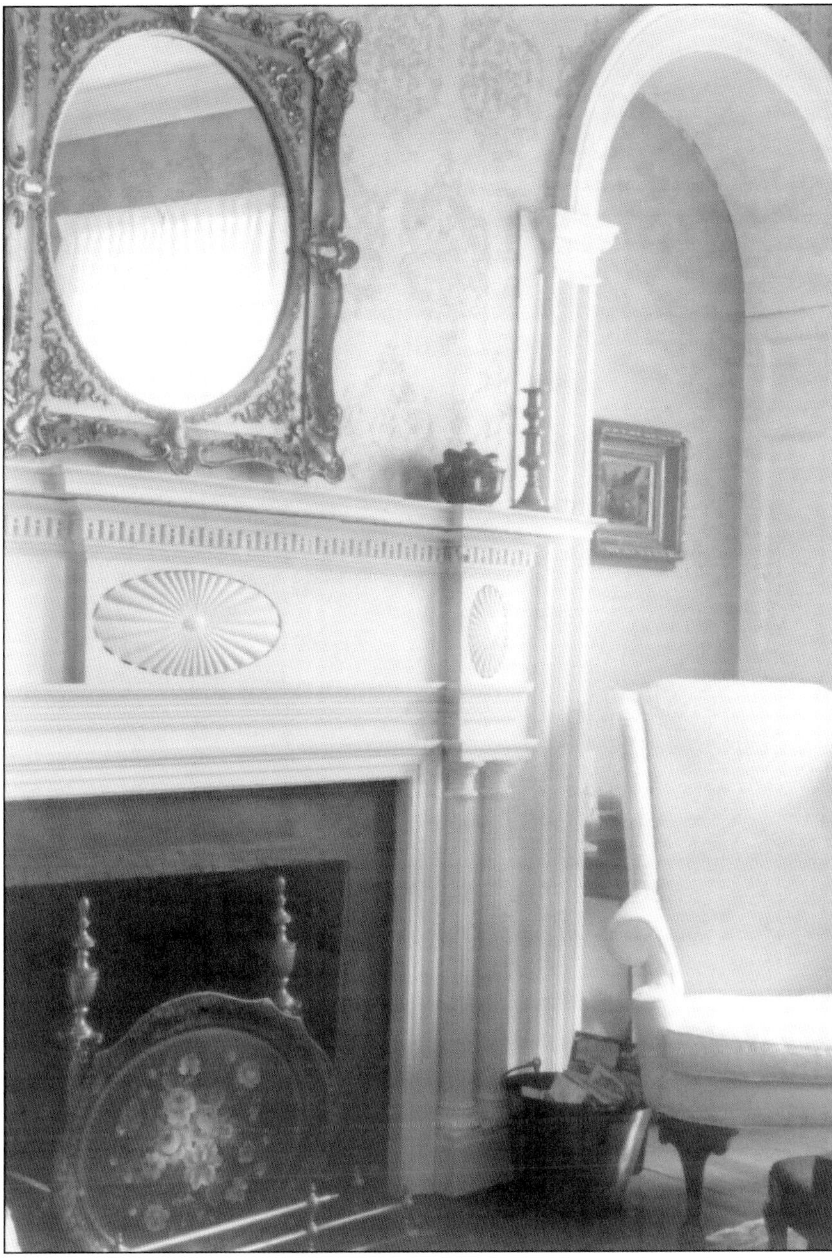

The plan of Hawthorne Hall was also influenced by Federal-period trends. It features a center hall with two rooms to either side. The center passage is divided into a front entry hall and a rear stair hall by an arched opening with side columns. The most detailed room in the house is the first-floor parlor, which would have been a public space and meant to impress visitors. Located at the front of the house, the parlor features an ornate fireplace flanked by arched niches with paneled reveals. The mantel incorporates numerous decorative elements, including paired fluted columnettes and sunburst motifs, which are hallmarks of the Federal style. Other rooms on the first floor include a study, a dining room, and a chamber (bedroom). The garret (half story) above holds four small bedrooms and a bathroom. (The exterior of Hawthorne Hall is shown in Images of America: *Botetourt County*.) (Photograph by Leslie A. Giles; courtesy of VDHR.)

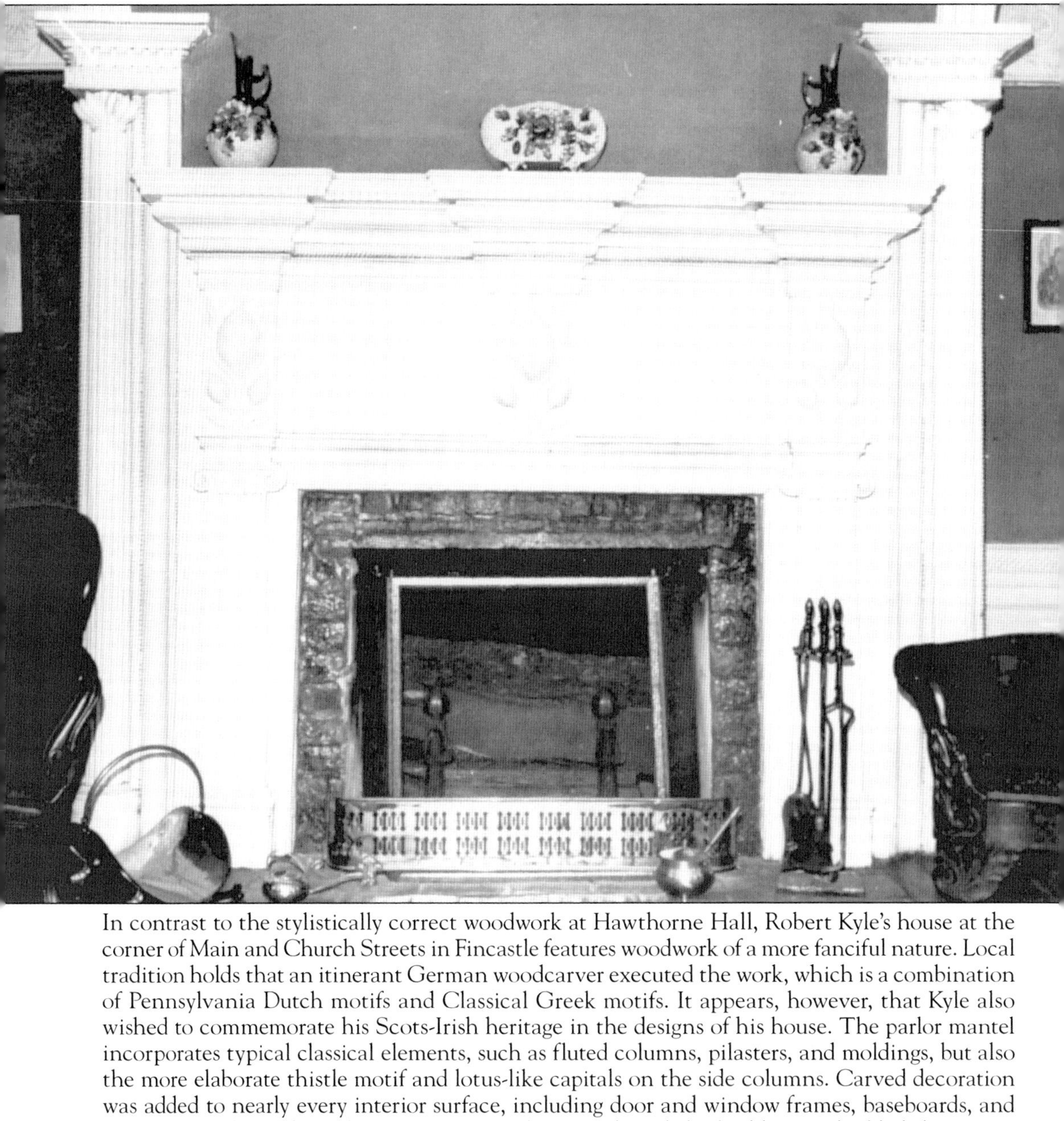

In contrast to the stylistically correct woodwork at Hawthorne Hall, Robert Kyle's house at the corner of Main and Church Streets in Fincastle features woodwork of a more fanciful nature. Local tradition holds that an itinerant German woodcarver executed the work, which is a combination of Pennsylvania Dutch motifs and Classical Greek motifs. It appears, however, that Kyle also wished to commemorate his Scots-Irish heritage in the designs of his house. The parlor mantel incorporates typical classical elements, such as fluted columns, pilasters, and moldings, but also the more elaborate thistle motif and lotus-like capitals on the side columns. Carved decoration was added to nearly every interior surface, including door and window frames, baseboards, and cornices. In the early 20th century, F.D. Bolton purchased the building and added the corner entrance for his store. (The exterior of the Kyle house is shown in Images of America: *Botetourt County*.) (Courtesy of VDHR.)

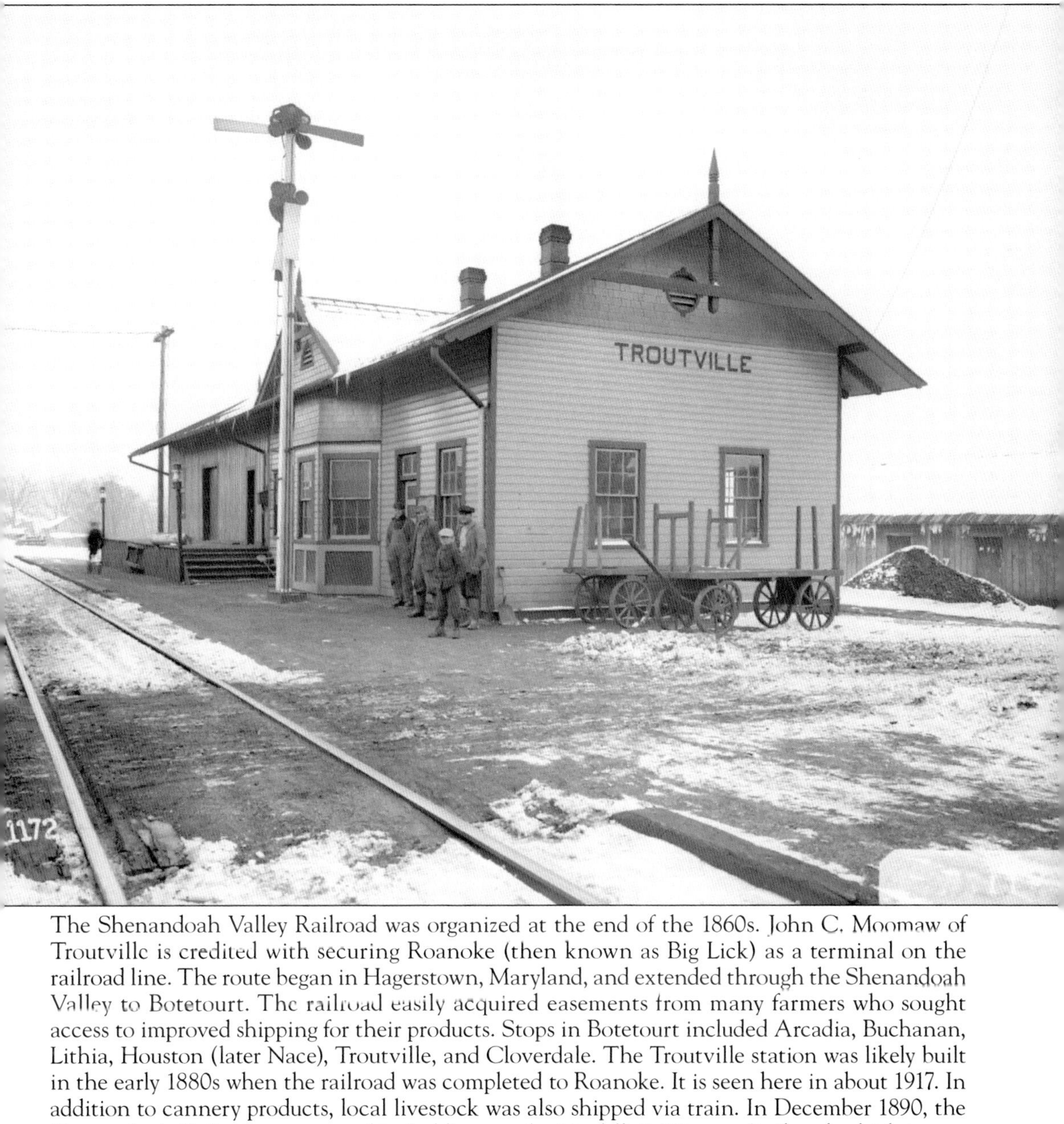

The Shenandoah Valley Railroad was organized at the end of the 1860s. John C. Moomaw of Troutville is credited with securing Roanoke (then known as Big Lick) as a terminal on the railroad line. The route began in Hagerstown, Maryland, and extended through the Shenandoah Valley to Botetourt. The railroad easily acquired easements from many farmers who sought access to improved shipping for their products. Stops in Botetourt included Arcadia, Buchanan, Lithia, Houston (later Nace), Troutville, and Cloverdale. The Troutville station was likely built in the early 1880s when the railroad was completed to Roanoke. It is seen here in about 1917. In addition to cannery products, local livestock was also shipped via train. In December 1890, the Shenandoah Valley line conveyed its holdings to the Norfolk & Western Railroad, which is now a part of the Norfolk & Southern system. (Courtesy of NWHP, DLA, VT.)

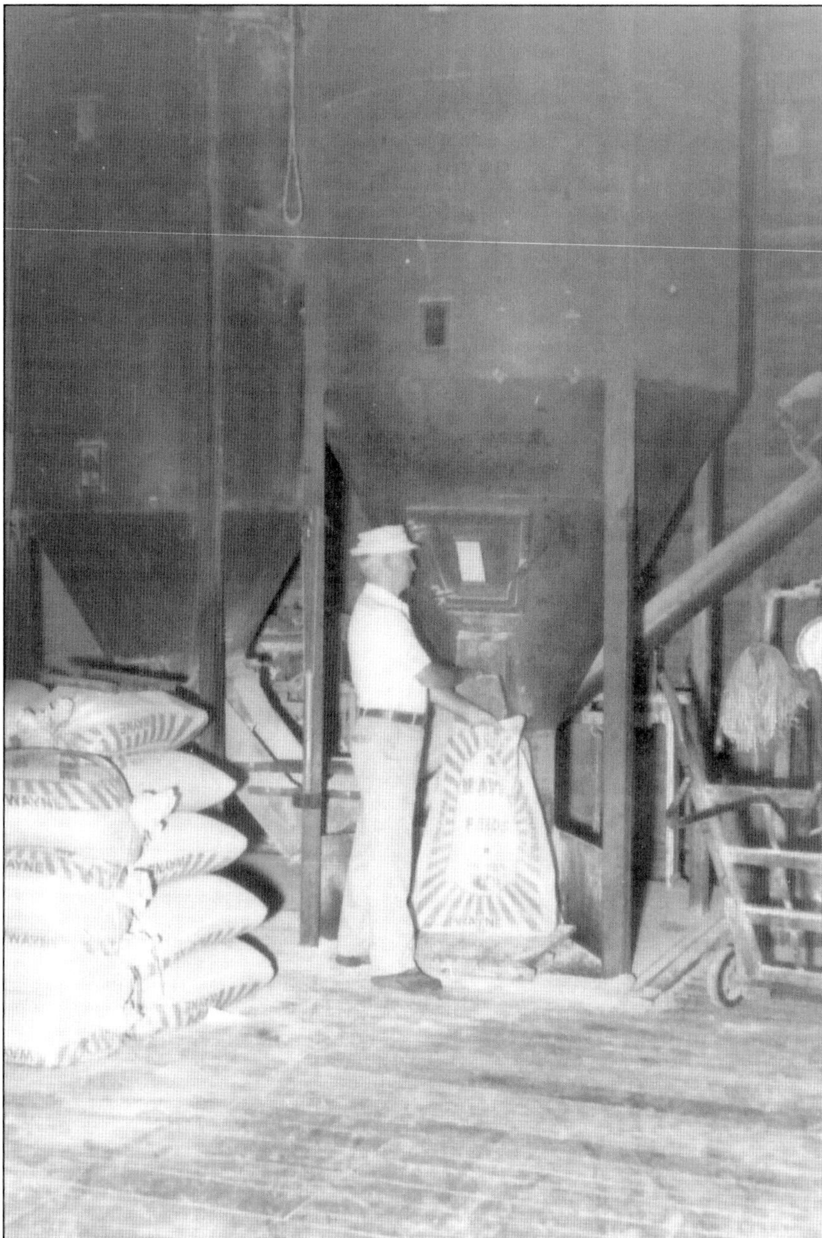

Numerous businesses that furnished farmers with supplies were located in Troutville. Along with the Virginia Can Company (originally Old Dominion Can), there were blacksmith shops, livery stables, and feed stores. In the 1920s, George A. Moomaw operated a feed store on the north side of Stoney Battery Road in Troutville. That store, also known as Wayne Feed Store, was torn down around 1950 to make way for the post office building. In the late 1940s, Jonathan and David Obenshain purchased land on the opposite side of the road, behind the train depot, and built another feed store. The Obenshains sold the enterprise to brothers Baron and George Beech in 1964. George is pictured here mixing feed at the store around 1977. The feed store remained in operation into the 1980s as Southern States Farm Supply. In 2013, the Pomegranate Restaurant occupied the building. (Courtesy of the *Fincastle Herald*.)

Whether considered an art or a craft, home cooking is a skill often handed down from generation to generation. Like her mother before her, Ann "Nannie" Godwin (right) of Fincastle kept a hardbound journal containing handwritten recipes. In 1859, Nannie married Charles Figgat, also of Fincastle, and the couple moved to Lexington. Her book includes recipes copied from Mary Randolph's 1824 book *Virginia Housewife*. Both family recipe books are now in the Peacock-Harper Culinary History Collections at Virginia Tech. In 1896, the Ladies' Aid Society of the Fincastle Presbyterian Church published *The Housekeeper's Friend* (below). The fundraising publication included recipes and everyday tips, such as what to do when one is struck by lightning and how to get rid of bugs. (Right, courtesy of the Smiley Collection, Special Collections, Washington & Lee University; below, courtesy of the Library of Virginia.)

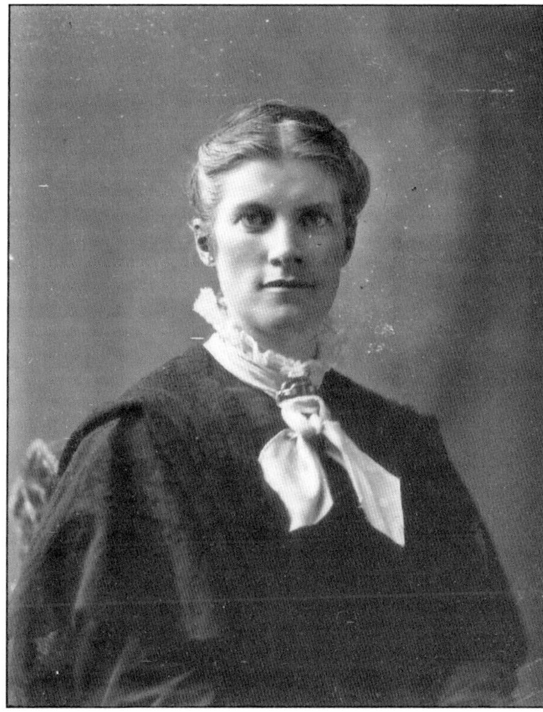

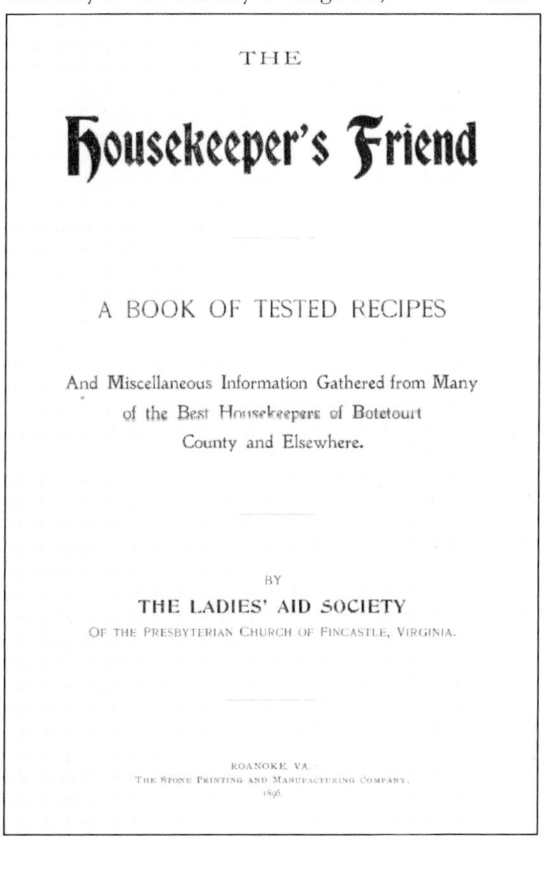

THE

Housekeeper's Friend

A BOOK OF TESTED RECIPES

And Miscellaneous Information Gathered from Many of the Best Housekeepers of Botetourt County and Elsewhere.

BY

THE LADIES' AID SOCIETY

OF THE PRESBYTERIAN CHURCH OF FINCASTLE, VIRGINIA.

ROANOKE, VA.:
THE STONE PRINTING AND MANUFACTURING COMPANY,
1896.

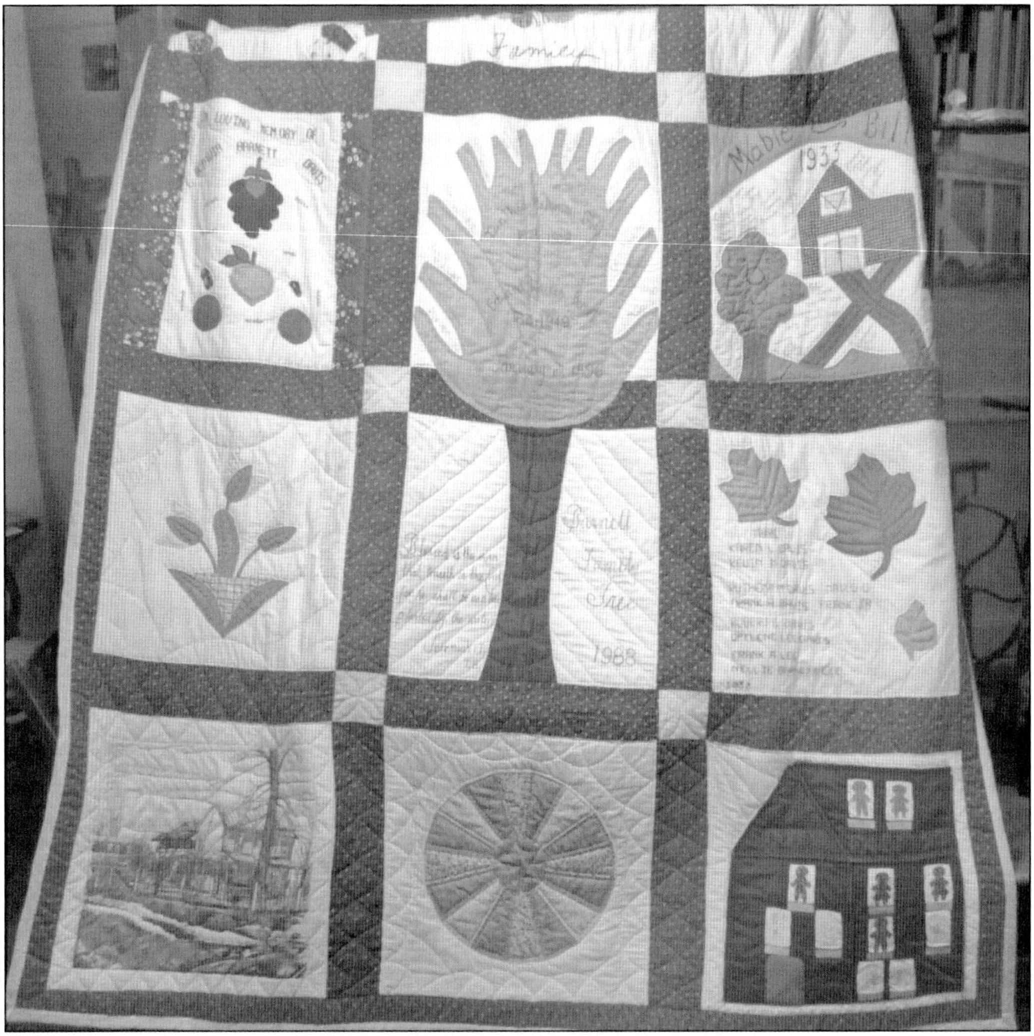

Early American households typically did not have quilts until the late 1700s. Imported material was expensive and scarce, and homespun fabric was used for other household items such as clothing. By 1800, with increased manufacturing that included cotton textiles, material became more affordable and social emphasis on domesticity made quilting popular. An individual generally did piecing or appliqué work, but quilting was often completed in a group gathering, sometimes called a quilting bee. "Flying geese," "winding blade," and "tree everlasting" are patterns that became popular during the 19th century. Quilts are also commemorative items. This quilt was completed in 1990 by the granddaughters of Edward and Ianthia Girty Barnett of Buchanan. The quilt squares represent the 10 children in the family. The quilters included Vivian Woody, Jeannette Brown, Betty Smith, Andrea Williams, Jackie Pierce, Judy Barnett, and June White. The quilt is now in the collections of the Botetourt County Historical Museum. The museum also has examples of candlewick bedcovers, an early-19th-century type of embroidery done with twisted cotton thread. (Courtesy of BCHM.)

In the 18th and 19th centuries, part of a young woman's training was learning to sew, often through completing embroidered or cross-stitched samplers. A marking sampler taught basic stitches, but also letters and numbers. Later, more decorative samplers were undertaken, and often framed. This 1798 sampler completed by Lydia Graybill is in the collections of the Botetourt County Historical Museum. (Courtesy of BCHM.)

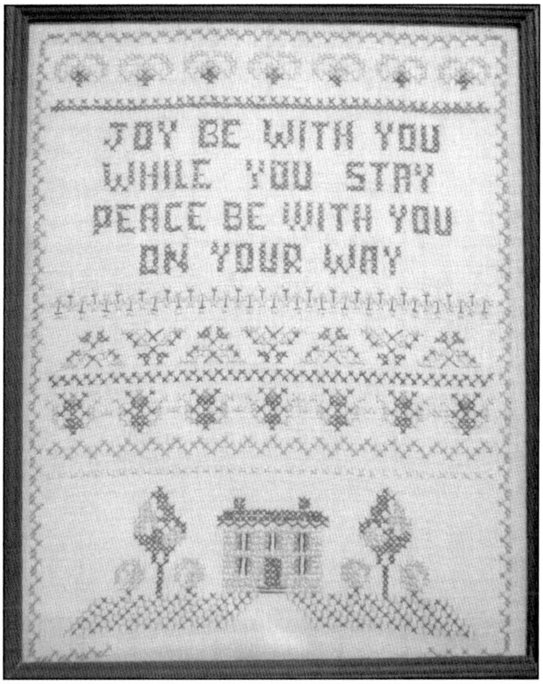

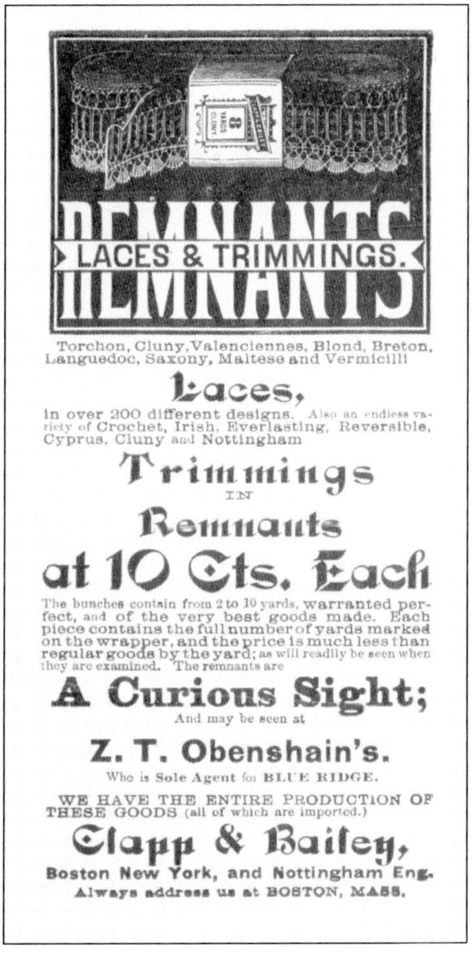

Zachary Taylor "Z.T." Obenshain, the son of "Hotel Sam" Obenshain, married Virginia Magdalene Thrasher in 1870. Z.T. operated a store, post office, and apothecary shop, as well as Arch Mill. In 1891, he built a new house, store, and post office at the corner of present-day Route 11 and Ridge Road. This advertisement lists the many fancy millinery trimmings carried at Obenshain's store. (Courtesy of BCHM.)

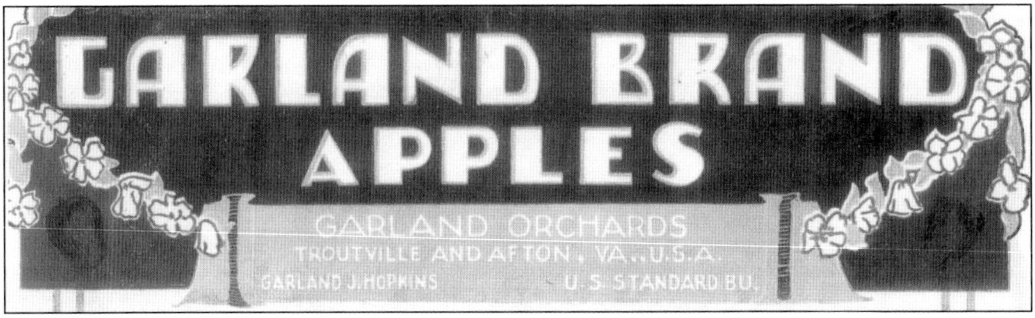

In 1911, Garland J. Hopkins started Garland Orchards under the name Garland Brand. He built a packinghouse in Troutville, purchased nearby apple orchards, and planted additional trees. Hopkins produced Delicious, York, Stayman, Winesap, Transparent, and Lowry (of Afton origin) varieties. After his death in 1949, his widow, Maude Logan Hopkins, and his son William began making cider and shipping apples to Winchester for cider. (Courtesy of BCHM.)

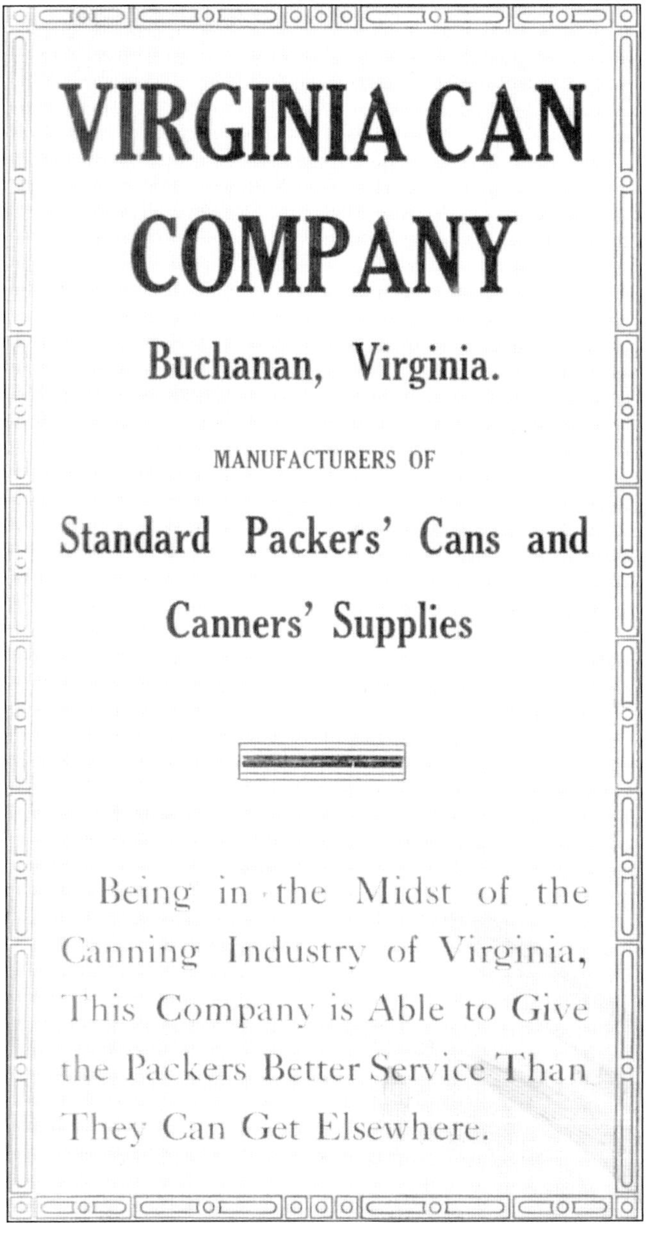

Canneries in Botetourt were able to acquire their supplies locally. Labels were available from the Piedmont Labeling Company in Bedford, and tins and wooden cases were available from the Virginia Can Company, which had plants in Buchanan, Troutville (formerly Old Dominion Can), and Roanoke. This advertisement ran in a 1910 county directory. (Courtesy of John E. Alderson Jr.)

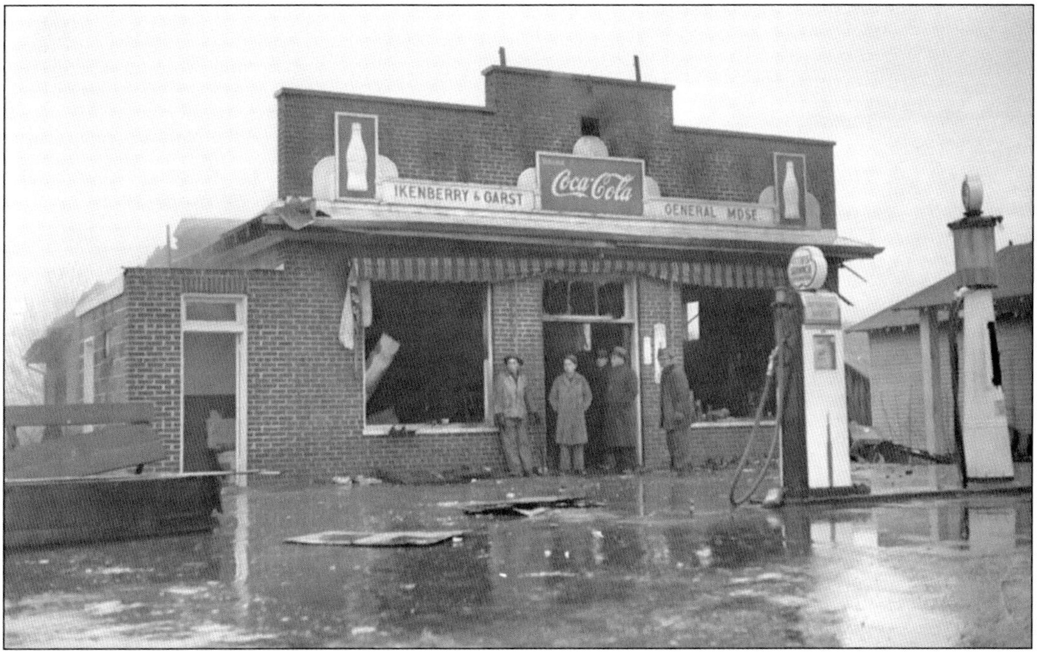

In 1934, Karl Ikenberry and Lawrence Garst opened their general merchandise store in Daleville. Garst married Karl's cousin Kathleen, the daughter of orchardist B.R. Ikenberry. Their store, at the corner of Routes 220 and 779, is seen above in 1941 after a fire gutted the building. The fire, likely cased by faulty wiring, occurred right before Christmas. Among the items lost in the fire were the Garst children's presents, which Lawrence had kept hidden there. Ikenberry and Garst then rebuilt the store larger than before. The photograph below shows the store in the late 1950s. Later, Jack Peck of Fincastle leased the store and ran it as The Village Market. Ben and Phyllis Garst operated the grocery store in the 1980s. The building still stands today and houses a variety of businesses. (Above, courtesy of JMU; below, courtesy of Phyllis Garst.)

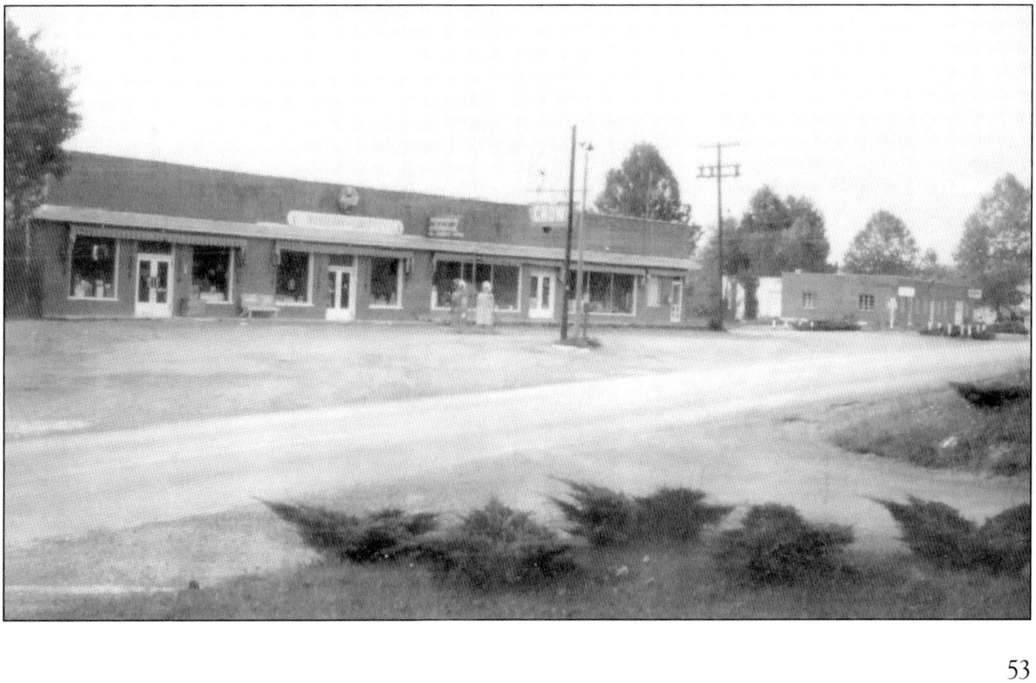

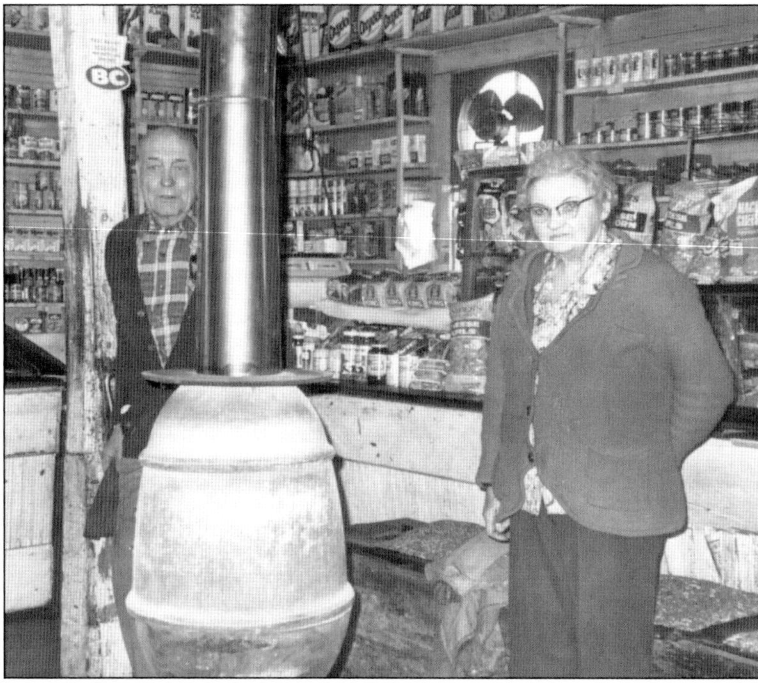

Herbert Marshall "Hub" Houseman's general mercantile store, located on Springwood Road, served much of the northern part of the county and even residents in neighboring Allegheny County. Although no longer in use, the building still stands in the bend of the road next to the old Houseman home place. Here, "Hub" and his wife, Lucille (née Camper), are seen inside the store in the mid-1980s. (Courtesy of the *Fincastle Herald.*)

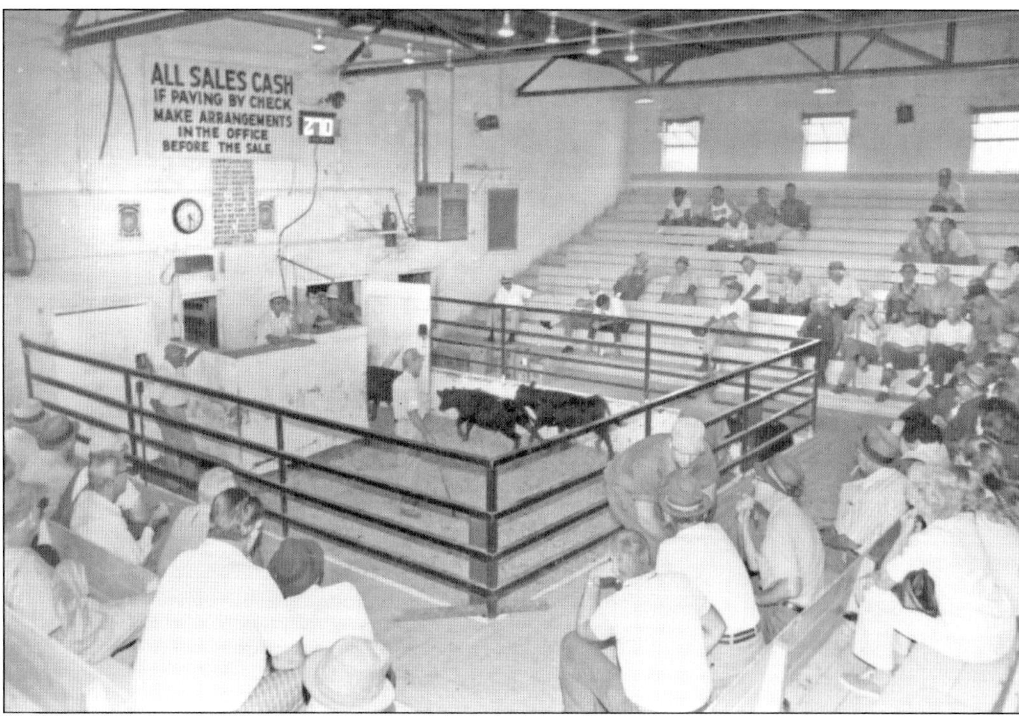

Organized cooperative marketing for beef cattle, a concept pioneered by lamb producers, began in the 1930s. Cattle auction sales first occurred at breeders' farms; then, in the 1940s, feeder calf auctions opened. The Roanoke-Hollins Stockyard, established at that time, began as a purebred sales pavilion. Morris Fannon of Lee County was the first auctioneer, retiring in 1959. This photograph shows the stockyard auction around 1975. (Courtesy of the *Fincastle Herald.*)

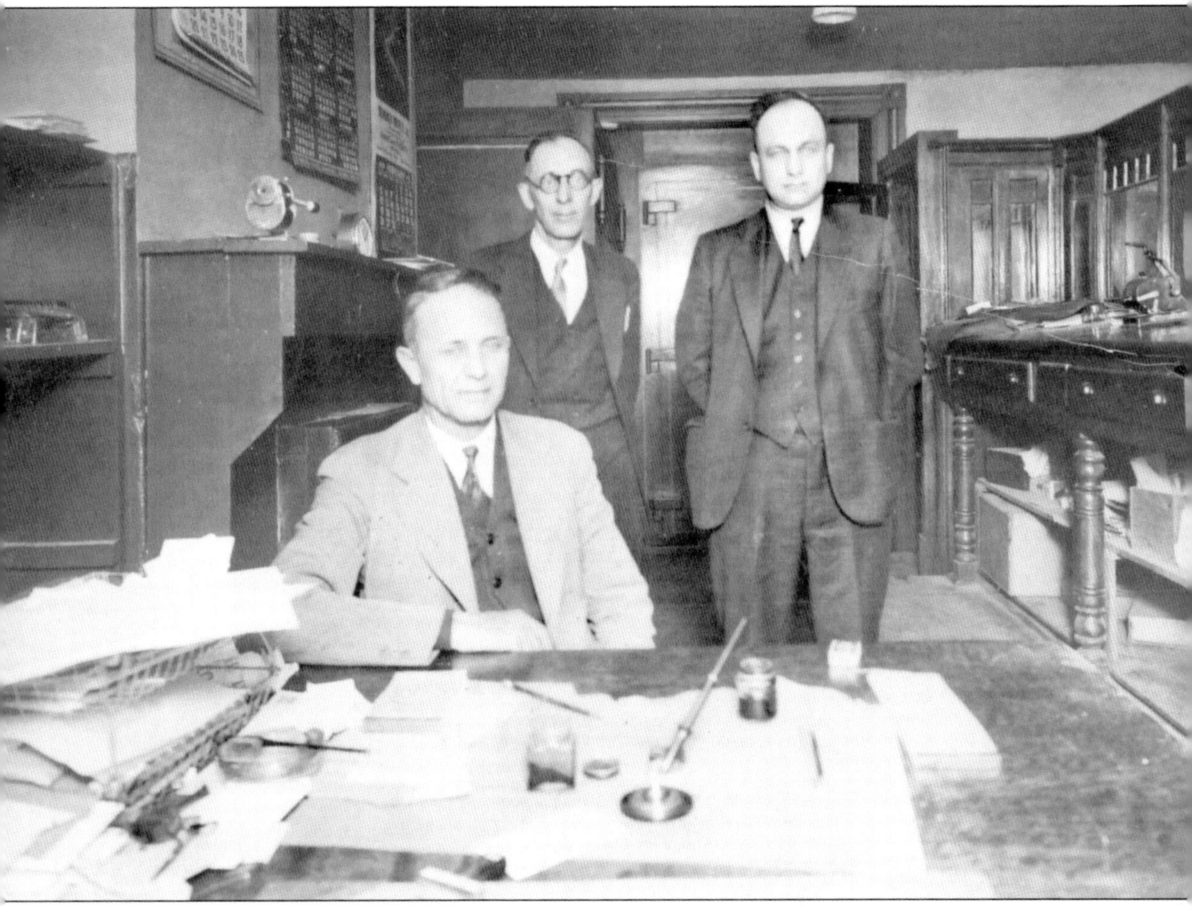

Dennis Urban Austin was the Botetourt County treasurer from 1924 to 1940. Austin was a World War I veteran and an honors graduate from Virginia Tech. He owned the D.U. Austin Lumber Company and D.U. Austin Canneries. In 1924, he married Mary Burger of Natural Bridge, and they had three children. Mary attended Daleville College and Madison College and was a charter member of the Fincastle Garden Club. Their son Dennis Jr. served with the Army's military police in Japan during World War II and went on to be a successful Roanoke realtor. Their other son, John William II, was active in local historical and genealogical groups and, with his wife, Rebecca, published *Related Families of Botetourt County* and other books pertaining to Botetourt history. Their daughter Katherine Parker worked for Life of Virginia and lived in Richmond. Dennis Sr. is seen here, seated in his office with deputy treasurer Otho Henry Brewbaker (left). Following Dennis Sr.'s death, his brother John (right) took the office of county treasurer, serving from 1940 to 1964. (Courtesy of BCHM.)

JOHN W. LAYMAN

TROUTVILLE, VA.

Grower and Packer of

FRUITS AND VEGETABLES

"Red Rose" Brand

Specialties: TOMATOES, APPLES and WHITE CHERRIES

Also Grower of fine Winter Apples. Any one in need of any of my productions I would be glad to correspond with them

John W. Layman was the first president of the Farmers and Canners Bank, founded in 1907. When the bank reorganized in 1910 as the First National Bank of Troutville, Layman again served as president. He was also a farmer and fruit grower and one of the county's pioneers in the cannery business. This advertisement for his farm products was in the 1910 county directory. (Courtesy of John E. Alderson Jr.)

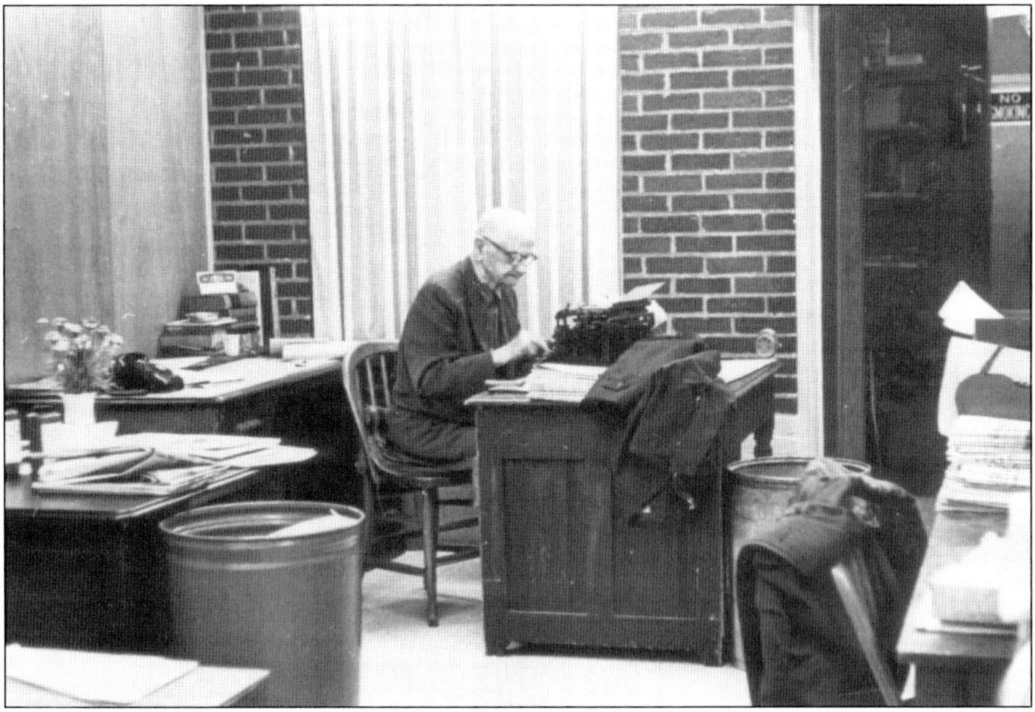

In January 1866, editors John T. James and Thomas D. Houston first published the *Fincastle Herald*. In the early 1800s, newspapers had been printed in Fincastle and Buchanan, but none survived. The *Herald*, however, proved successful. The Camper family edited the paper from 1869 to 1932, when Clyde Hubert Rieley purchased it. Seen here at his *Herald* desk, Rieley remained editor until 1970. (Courtesy of the *Fincastle Herald*.)

Three

Students and Teachers, Schools and Churches

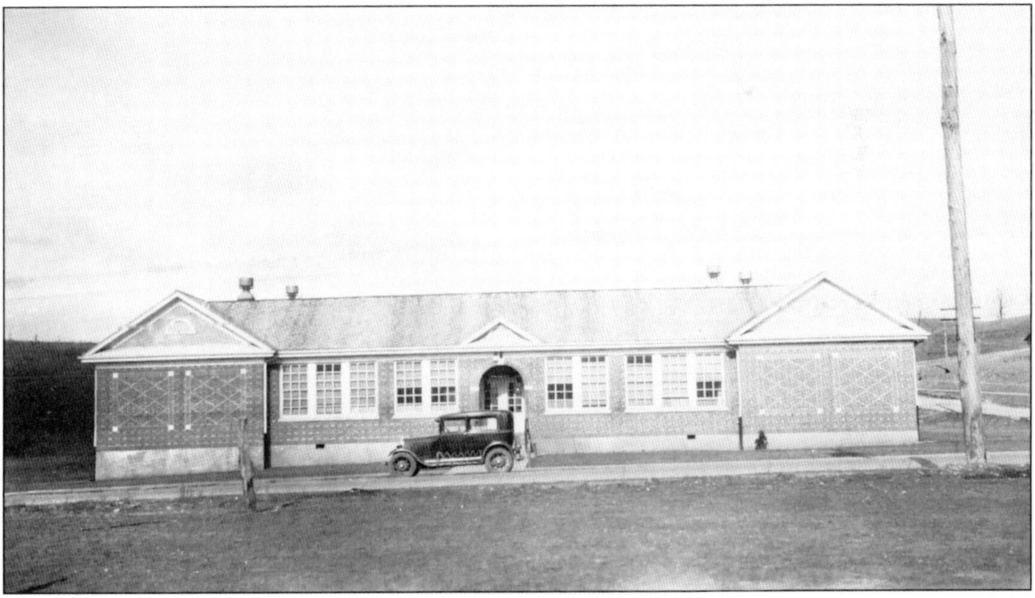

This photograph shows Troutville High School in 1930, soon after its completion. The land for the school was deeded by John W. and Elizabeth Layman. Land on the opposite side of Route 11 held the baseball field and other sports facilities. That area is now Troutville Town Park. The class of 1959 was the last to graduate from Troutville. Afterward, students attended Lord Botetourt High School in Daleville. (Courtesy of the Library of Virginia.)

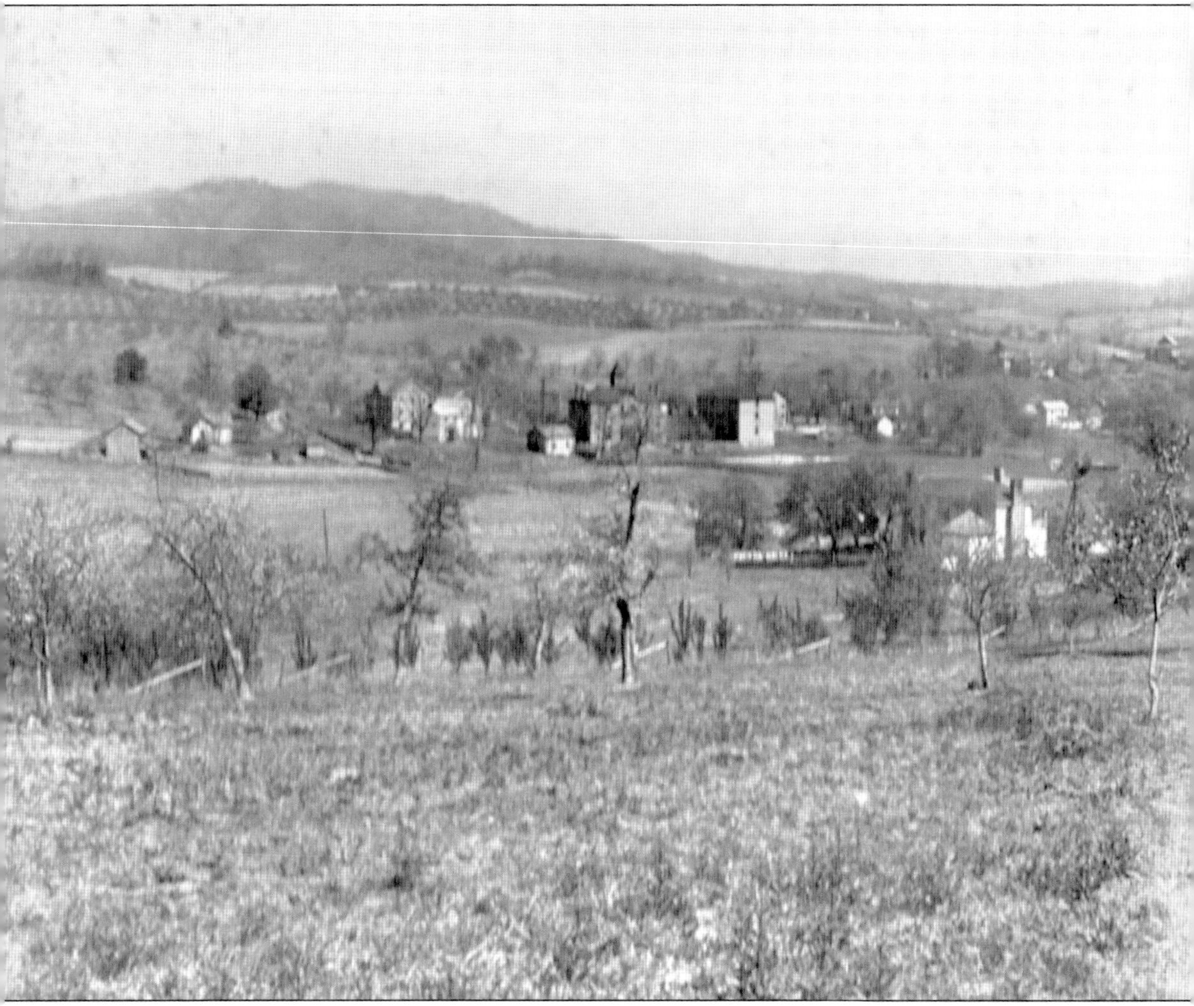

The community of Daleville, in the southern part of Botetourt, grew up around Peter Nininger's late-18th-century mill, located along the waters of Tinker Creek. Initially known as New Amsterdam, members of the Dunkard faith moved there, including the Layman, Moomaw, and Gish families. In addition to becoming the site of Botetourt's only four-year college, Daleville was an important area for orchards, including those of the Nininger, Layman, Moomaw, and Ikenberry families. This image looking east toward Daleville dates to about 1905. It shows buildings of Daleville College in the center and the orchards of Benjamin Nininger in the foreground and on the hills beyond, where the Orchard subdivision is now located. Today, Lord Botetourt High School is located just north (left) of the Daleville College site. Ikenberry Orchards, about one mile north of this site, continues to operate today. (Courtesy of Bridgewater College Special Collections.)

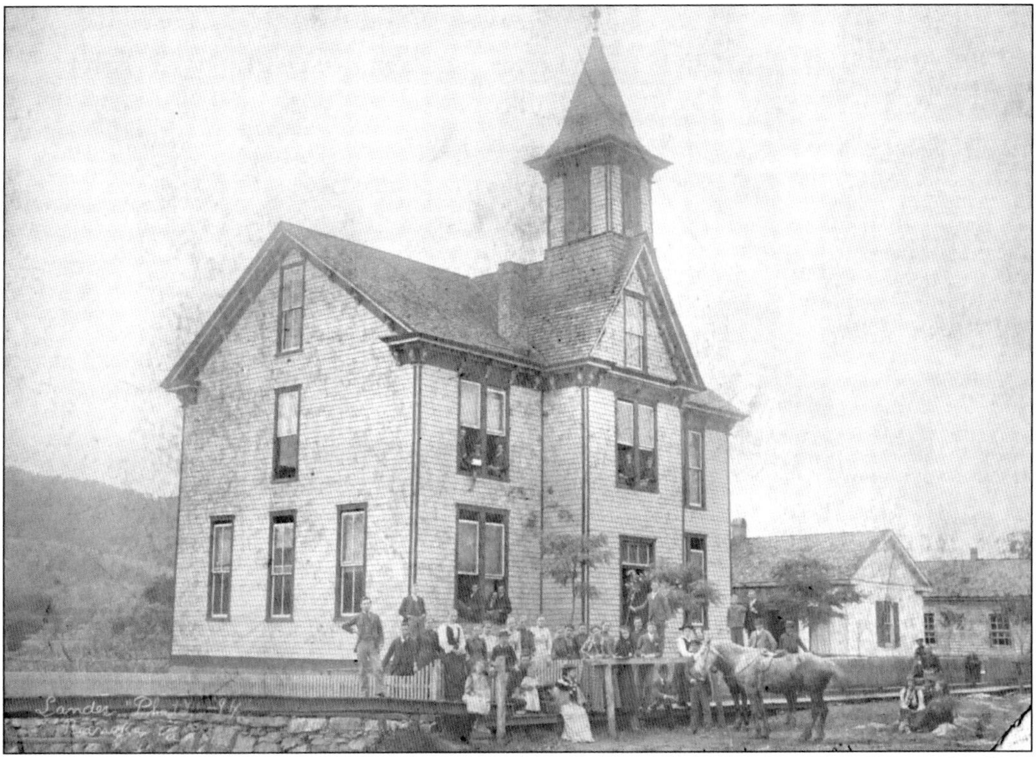

In 1890, the Layman and Nininger families of Daleville began a "select," or private, school for their children. The school was soon open to students outside of the two families. In 1893, it became the Botetourt Normal School and began offering more courses and training for teachers. According to school histories, the Daleville school served a local need for educators and was met with a warm response. The first school building is seen above in 1891; it later became the boys' dormitory before burning down in 1903. The principal's frame house is visible to the right. The photograph below shows students and faculty in 1892. At the time, the school had 73 students and four teachers. (Both courtesy of Bridgewater College Special Collections.)

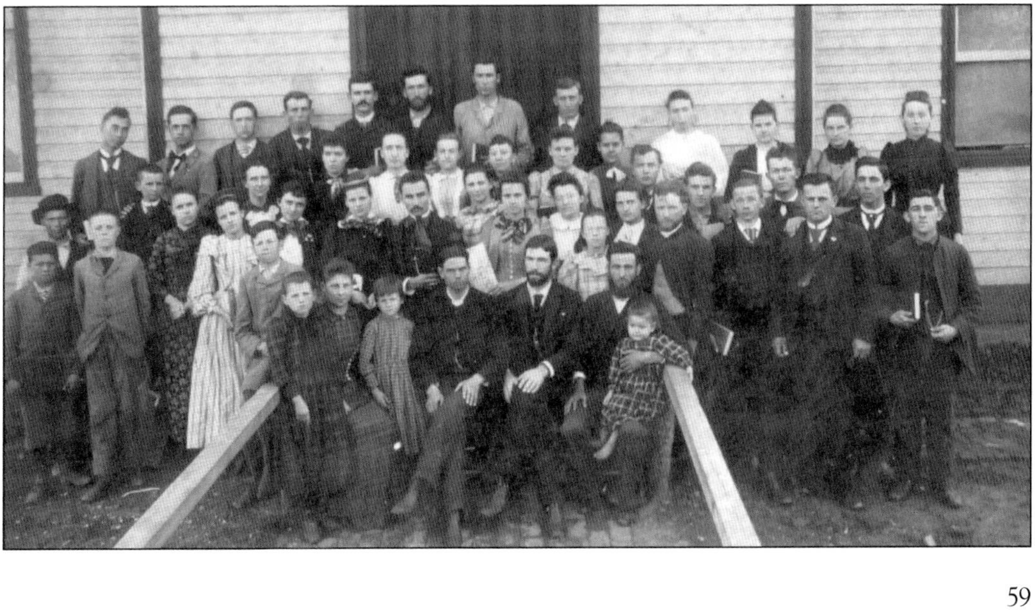

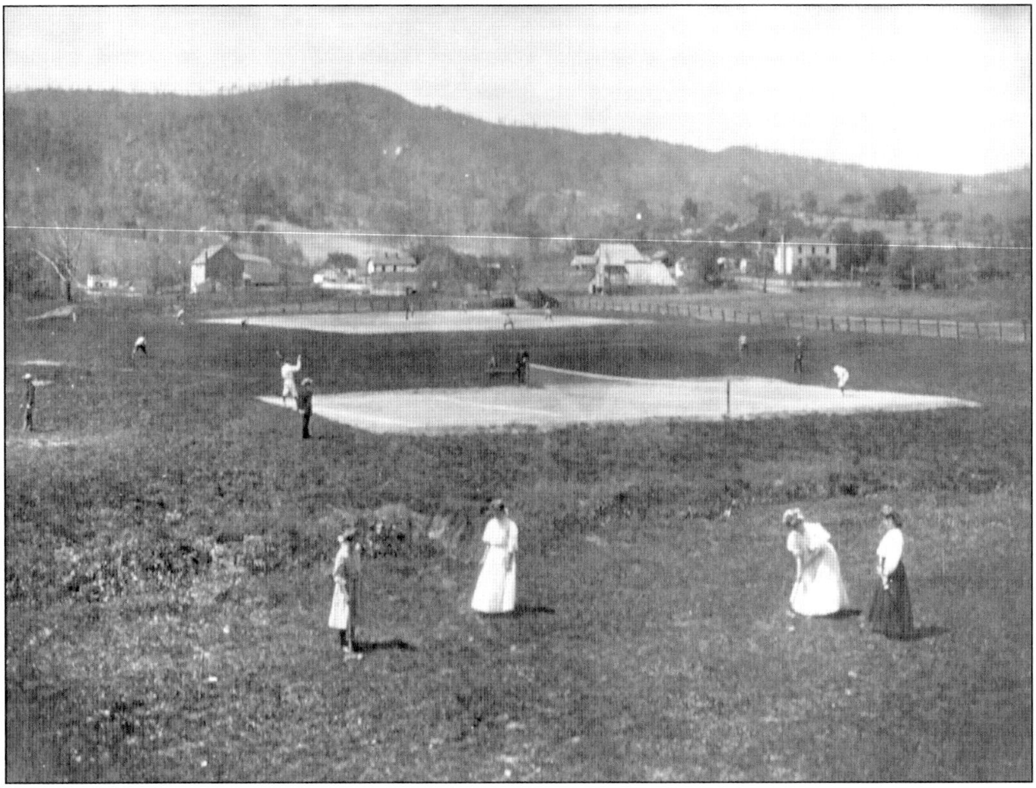

This view looking west toward Tinker Mountain shows the athletic fields at Daleville College. The fields included croquet and tennis courts and baseball diamonds. Physical activity was always part of the curriculum, and the school offered numerous organized sports. In 1911, a gymnasium was constructed that was also used for the school's many lectures, plays, and public-speaking presentations. (Courtesy of Bridgewater College Special Collections.)

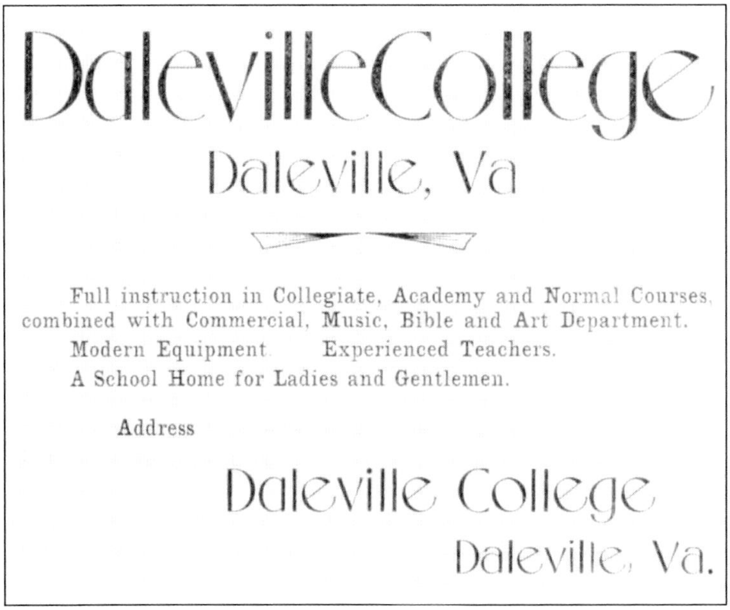

This 1910 advertisement for Daleville College outlined the advantages of the school and its curriculum. The school aimed to provide an education based on "moral and religious principles, as well as by good scholarship." The college offered courses in English, Latin, elocution, the Bible, music, commercial (law and salesmanship), and art. Later, courses included foreign languages, home economics, history, and business. (Courtesy of John E. Alderson Jr.)

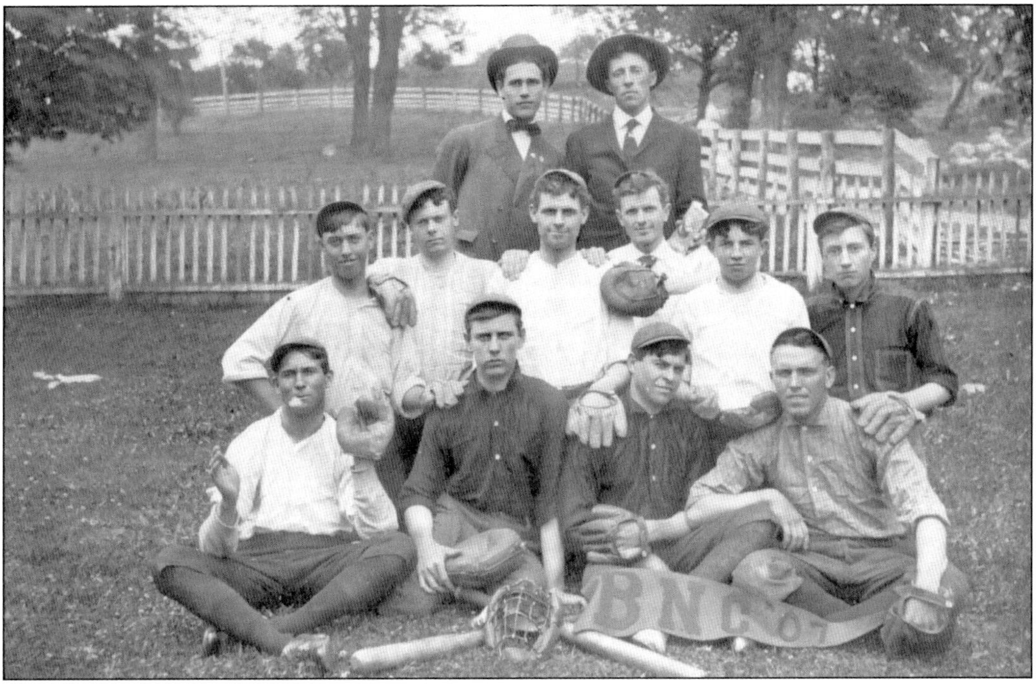

The Botetourt Normal School enjoyed great success during its first decade. As its student population grew, buildings were added to the campus. Nininger Memorial Hall, a dormitory for girls, was completed in 1909. A new home for the president and new electrical systems were also installed. As students desired more advanced classes, the decision was made to extend the curriculum to include college-level studies. Between the spring and fall of 1910, the school became Daleville College and began conferring college degrees. The 1907 baseball team (above) sports the BNC (Botetourt Normal School) pennant. Below is the 1911 ladies' tennis team from Daleville College. (Both courtesy of Bridgewater College Special Collections.)

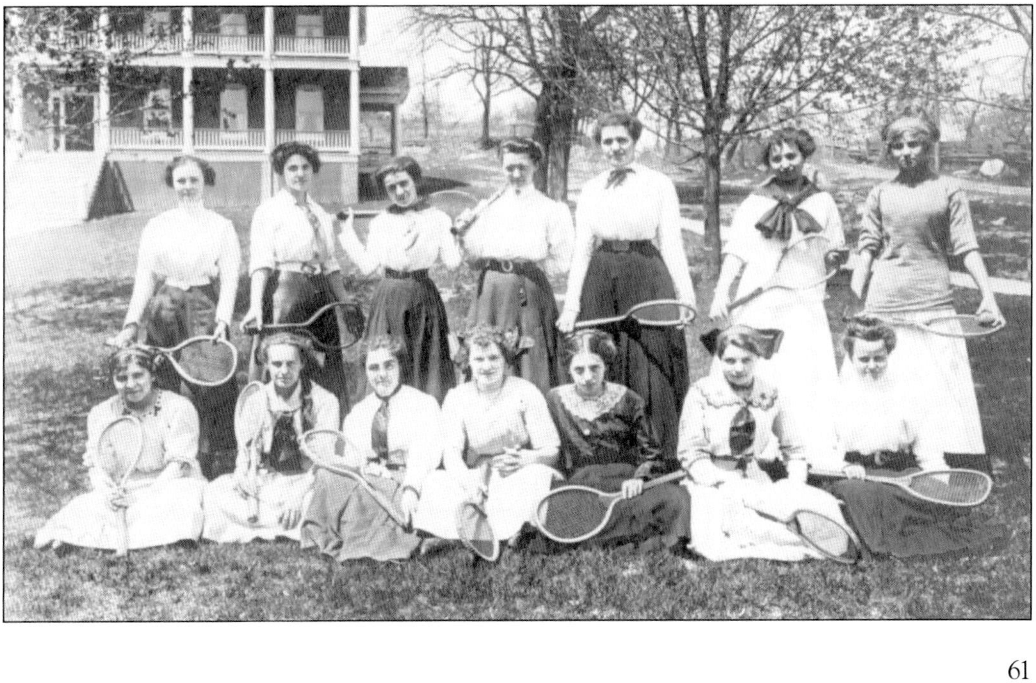

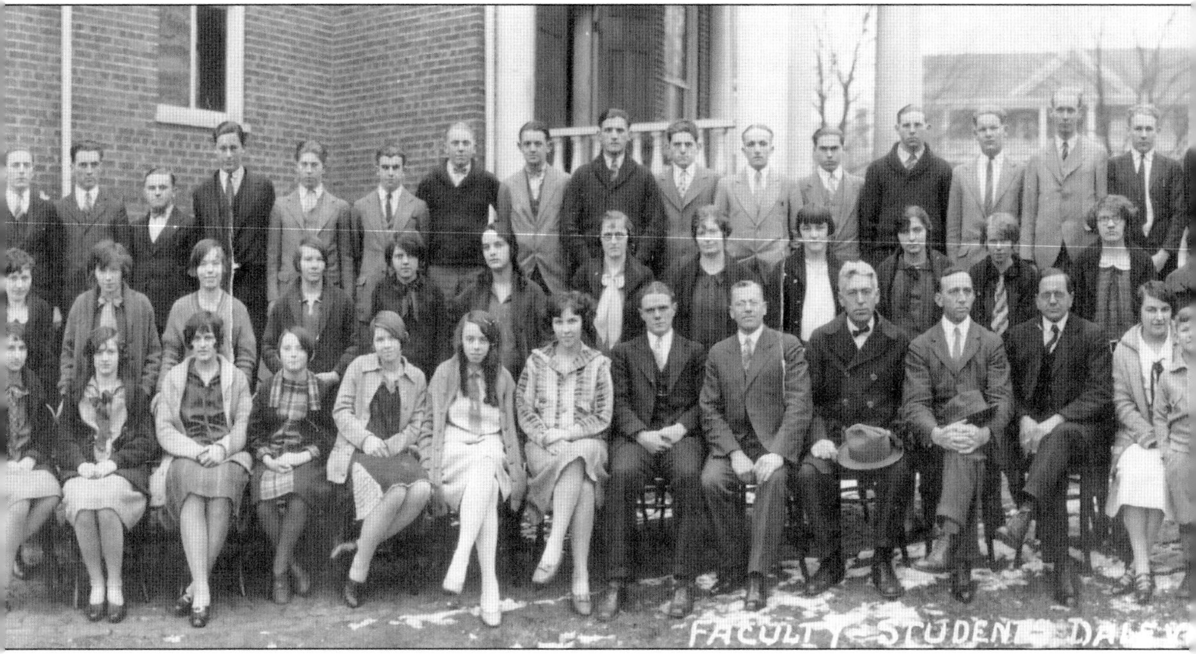

In 1912, Daleville College became associated with the Virginia Church of the Brethren. In 1914, the school was accredited as a full junior college. As early as 1918, negotiations had begun between Daleville College and Bridgewater College, also a Church of the Brethren affiliate. In 1923, the final consolidation was completed. The reorganization standardized the departments of the school, and it operated under the same management. By 1924, high school courses were

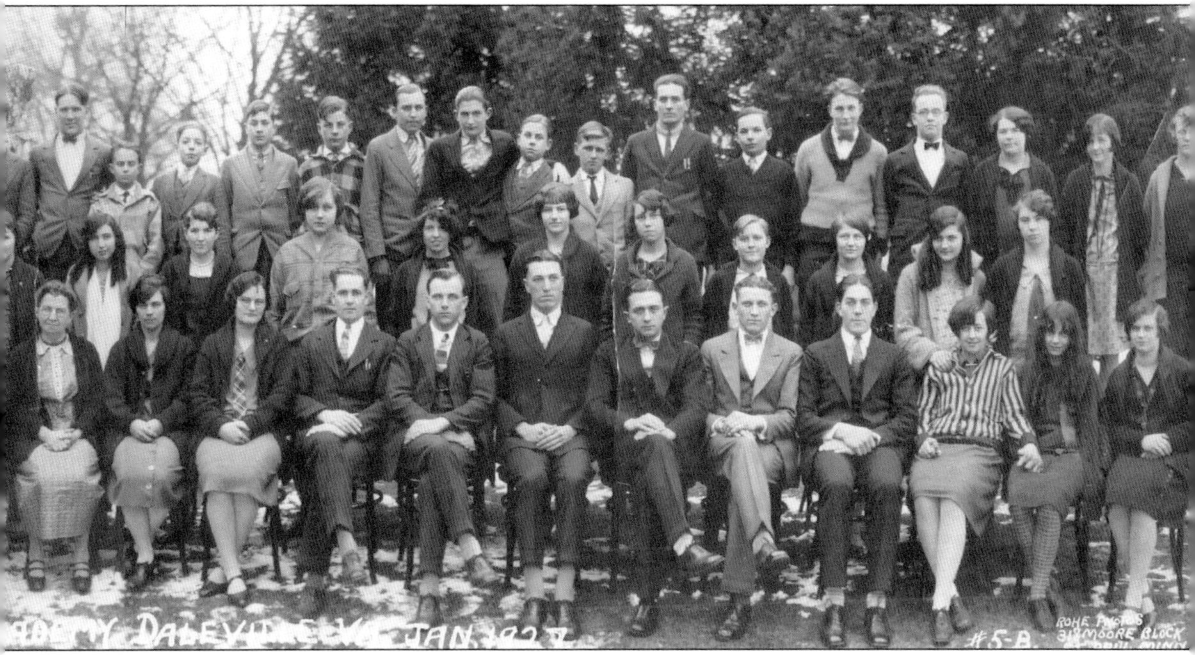

taught at Daleville and all college courses were taught at Bridgewater. This photograph shows the faculty and students in 1927 in front of the Central Building (left) and Nininger Memorial Hall (center). Among the faculty seated in the first row is Charles S. Ikenberry (center, left of the woman and child), who was a graduate of Daleville and Boston University and was the dean of the Department of Bible and Religious Education at Daleville. (Courtesy of BCHM.)

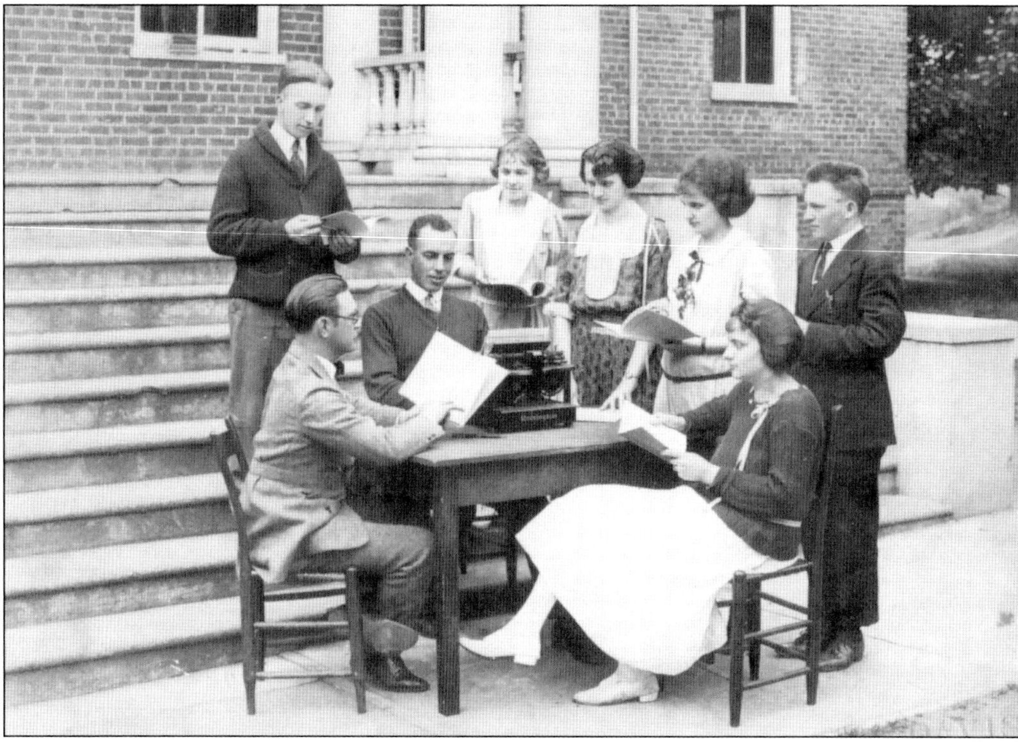

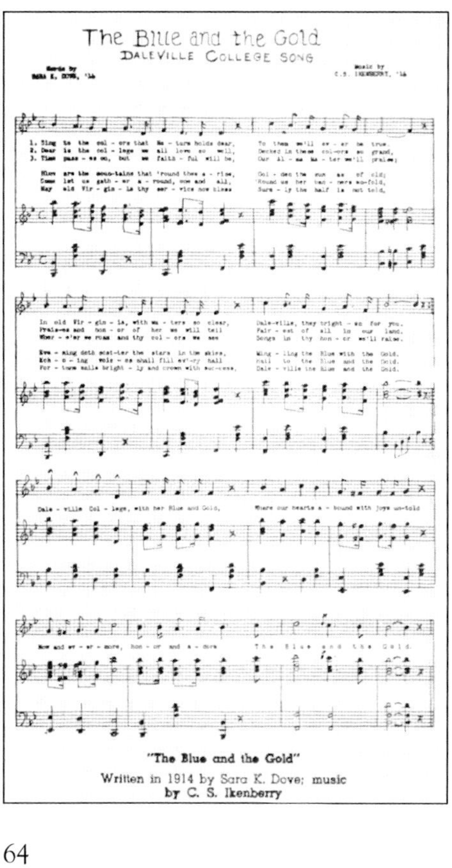

The *Daleville Leader* was a periodic anthology published by the Columbian and Aristotelian Literary Societies at Daleville College beginning in June 1908. Here, the 1921–1923 staff of the *Leader* poses outside of the Central Building. From left to right are (seated) Newton Akers, Benton Alderman, and Kathryn Ellen Peters; (standing) unidentified, Katie Bowman, Elizabeth Brubaker Clingenpeel, Miriam Ikenberry Duffy, and unidentified. (Courtesy of Bridgewater College Special Collections.)

School spirit seems to have always run high at Daleville College. Charles S. Ikenberry (music) and Sara K. Dove (words) composed the Daleville College song, "The Blue and the Gold." Both musicians were graduates of the 1914 class. When the school merged with Bridgewater College, a new joint seal was designed. The Bridgewater seal bore the Latin inscription *bonitas, veritas, pulchritudo, concordia* ("goodness, truth, beauty, harmony"), and the Daleville seal was inscribed with *aedificans in saxo veritatis* ("building on the rock of truth"). (Courtesy of Bridgewater College Special Collections.)

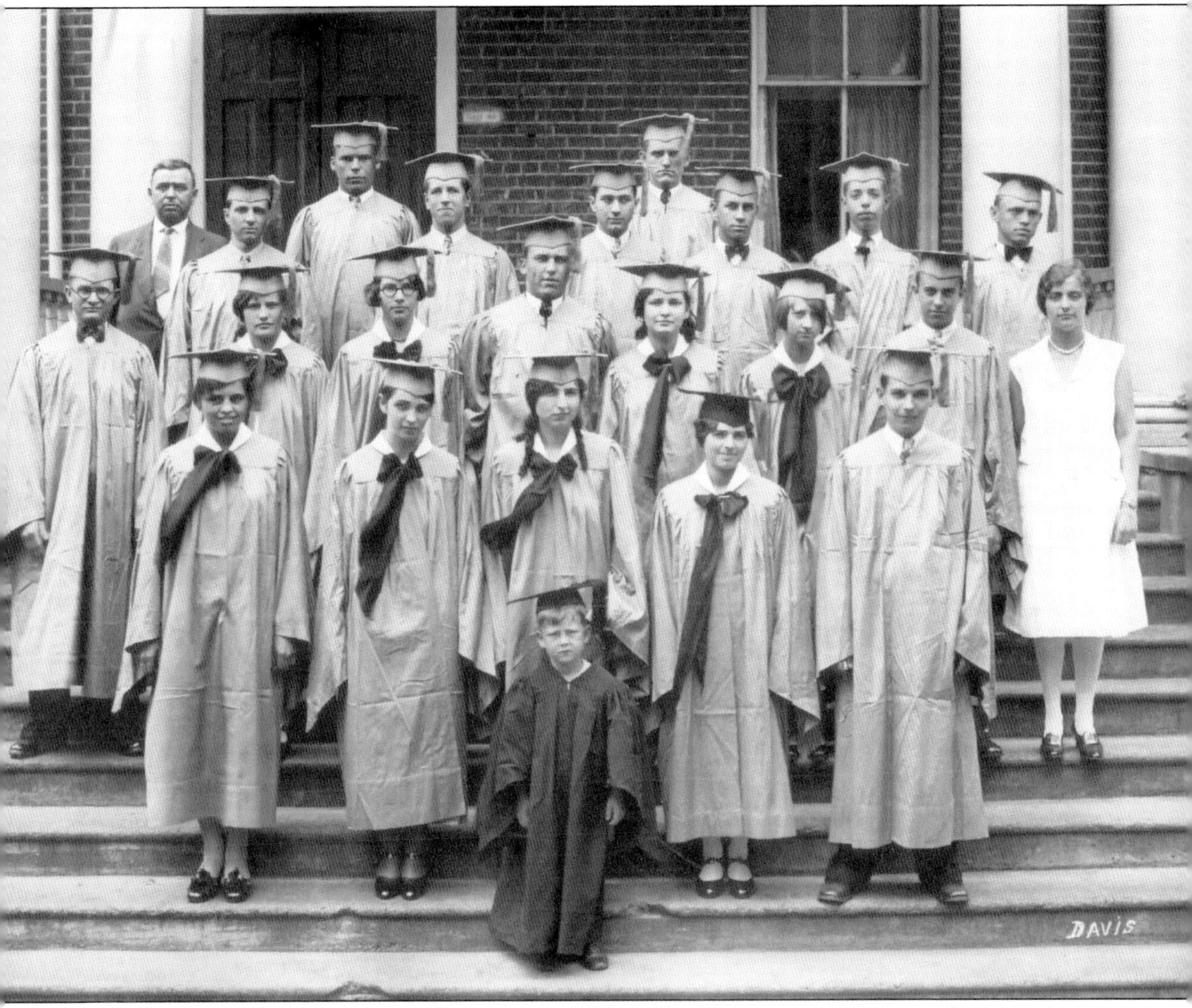

This photograph shows the 1930 class at Daleville College. Norman A. Seese, who served as principal from 1928 to 1930, stands on the far left in the back row. At the commencement, an announcement was made that the school would be closing. A group of alumni and friends leased the Daleville property for three more years, operating the Daleville Academy as a part of the Bridgewater College system. The Great Depression and accessible public schools brought an end to the academy, and it closed for good at the end of the 1932–1933 session. In the late 1950s, Lawrence Garst and Karl Ikenberry purchased several of the school buildings and converted them into residential apartments. Many of the buildings still stand behind the Bank of Fincastle, which is in the stone B.F. Nininger house that had served as the college president's home. (Courtesy of Bridgewater College Special Collections.)

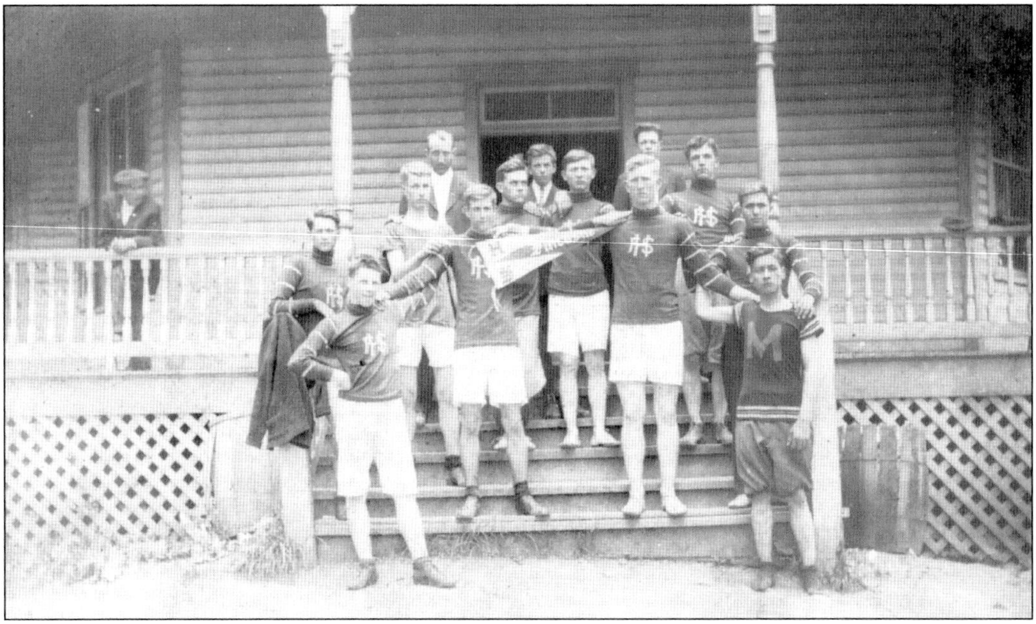

The Fincastle High School basketball team stands proudly with its school pennant around 1915. The team members seen here are, from left to right, (first row) James McDowell and Fulton T. Waid; (second row) Collins Noffsinger, K.B. Stoner, Hub Howell, and John W. Austin; (third row) Thomas Scott, Norman Bolton, Gil Slusser, and Claude Huffman; (fourth row) Coach Sasman, Bob Stoner, and Frank Slusser. The man on the left on the porch is unidentified. (Courtesy of BCHM.)

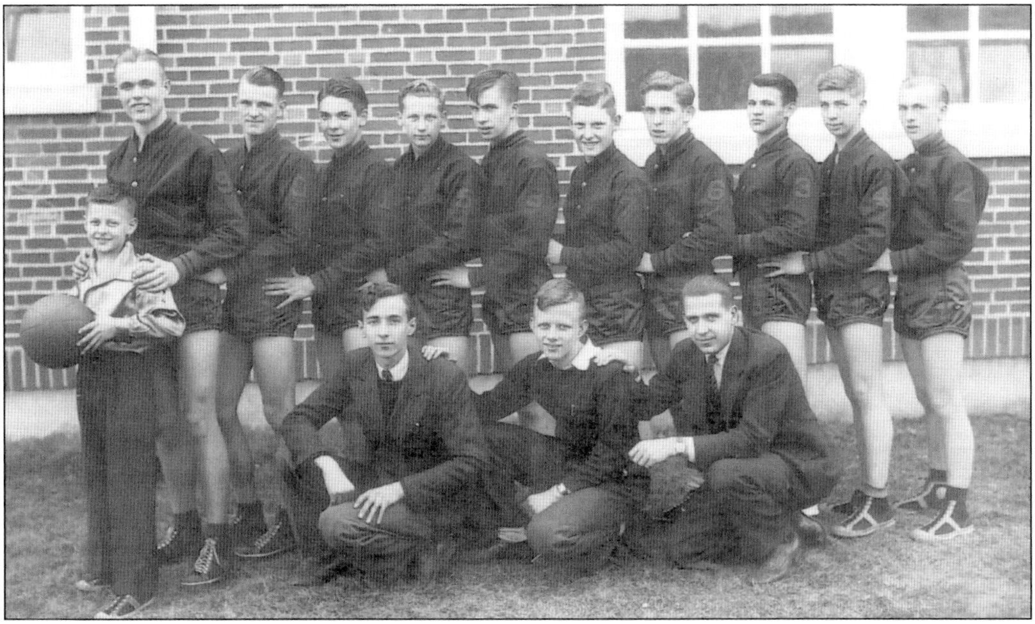

The yearbook identifies the members of the 1941 Troutville High School Warriors basketball team as, from left to right, (kneeling) Sam Crumpacker (scorekeeper), Bland Painter (manager), and Harold Barron (coach); (standing) Dick Painter (mascot), David Brillhart, Al Dooley, Milton "Tinky" Hicks, F.E. Bishop, Bill Stevens, Joe Kinzie, Jimmie Bramblett, George Graybill, Rex Kelly, and Troy Wiley. (Courtesy of BCHM.)

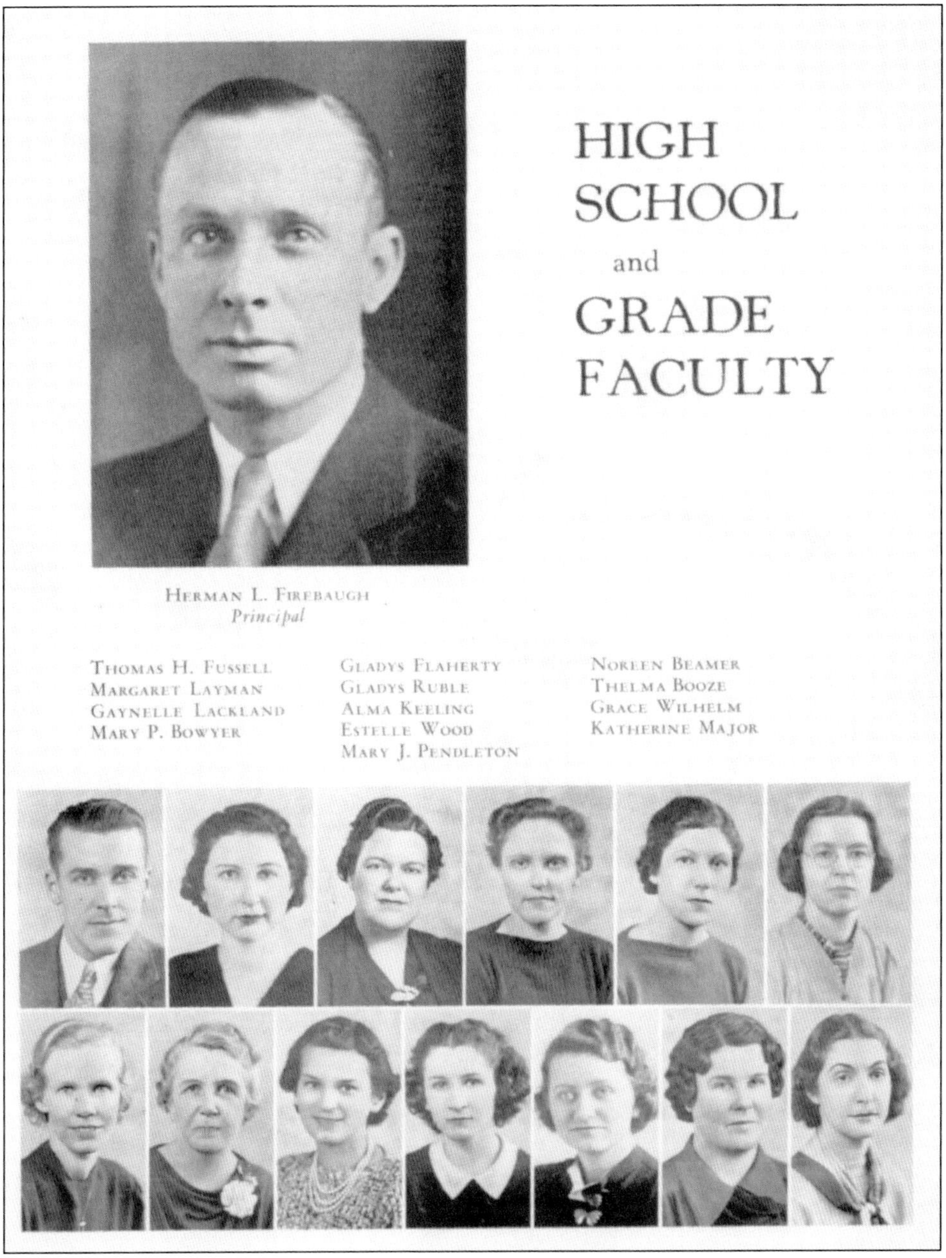
HIGH SCHOOL and GRADE FACULTY

HERMAN L. FIREBAUGH
Principal

THOMAS H. FUSSELL
MARGARET LAYMAN
GAYNELLE LACKLAND
MARY P. BOWYER

GLADYS FLAHERTY
GLADYS RUBLE
ALMA KEELING
ESTELLE WOOD
MARY J. PENDLETON

NOREEN BEAMER
THELMA BOOZE
GRACE WILHELM
KATHERINE MAJOR

In the early 20th century, one-room schoolhouses, which were often separate for white and black children, served the rural areas of the county. In the northern part of the county, such schools were located in Iron Gate, Glen Wilton, Gala, Salt Petre Cave, and Lapsley's Run, among others. In the 1930s, these schools were consolidated, and students were sent to the Eagle Rock and Oriskany schools, which held grades one through twelve. Glen Wilton students attended school in that community through fourth grade, then completed schooling in Eagle Rock. African American students attended separate schools in Glen Wilton, Oriskany, and Eagle Rock. The 1938 Eagle Rock high school and grade school faculty are shown here in the yearbook. In 1959, James River High School was built for grades eight through twelve, and Central Academy was built for all black students in the county, grades one through twelve. (Courtesy of BCHM.)

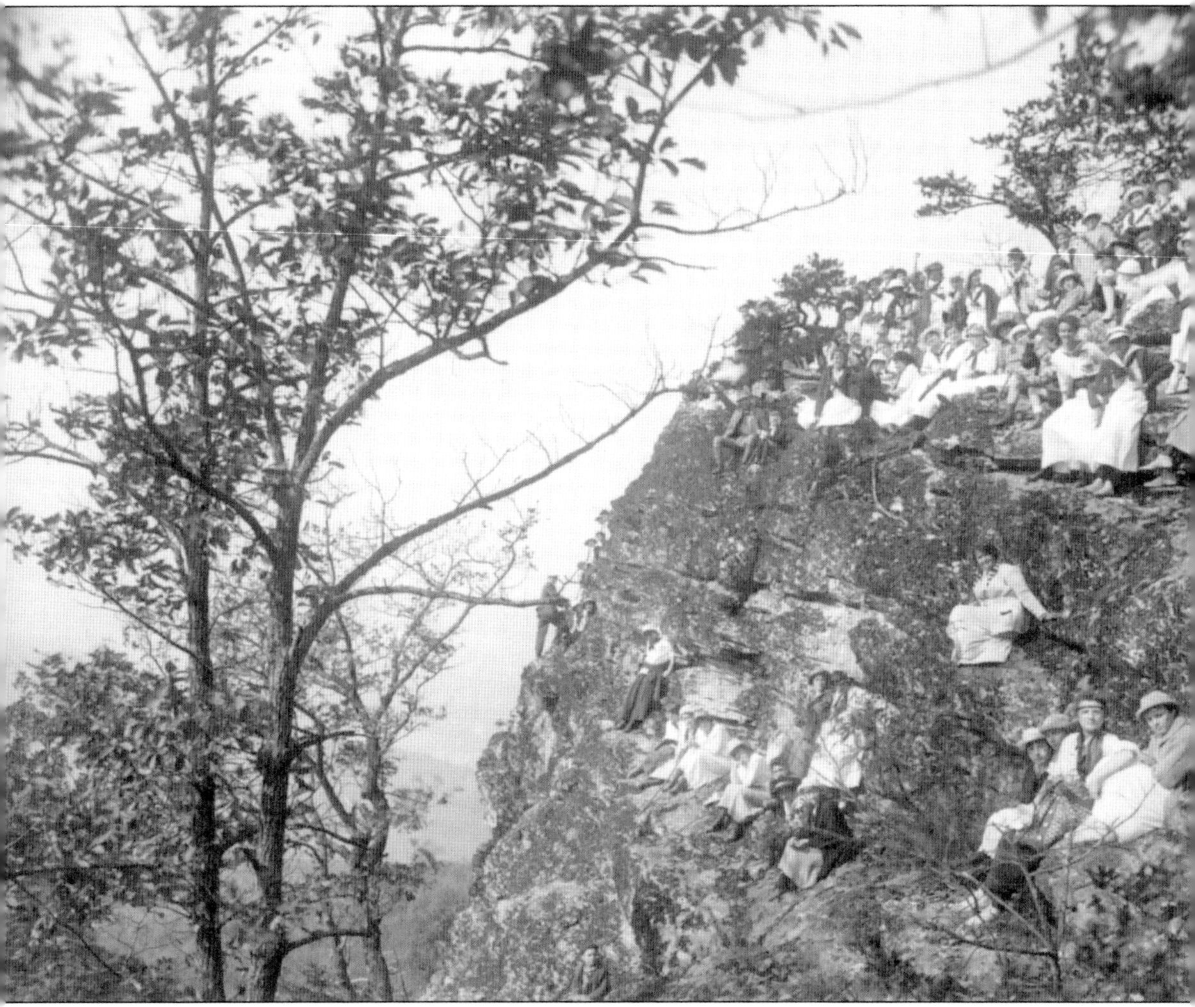

Begun by Charles Johnston in the early 1830s, the resort springs, which were then located in Botetourt County, evolved into an educational institution, first associated with a Baptist seminary and then becoming a secular school. In 1842, the Valley Union Seminary hired Charles Lewis Cocke to head the coeducational school. In 1852, Cocke dissolved the men's department, and the school became the Roanoke Female Seminary. In 1855, the school was renamed Hollins Institute, after a generous donor. In 1895, Hollins Institute began the tradition of declaring Tinker Day an official holiday when classes are canceled and the student body hikes to the top of Tinker Mountain with a picnic. In the 1880s, this event was observed in both the spring and fall, but it later became a fall-only event, with May Day celebrated in the spring instead. This photograph shows Hollins students and faculty on Tinker Mountain in 1915. Tinker Day remains a revered school holiday, with the exact date kept secret until the president's official announcement. (Courtesy of Hollins University, Wyndham Robertson Library Special Collections.)

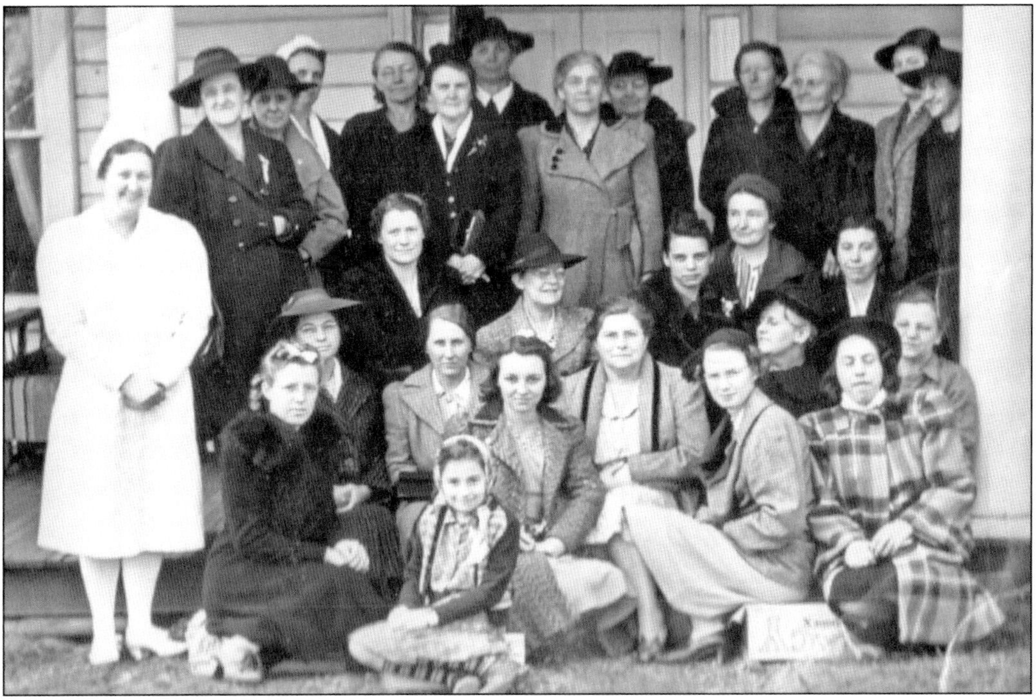

The Home Demonstration Clubs of the Virginia Cooperative Extension Service traveled throughout rural areas encouraging modernization of domestic practices. Mrs. Bolton, the nurse who was the teacher, led this 1940s meeting in Nace. The young girl in front is Maggie Roberson, and the ladies in attendance were members of the Brugh, Deel, Obenshain, Rader, Simmons, Simpson, and Stevens families. (Courtesy of John W. Rader.)

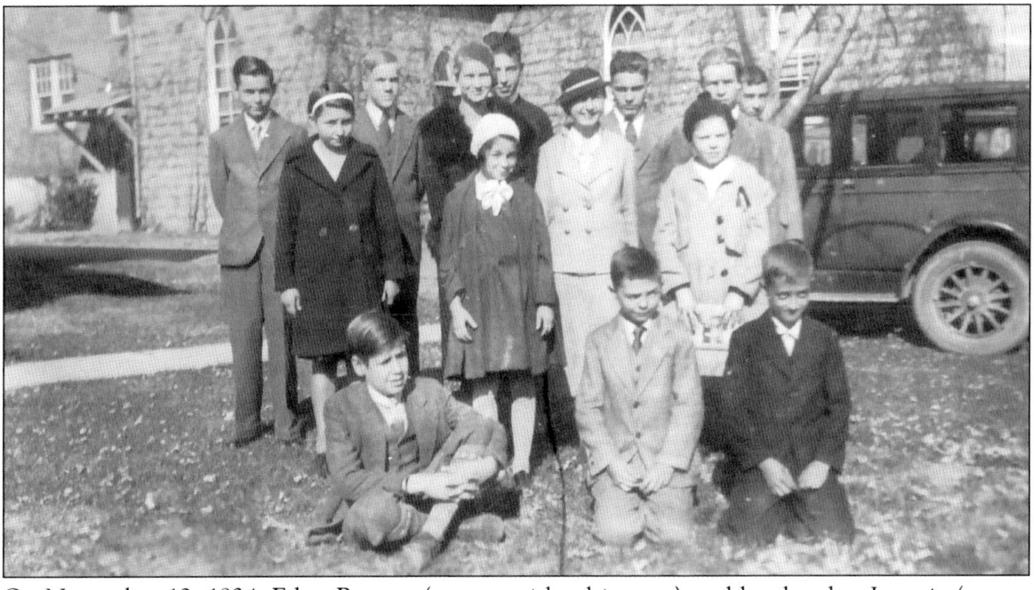

On November 12, 1934, Edna Brogan (center, with white cap) and her brother Lonnie (center back) were baptized by Rev. McKinley Coffman, the pastor of the Troutville Church of the Brethren. The Brogans attended the Troutville church until 1954, when the family transferred its membership to the Trinity Church of the Brethren. (Courtesy of Edna Brogan Bolton.)

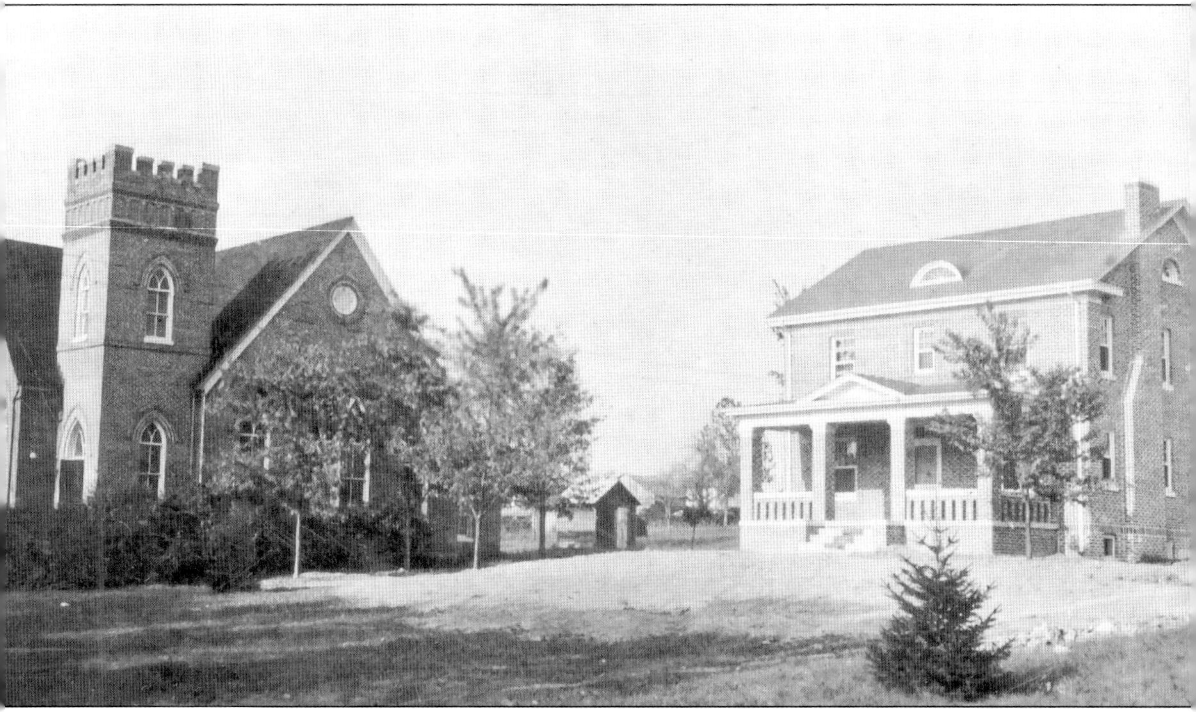

The Cloverdale Church of the Brethren was organized in 1913 when the Botetourt Congregation was divided into three sections—the other two being Valley (now Daleville) and Troutville. The Botetourt Congregation first met in the frame structure located south of the present church parking lot. This building, the Cloverdale Union Chapel, was shared with area Baptist and Methodist congregations. When the congregation was divided, a new building was constructed. On December 21, 1913, Dr. T.S. Moherman, then president of Daleville College, gave the dedication address at the new Cloverdale Church of the Brethren. Stained-glass windows and musical instruments were added later. In 1954, an educational wing was constructed and the entrance tower was enlarged. The handsome brick parsonage (right) was built in 1929. Pastor Frank A. Myers and his family were the first to live there. Around 1930, a telephone was installed in the parsonage. Roanoke-based architect Homer Miller is credited with the design for both the church building and the parsonage. (Courtesy of Paul Garber.)

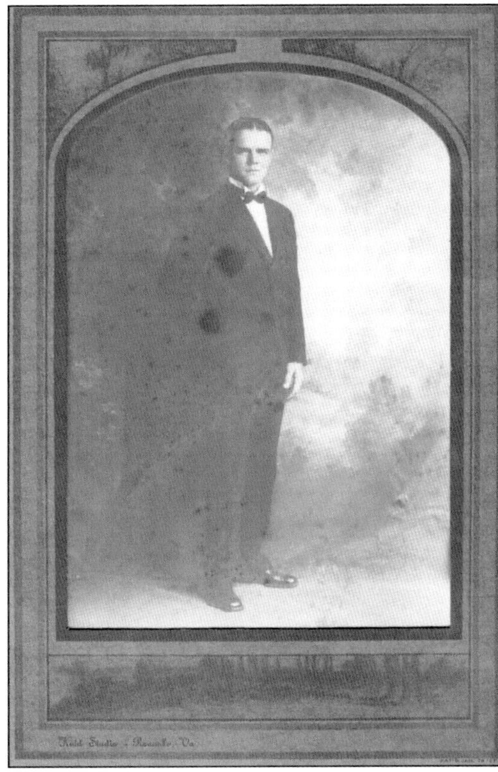

The marriage of Orval Samuel Garber (right) to Mary Crumpacker (below) in 1928 was the first wedding held at the Cloverdale Church of the Brethren's sanctuary. Pastor Myers conducted the ceremony. Orval was born in Rockingham County and attended Bridgewater College, where he participated in numerous sports and clubs. He was a teacher and administrator for over 30 years at Roanoke's Monroe Junior High School and was also an ordained minister in the Church of the Brethren. In 1958, he was elected vice president of the Roanoke-Botetourt Farm Bureau. Mary, the daughter of Emory and Daisy Crumpacker of Bonsack, was a schoolteacher at Preston Park Elementary and, later, authored three books and numerous articles on historical and religious topics. (Both courtesy of Paul Garber.)

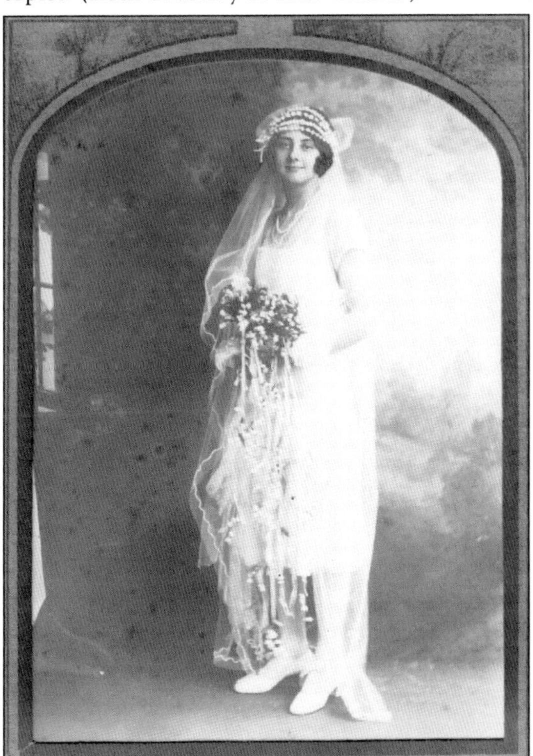

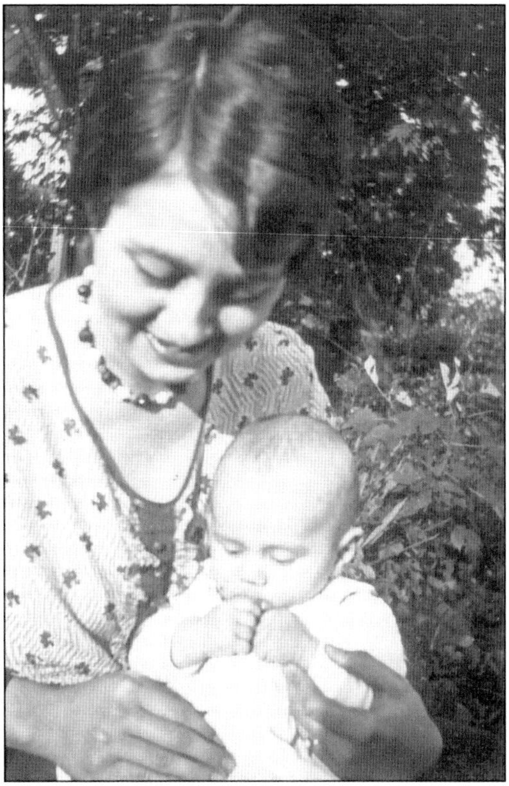

In 1931, Paul S. Garber was the first baby dedicated at the Cloverdale sanctuary. He is pictured here with his mother, Mary. She wrote the first history of the Cloverdale church, covering the period from its founding in 1912 to 1978. In 2013, Paul and church member Rebecca Wilson authored a second volume of the history for the church's 100th anniversary. (Courtesy of Paul Garber.)

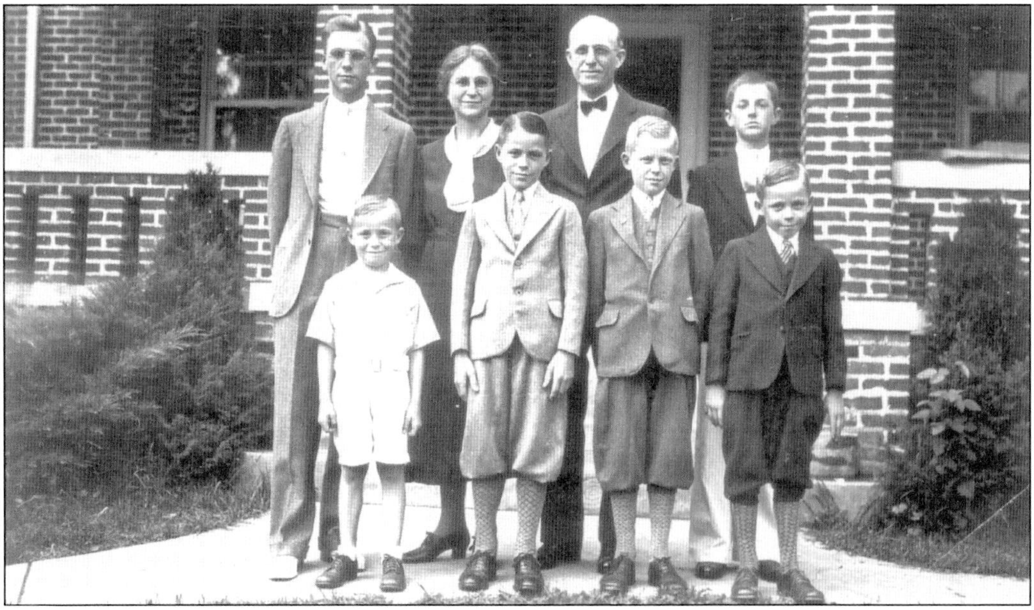

In 1920, the Cloverdale congregation appointed a committee to secure a full-time pastor. The committee searched for a year but was not successful. Seven years later, a second committee named Frank A. Myers the church's first full-time pastor. Here, Pastor Myers, who served from 1929 to 1934, poses with his wife, Dorothy, and their six boys in front of the church parsonage. (Courtesy of Paul Garber.)

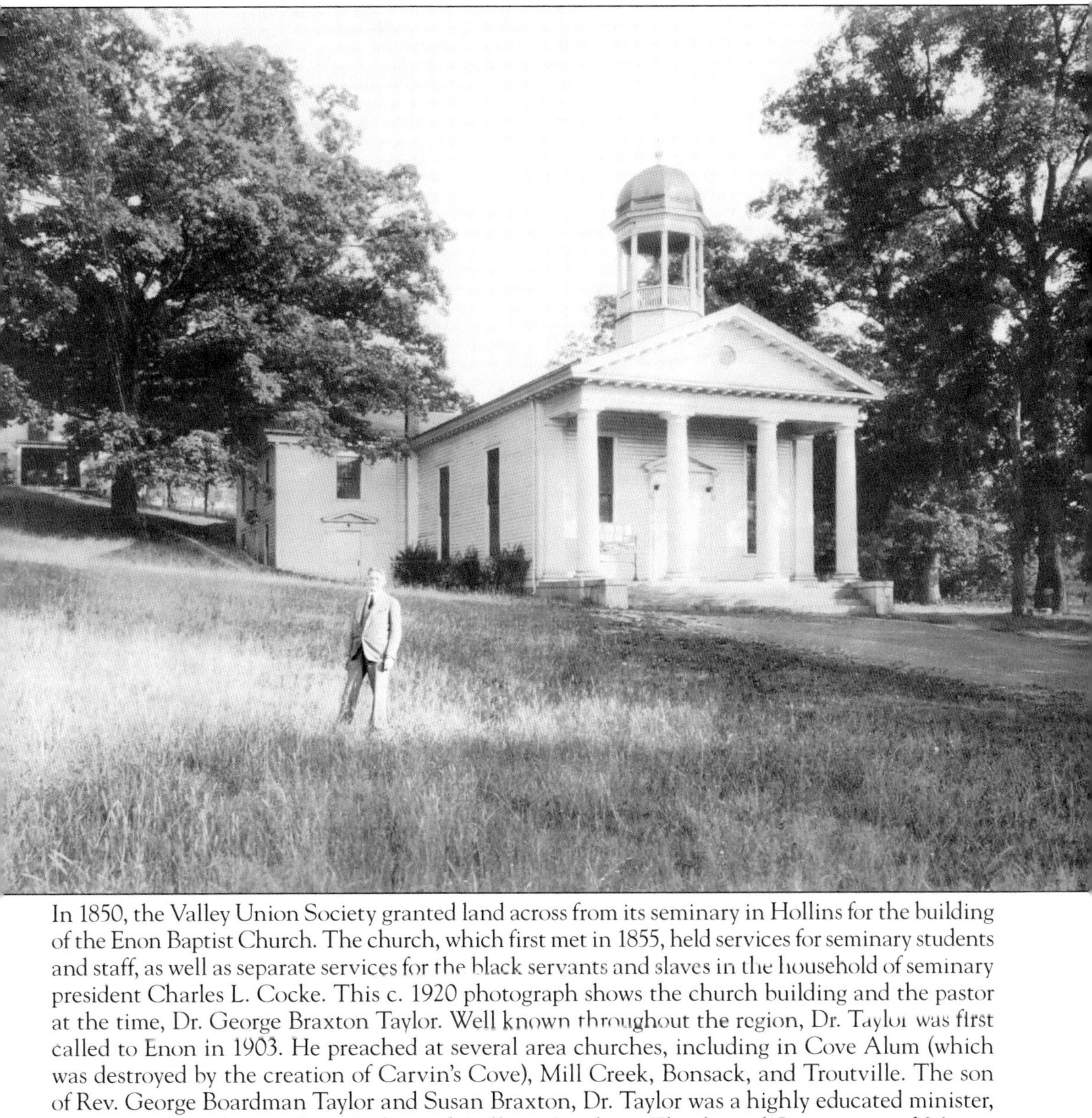

In 1850, the Valley Union Society granted land across from its seminary in Hollins for the building of the Enon Baptist Church. The church, which first met in 1855, held services for seminary students and staff, as well as separate services for the black servants and slaves in the household of seminary president Charles L. Cocke. This c. 1920 photograph shows the church building and the pastor at the time, Dr. George Braxton Taylor. Well known throughout the region, Dr. Taylor was first called to Enon in 1903. He preached at several area churches, including in Cove Alum (which was destroyed by the creation of Carvin's Cove), Mill Creek, Bonsack, and Troutville. The son of Rev. George Boardman Taylor and Susan Braxton, Dr. Taylor was a highly educated minister, having received degrees from Richmond College, Southern Theological Seminary, and Mercer University. He was the first resident chaplain and a teacher of the Bible at Hollins Institute, and later served as chaplain emeritus. He retired from active ministry in 1940, preaching his last sermon at Enon. (Courtesy of Hollins University, Wyndham Robertson Library Special Collections.)

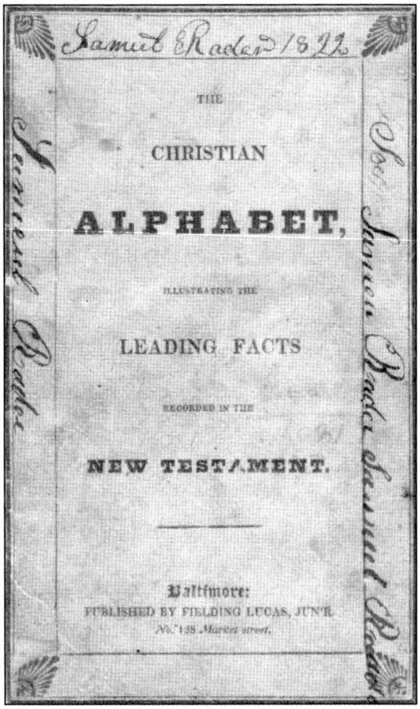

Samuel Rader 1822

THE

CHRISTIAN

ALPHABET,

ILLUSTRATING THE

LEADING FACTS

RECORDED IN THE

NEW TESTAMENT.

Baltimore:
PUBLISHED BY FIELDING LUCAS, JUN'R.
No. 138 Market street.

Samuel Rader owned this *Christian Alphabet* book written in 1822. These books, published by Fielding Lucas Jr. of Baltimore, were printed for children, "illustrating the leading facts recorded in the New Testament" in alphabetical order. They were, therefore, intended to be instructive in both education and religion. Lucas, an artist and cartographer, likely drew and painted the watercolor illustrations for the book, which were printed on one side of the interior pages. Samuel Rader used the blank pages to record family events. The pages below show the illustrations for the letters *A*, *B*, *G*, and *H*, which are executed in full color in the original book. (Both courtesy of John W. Rader.)

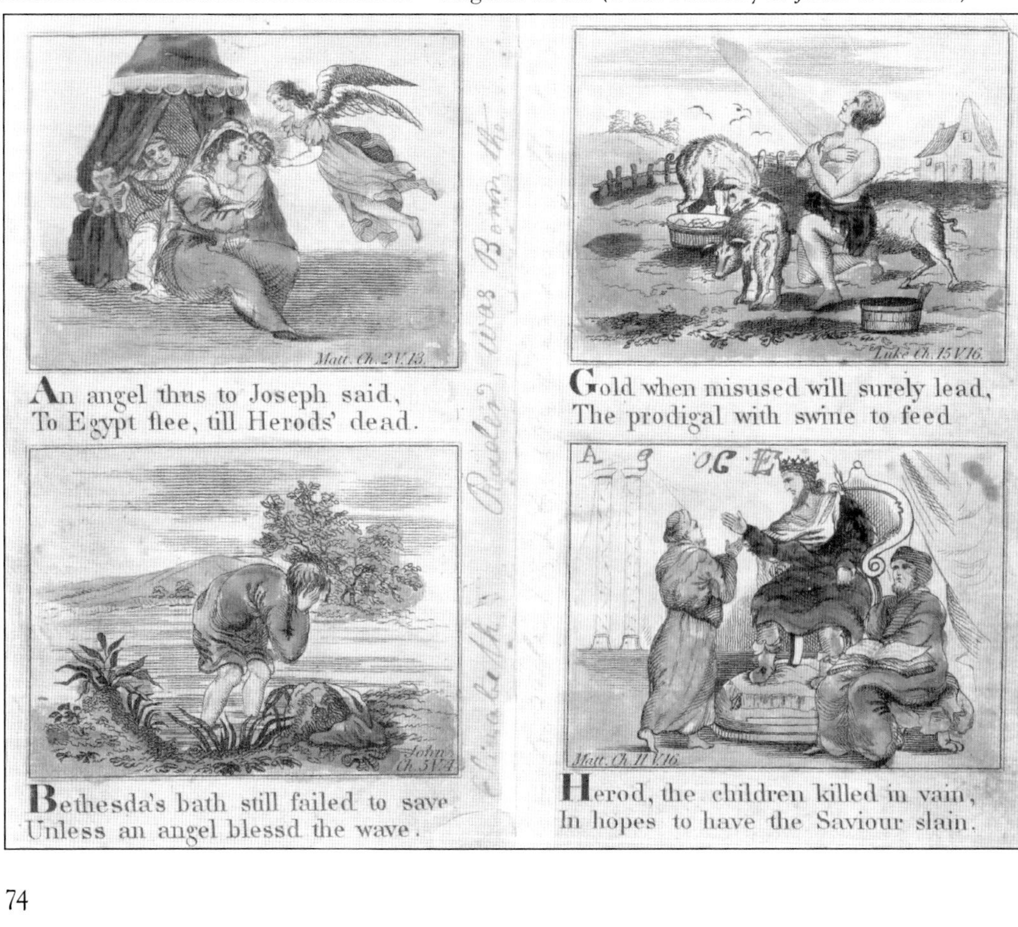

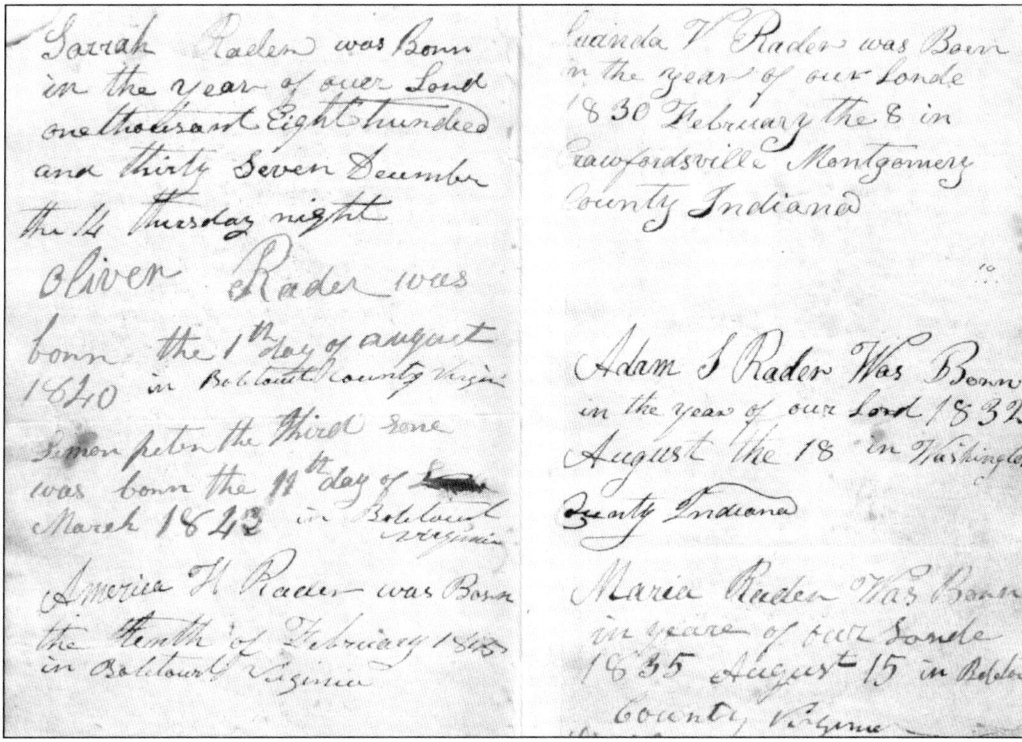

Sarrah Rader was Born
in the year of ouer Lord
one thousand Eight hundred
and thirty Seven December
the 14 thursday night

Oliver Rader was
born the 1th day of august
1840 in Botetourt County Virginia

Simon peter the Third Sone
was born the 11th day of
March 1843 in Botetourt
Virginia

America H Rader was Born
the tenth of February 1845
in Botetourt Virginia

Lucinda V Rader was Born
in the year of our Londe
1830 February the 8 in
Crawfordsville Montgomery
County Indiana

Adam S Rader Was Born
in the year of our Lord 1832
August the 18 in Washington
County Indiana

Maria Rader Was Born
in yeare of our Londe
1835 August 15 in Botetourt
County Virginia

In 1825, Samuel Rader married Sarah Brugh, and, in 1829, they moved to Indiana, where Samuel served as a militia captain. In 1832, they returned to Botetourt, where Samuel became an accomplished brick maker and builder. These pages, from Samuel's *Christian Alphabet* book, record the births of children Sarrah, Oliver, Simon Peter, America, Lucinda, Adam, and Maria. Both Oliver and Adam were killed during the Civil War. (Courtesy of John W. Rader.)

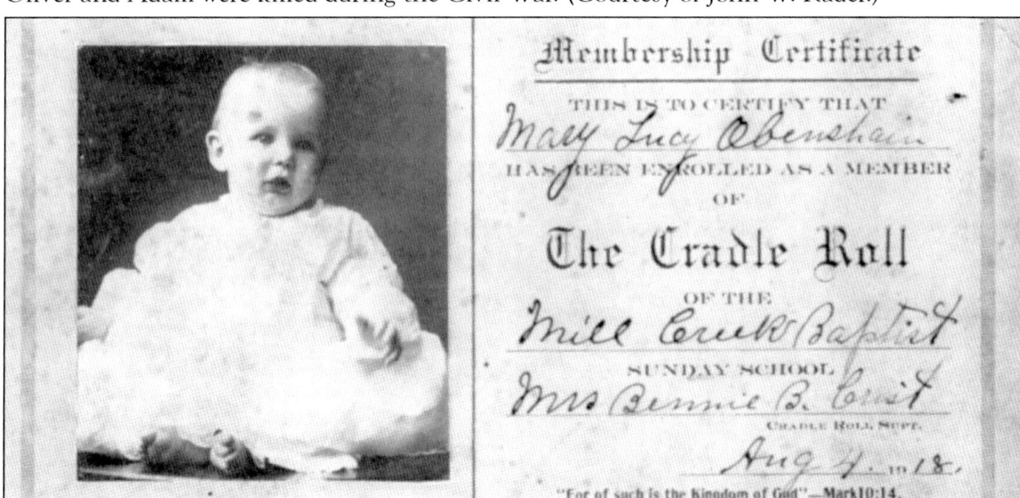

Membership Certificate
THIS IS TO CERTIFY THAT
Mary Lucy Obenshain
HAS BEEN ENROLLED AS A MEMBER
OF
The Cradle Roll
OF THE
Mill Creek Baptist
SUNDAY SCHOOL
Mrs Bennie B. Crist
CRADLE ROLL SUPT.
Aug 4. 1918.
"For of such is the Kingdom of God"—Mark 10:14.

On August 4, 1918, four-month-old Mary Lucy Obenshain was enrolled in Mill Creek Baptist Church's Cradle Roll, a class for children from infancy to four years old. Mary Lucy was the daughter of Edith Stevens and Elmer Peyton "E.P." Obenshain. She married Russell Deel in 1939. They remained lifelong members of the church, where they are buried. Mary Lucy was a well-known baker, especially for her cakes. (Courtesy of Judy Deel.)

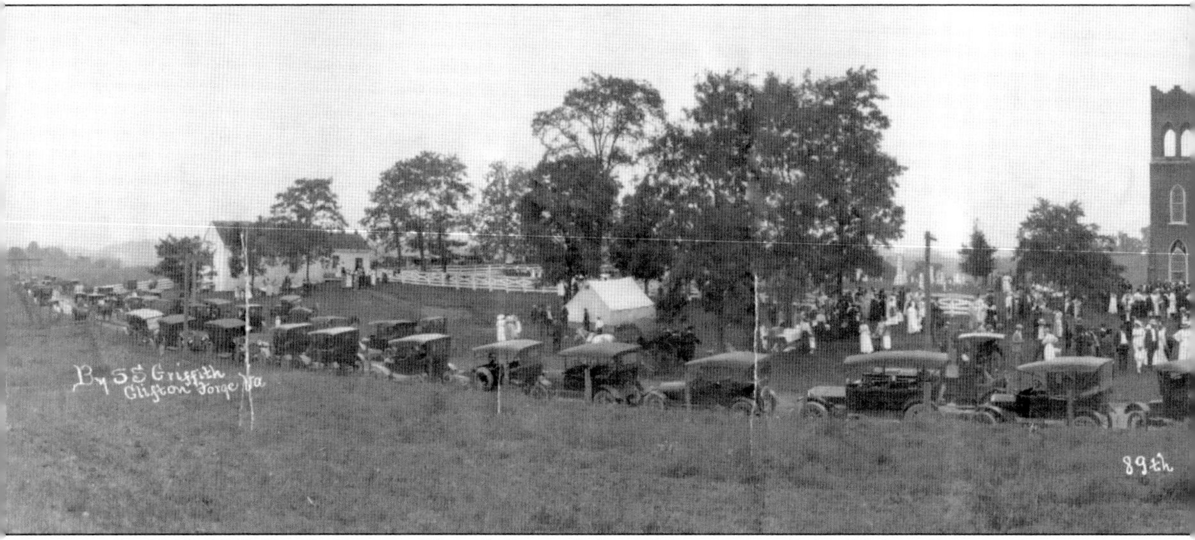

In 1916, Mill Creek Baptist Church hosted the 89th session of the Valley Baptist Association conference. In 1862 and 1904, the conference had met at the church's previous building. The brick building pictured here was the third church building, dedicated on May 7, 1911. Church records indicate that A.J. Miller was the builder. The total construction cost was $8,501.96. In 1956, a parsonage was constructed north of the church (site of the cornfield in this photograph),

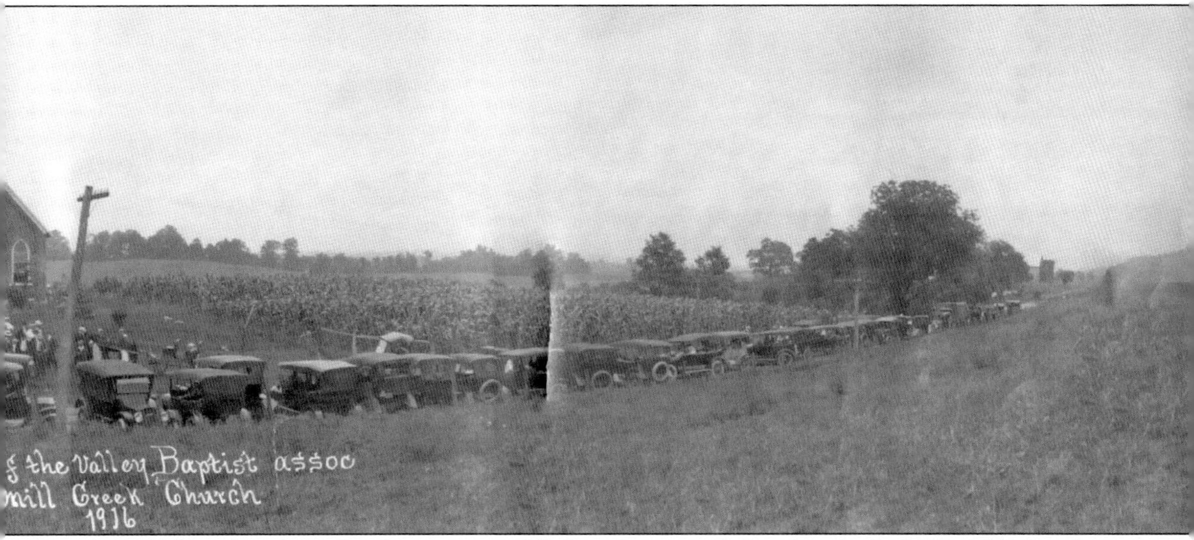

and, in 1964, a Sunday school wing was added to the rear of the church. In 2004, Mill Creek celebrated its 200th anniversary. It is the oldest active congregation in the Roanoke Valley Baptist Association. Located at the intersection of Route 11 and the Blue Ridge Turnpike, the church remains active in missions at home and abroad. (Courtesy of Judy Deel.)

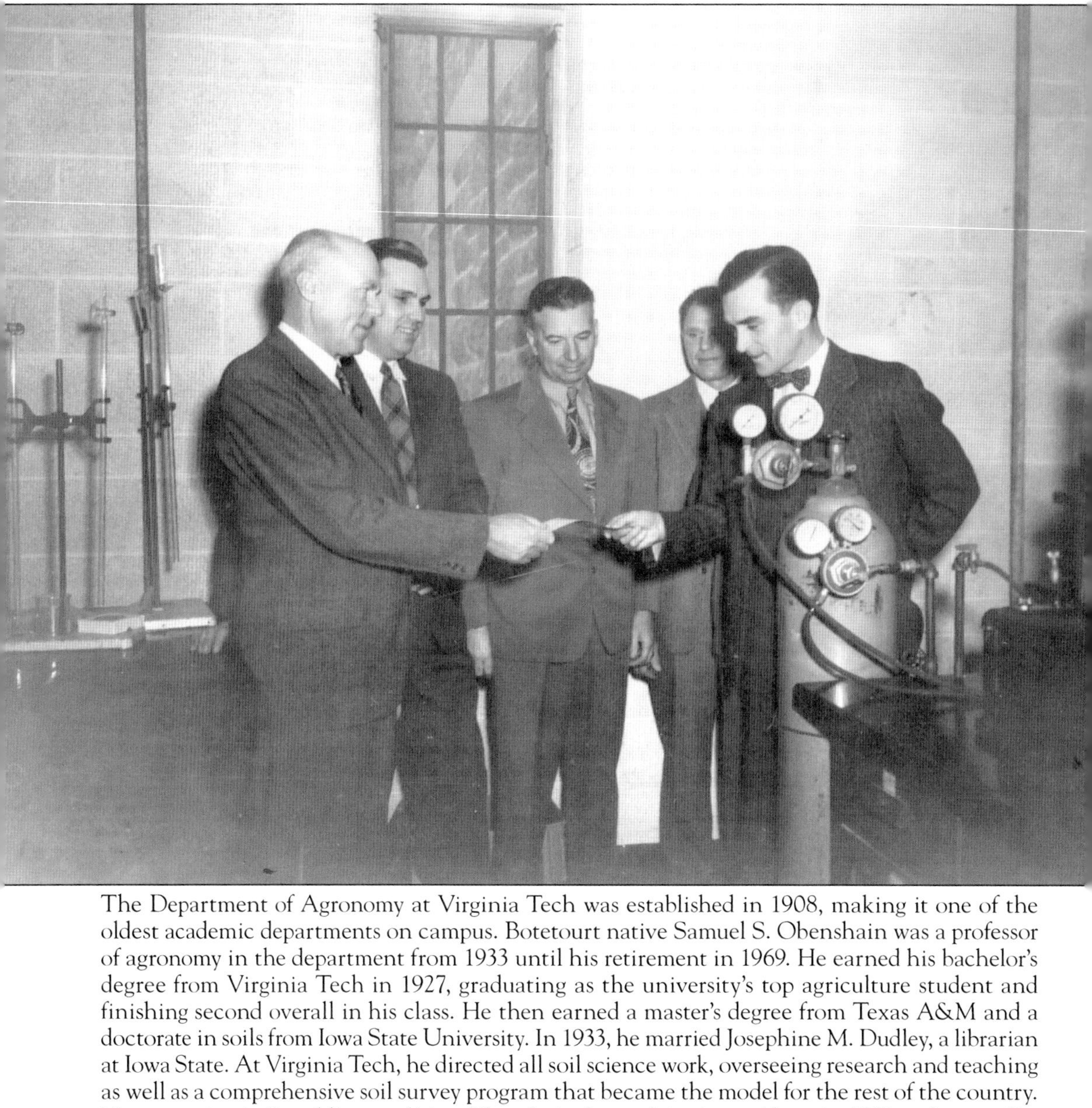

The Department of Agronomy at Virginia Tech was established in 1908, making it one of the oldest academic departments on campus. Botetourt native Samuel S. Obenshain was a professor of agronomy in the department from 1933 until his retirement in 1969. He earned his bachelor's degree from Virginia Tech in 1927, graduating as the university's top agriculture student and finishing second overall in his class. He then earned a master's degree from Texas A&M and a doctorate in soils from Iowa State University. In 1933, he married Josephine M. Dudley, a librarian at Iowa State. At Virginia Tech, he directed all soil science work, overseeing research and teaching as well as a comprehensive soil survey program that became the model for the rest of the country. He was active in Republican politics. Obenshain (center) is pictured here in 1951 as director Dr. H.N. Young (far left) receives a prize check for the Virginia Agricultural Experiment Station's work on radioactive fertilizer. Others pictured are, from left to right, Dr. Charles Rich, Dr. Roy Blaser, and Dr. Henry L. Dunton. (Courtesy of the Virginia Cooperative Extension, DLA, VT.)

Four

Roads and Places along the Way

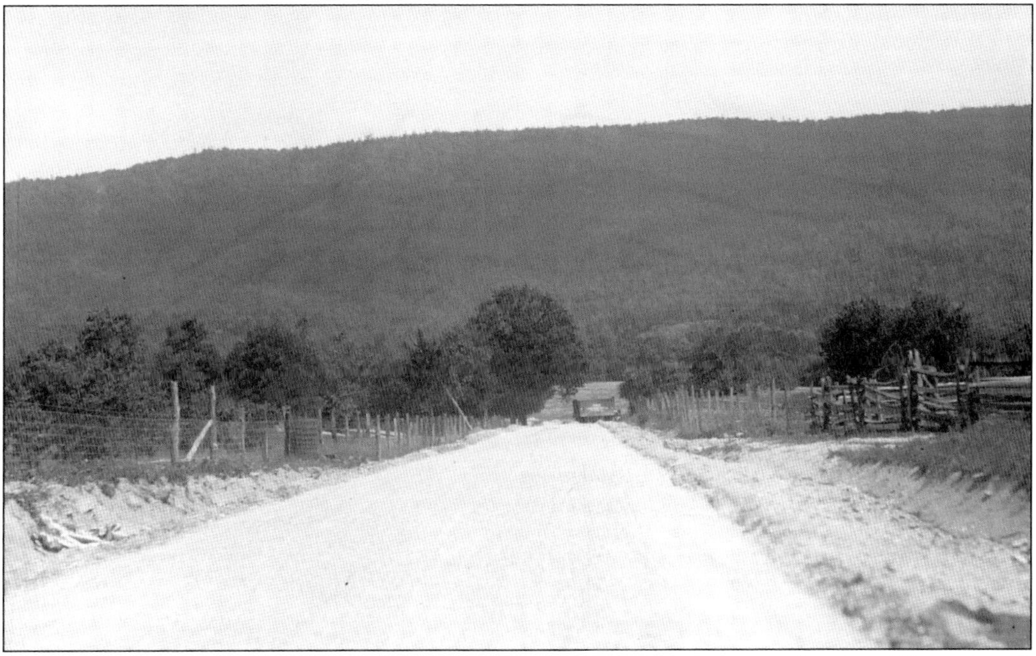

The main transportation artery through the county in the 18th century was the Great Wagon Road, which generally followed earlier Native American trails. It was the migratory path for numerous Scots-Irish, German, and English settlers into the Shenandoah Valley. At Amsterdam, the road connected to the western Wilderness Road. This photograph shows a macadamized road, a type of semi-pavement not introduced until the 1800s. (Courtesy of the Library of Congress.)

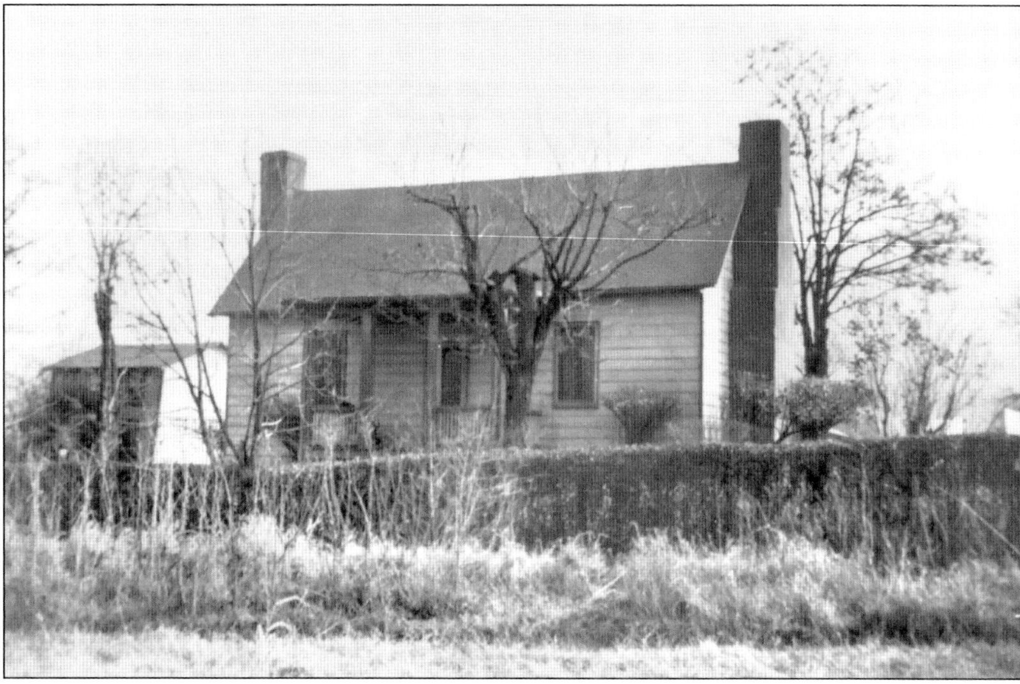

The Black Horse Tavern (c. 1790) was located along the Old Carolina Road (now Old Mountain Road) about two miles from the Botetourt Springs in Hollins. In 1815, John Luck purchased the land and operated the tavern. In 1854, William Kyle purchased it and built his home, Bellevue, behind the old log tavern. Only the stone chimneys from the old tavern building remain today. (Courtesy of the *Fincastle Herald*.)

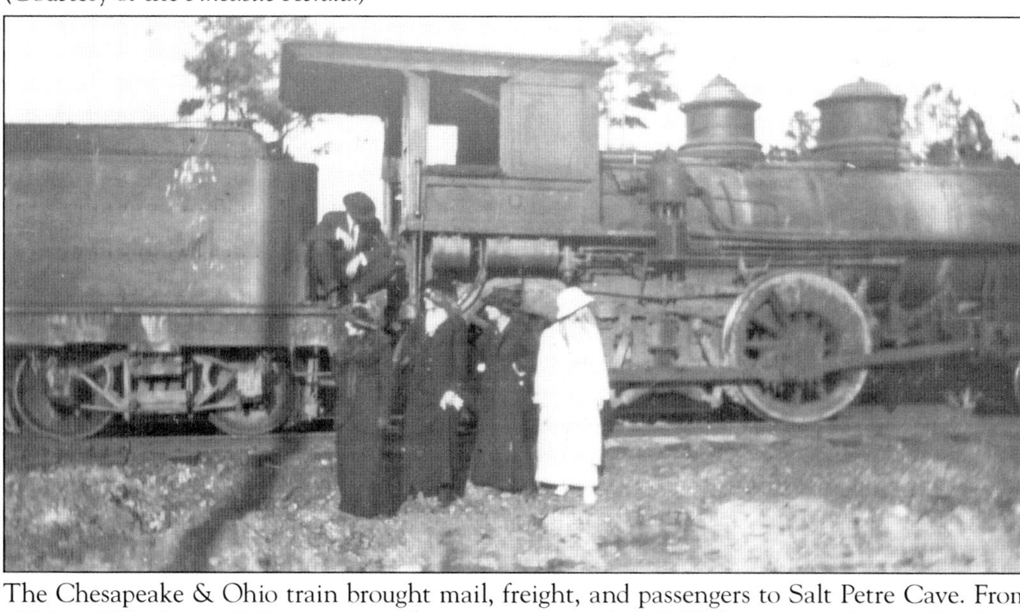

The Chesapeake & Ohio train brought mail, freight, and passengers to Salt Petre Cave. From 1886 to 1896, George P. Persinger was the postmaster, and, in 1902, his nephew Joseph "Joe Sam" Persinger, assisted by his son D.I. "Peck," became postmaster. The office closed in 1923, and Peck later served as postmaster in Eagle Rock. This unidentified group stands in front of a train stopped in Salt Petre Cave around 1907. (Courtesy of Anna Noel Damerel.)

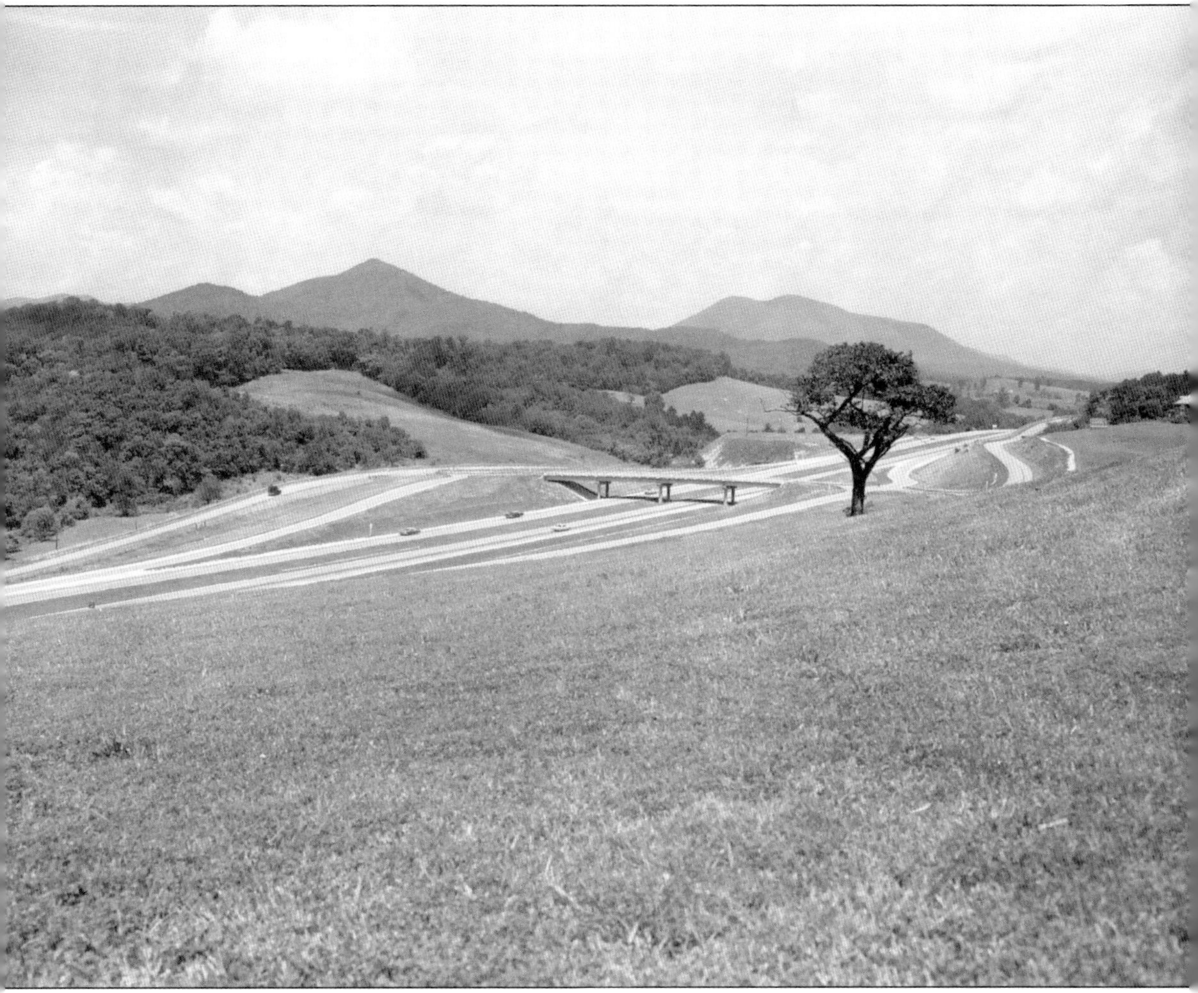

Federal highway agencies studied the feasibility of a system of interstate highways as early as 1938. In 1944, Congress passed the Federal Highway Act to establish such a system. Implementation was delayed by World War II, and financing did not become available until 1956. According to the Virginia Department of Transportation, an 11-mile stretch south of Buchanan was constructed in November 1953, and, in December 1957, construction started on a stretch of Interstate 81 from one mile north of Buchanan to one mile south of the Rockbridge County line. By December 1964, the interstate between Dixie Caverns and Fancy Hill was opened to the public. This 1962 image looks northwest at the finished interstate north of Buchanan. The bridge carries Route 614 across the interstate at the Arcadia exit. (Courtesy of the Virginia Department of Transportation, Office of Communications.)

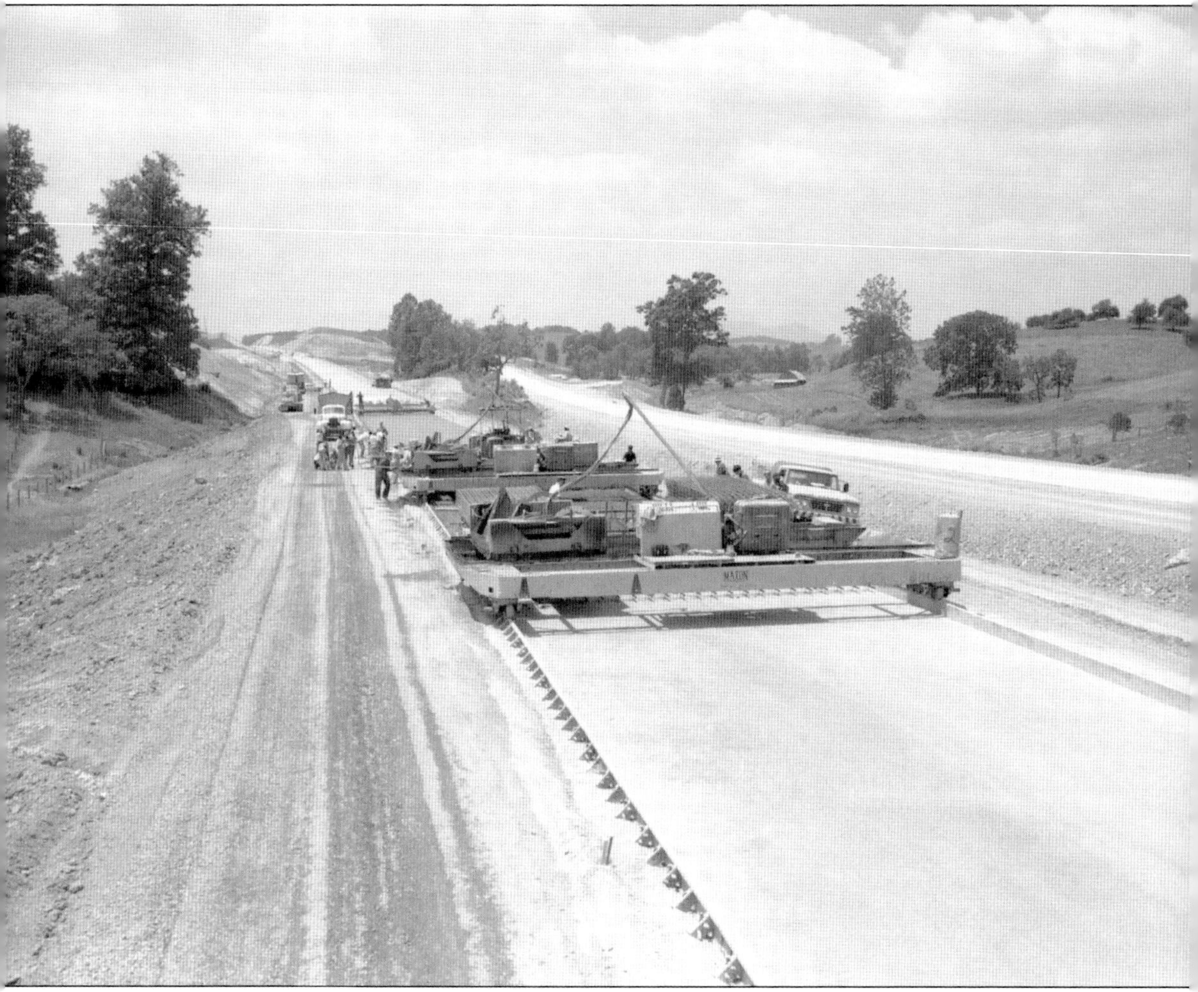

Built through Botetourt in the 1960s, Interstate 81 generally parallels Route 11, which, in turn, generally follows the route of the Great Wagon Road. The interstate highway has five exits in the county: three in the northern part of the county, one near Troutville, and one at its intersection with Route 220. This 1964 construction view shows the interstate near the Troutville exit. The Brugh farm is visible on the right. (Courtesy of the Virginia Department of Transportation, Office of Communications.)

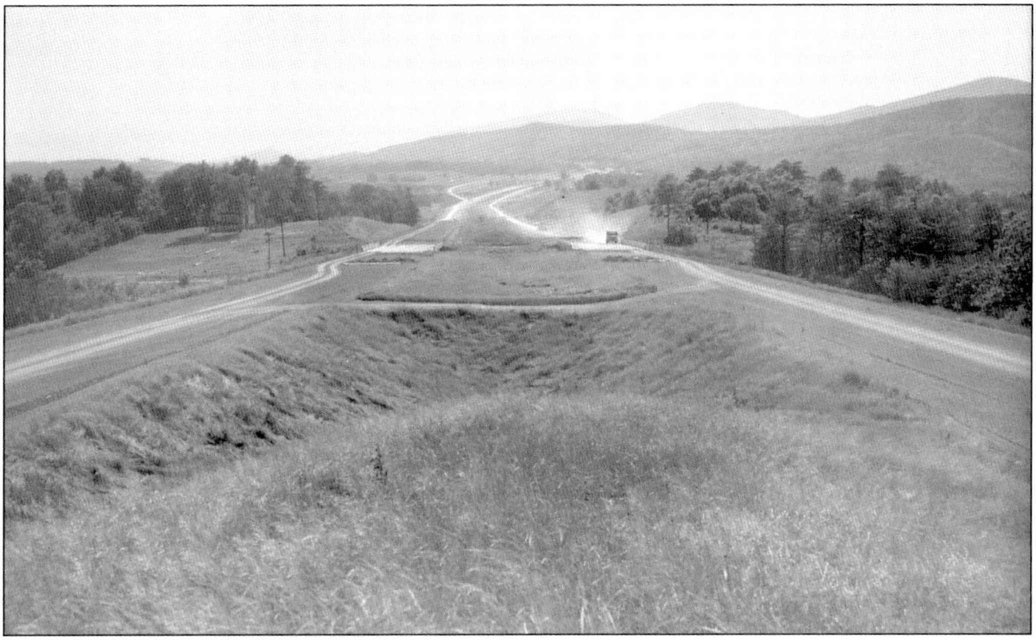

The view above of Interstate 81 construction shows the roadway at the southern end of the county, near the Hollins exit. Some historic buildings in the area were destroyed to build the interstate, including the Garst Fort, an early-19th-century dwelling made of logs. The development of Carvin's Cove reservoir in the 1970s destroyed many other homes and churches in the Hollins area. In 1973, the Virginia Department of Transportation (VDOT) widened Route 220 to four lanes through the county. The view below shows construction of new parallel lanes at the intersection of Route 665 (Country Club Road). The photograph was taken from the corner of the Bolton property. Tinker Mountain is visible in the background, and Trinity Cemetery is located to the left, out of view. (Both courtesy of the Virginia Department of Transportation, Office of Communications.)

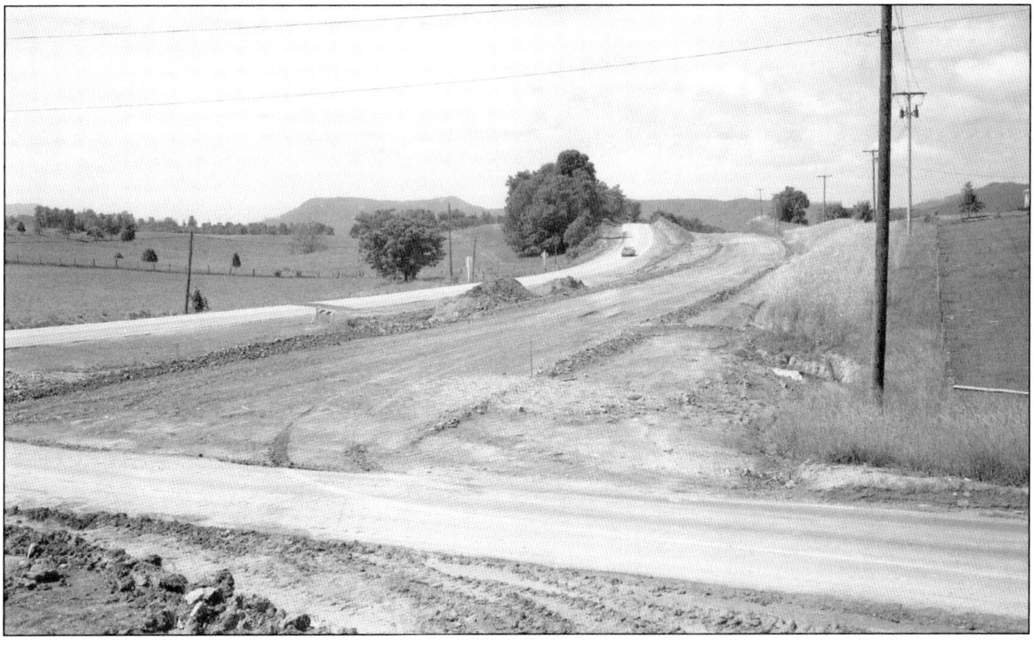

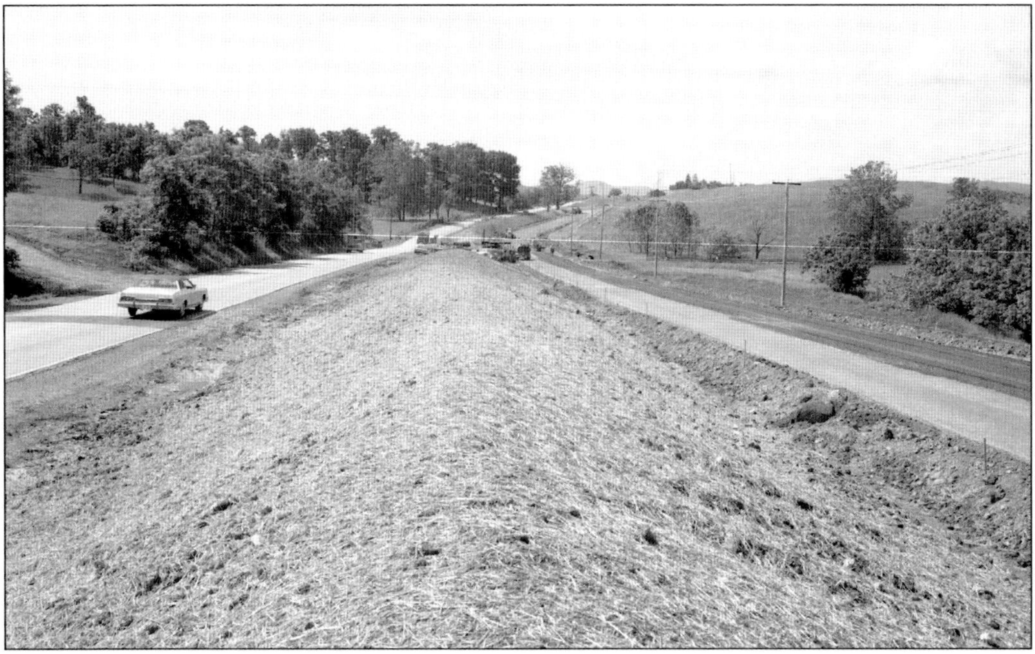

The 1973 view above shows the parallel, but unfinished, lanes on the west side of Route 220, when it was widened to four lanes. Two-way traffic continues to travel on the lanes to the left. The trucks in the center of the photograph are parked approximately where the entrances to Greenfield (right) and Ashley Plantation (left) are today. The construction view below, taken on the same day, shows crews working in the Trinity area, near Route 220's intersection with Route 670. Visible in this image are the old Trinity school, on the hill to the left, the Carl Snyder barn, at the foot of the hill, and the H.B. Layman house, at the intersection. The Rachel Layman barn is seen on the right. (Both courtesy of the Virginia Department of Transportation, Office of Communications.)

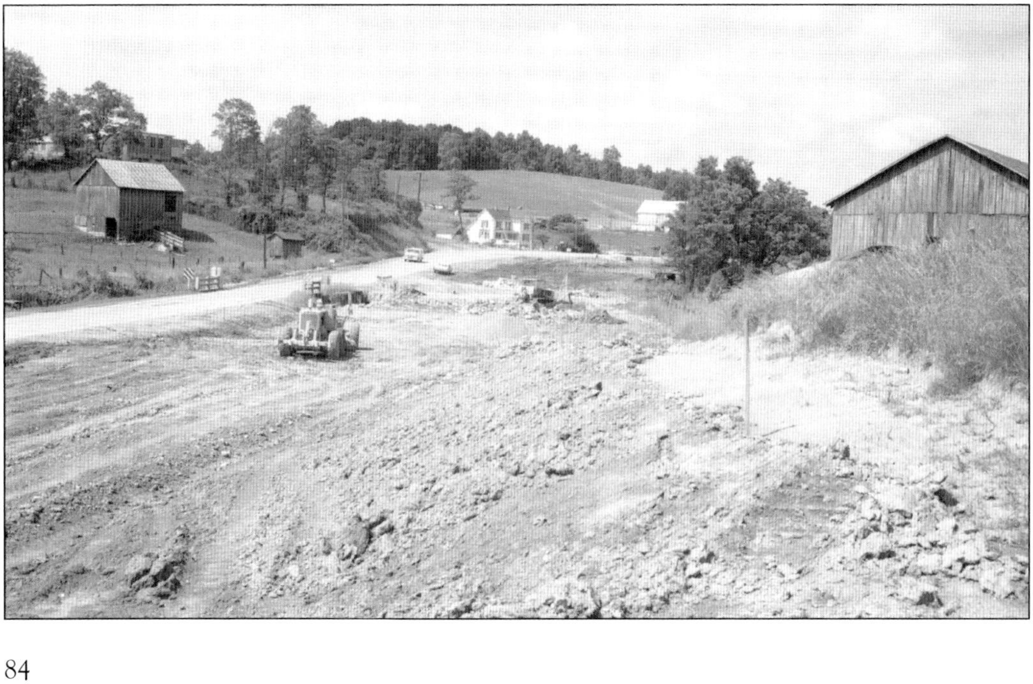

In 1957, Leonard Mitchell purchased the 17-acre Wills farm, at the intersection of Routes 11 and 220, at auction. When Interstate 81 was built, Mitchell realized a considerable return on his investment, selling part of the property to Truckstops of America. Motels, service stations, and restaurants followed. Here, in 1992, VDOT engineer Fred Altizer discusses proposed changes to Exit 150, where access improvements are ongoing. (Courtesy of the *Fincastle Herald*.)

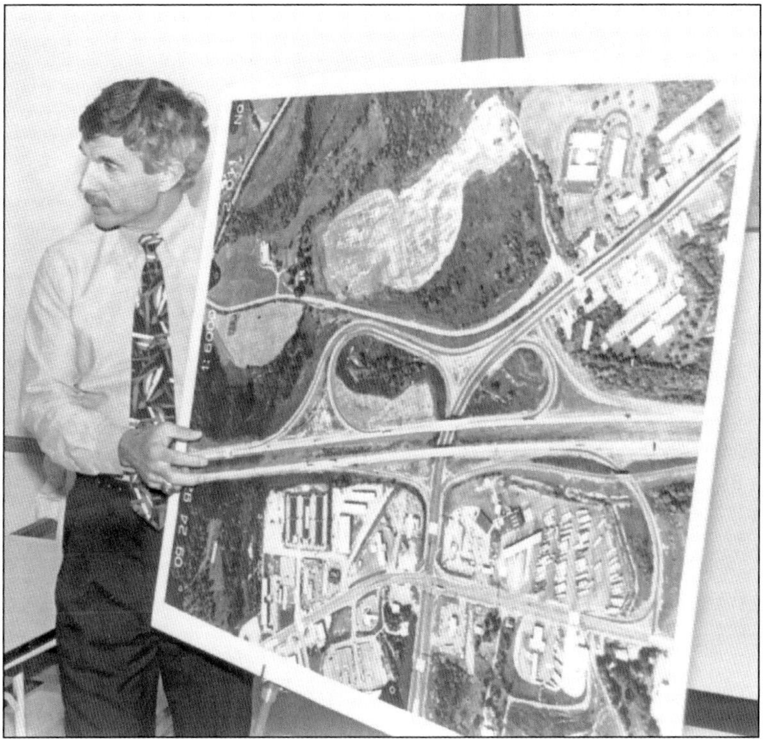

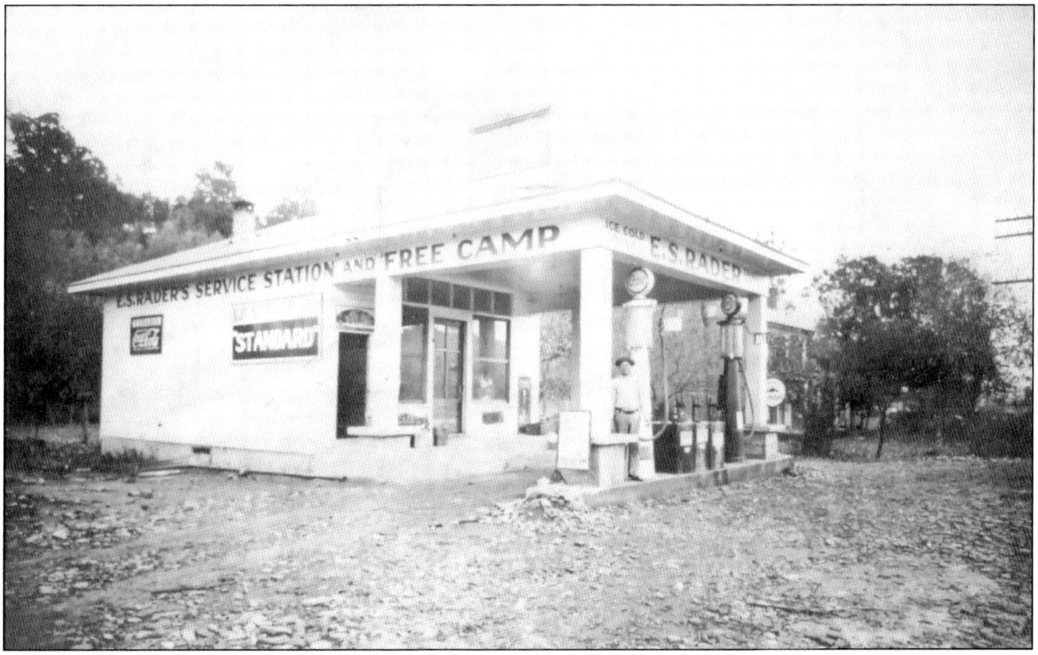

Ewell S. "Boney" Rader operated this service station during the 1920s. Located along the still-unpaved Route 11, the Rader station also offered free camping for travelers who wished to stay overnight. Later, Boney's granddaughter Eunice and her husband, Joe Parks, operated a general store there. The 1840s brick home of Samuel Rader (Boney's grandfather) is visible in the background. Both buildings are still standing. (Courtesy of John W. Rader.)

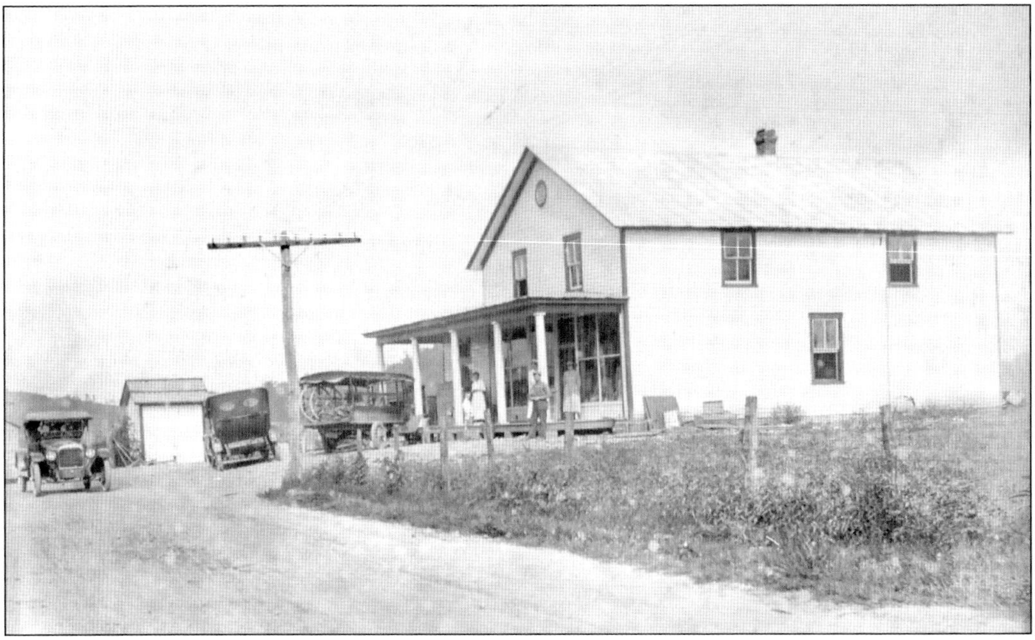

The Sifford general merchandise store (above) was located on the east side of Route 11, just across from its intersection with the Blue Ridge Turnpike. The store, which was located on the first floor of the house, was operated by Chester L. Sifford. It later became Sifford & Stevens when Frank Stevens partnered with Sifford. This 1920s view is looking northeast toward the house from the still-unpaved Route 11. Pictured below inside the store are, from left to right, Halley Sifford, Chester's wife, who worked as the store clerk, and Julia and Eunice, the two oldest Sifford daughters. (Both courtesy of Lewis Sifford.)

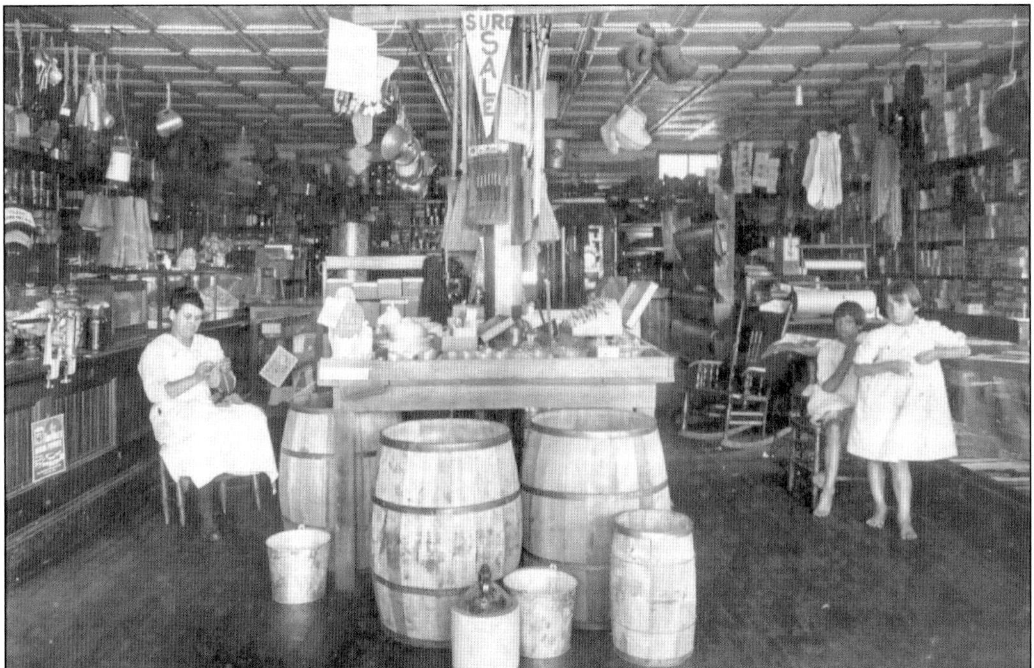

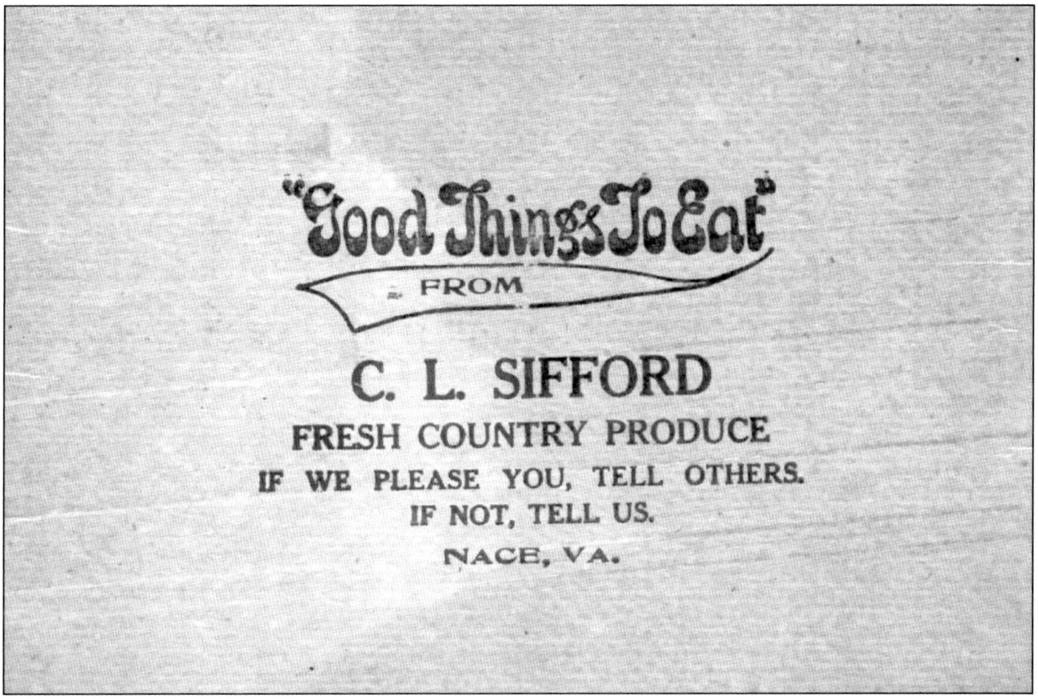

Chester Sifford married Halley Stevens in a double ceremony with Halley's brother Tilghman, who married Vinnie Spangler. Sifford was a dairy farmer, canner, and local merchant. He used to set his milk cans along the top of a concrete wall at the front of the property for pickup by the creamery trucks. Halley's recipes made good use of the cream, butter, and milk from the family's dairy farm. Blackberry cake and apple pie with caramel frosting were two of Halley's specialties. The label above came from a cardboard takeout box from the Sifford store, which sold some of Halley's fare. Later, the Siffords operated the Shady Nook Home, a tourist home that catered to automobile travelers along Route 11. Beds were $1 a night and meals were 50¢. (Above, courtesy of Judy Deel; below, courtesy of Lewis Sifford.)

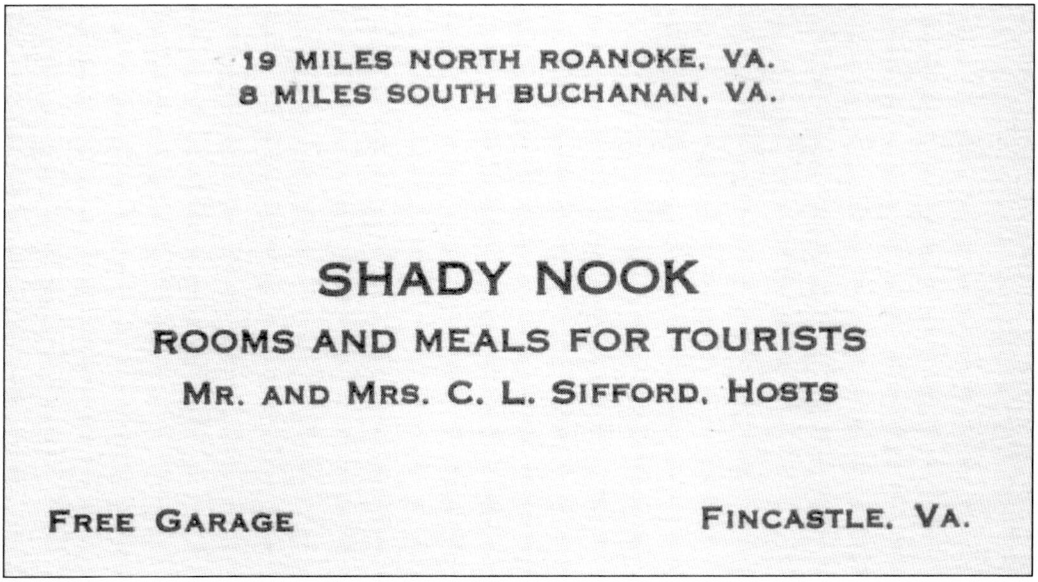

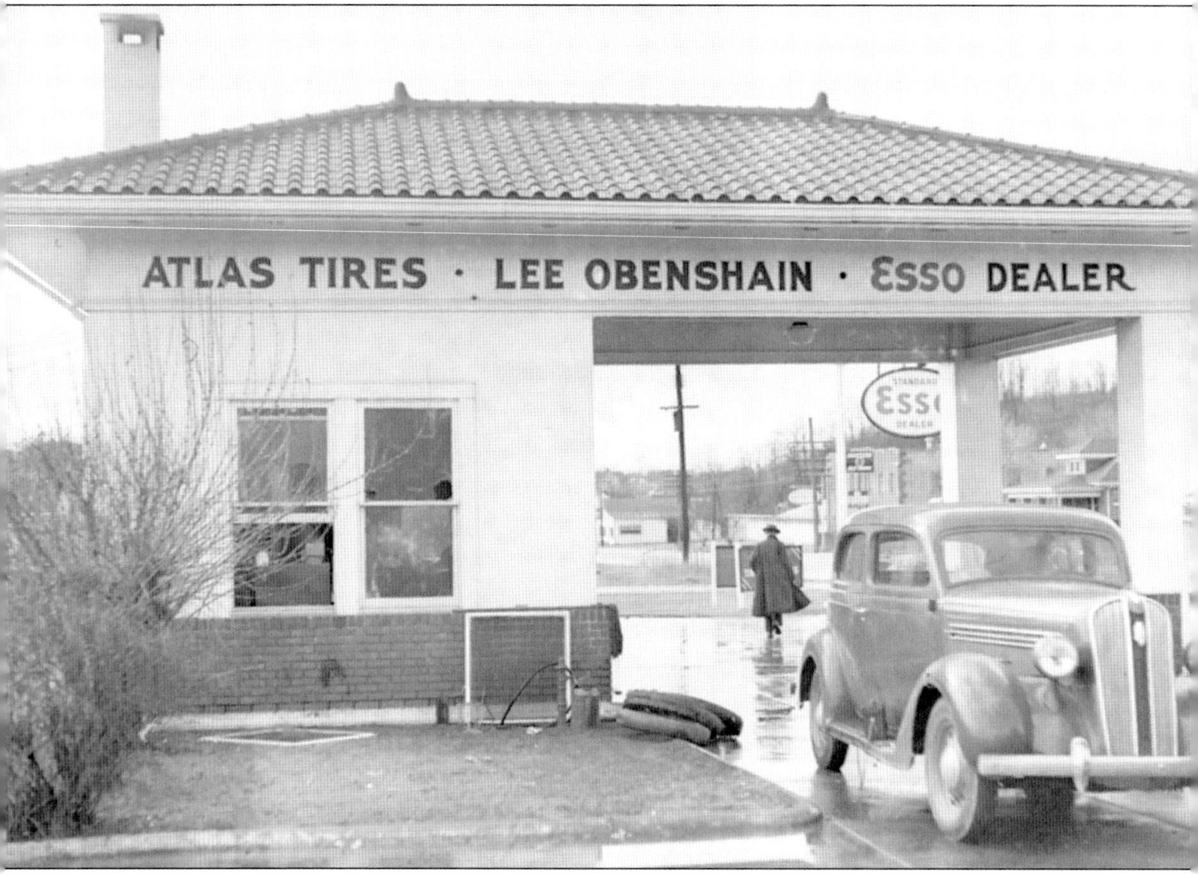

The Troutville Esso station, built around 1920, catered to the increased automobile travel along Route 11. The station is an example of the house-type design, which was the first significant new service station style to appear in the 1920s. The design featured the scale, materials, and appearance of domestic architecture in an effort to blend with its surroundings, since these buildings were often constructed in neighborhoods. This example featured a canopy that extended over the gas pump island, a distinctive tile-clad hipped roof, and highly visible signage. (Courtesy of JMU.)

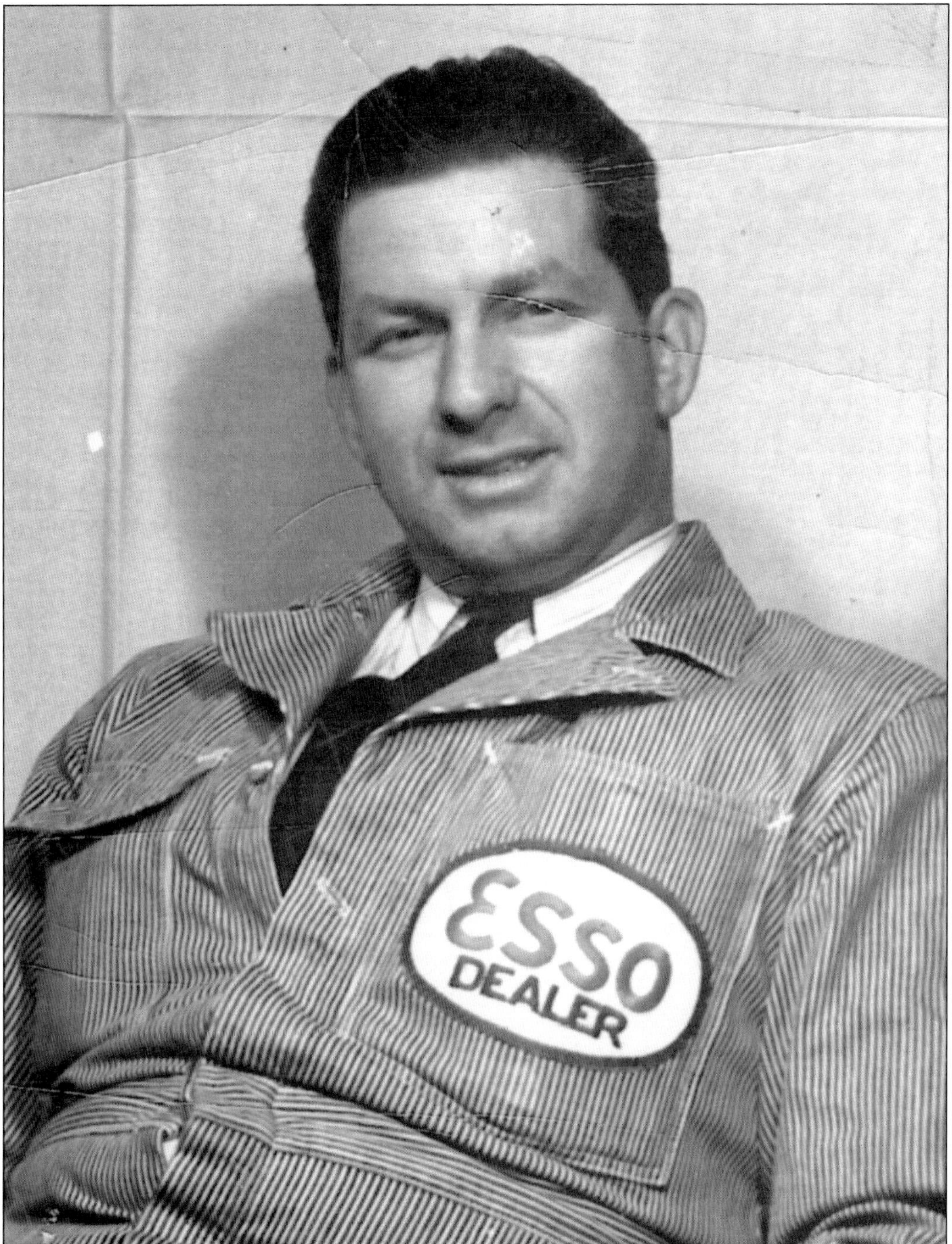

For many years, John V. Rader and Braxton Landers ran the Troutville Esso station, but Lee Obenshain began leasing it around 1937, and operated it for about 40 years. In 1952, Obenshain also bought John Kelly's garage at Mill Creek, which he later sold to Donny Spencer. Lee was the son of E.P. and Edith Stevens Obenshain. He worked on the farm and in the Obenshain cannery prior to purchasing the service station. He also served on the board of the Bank of Fincastle. (Courtesy of Sarah Spencer.)

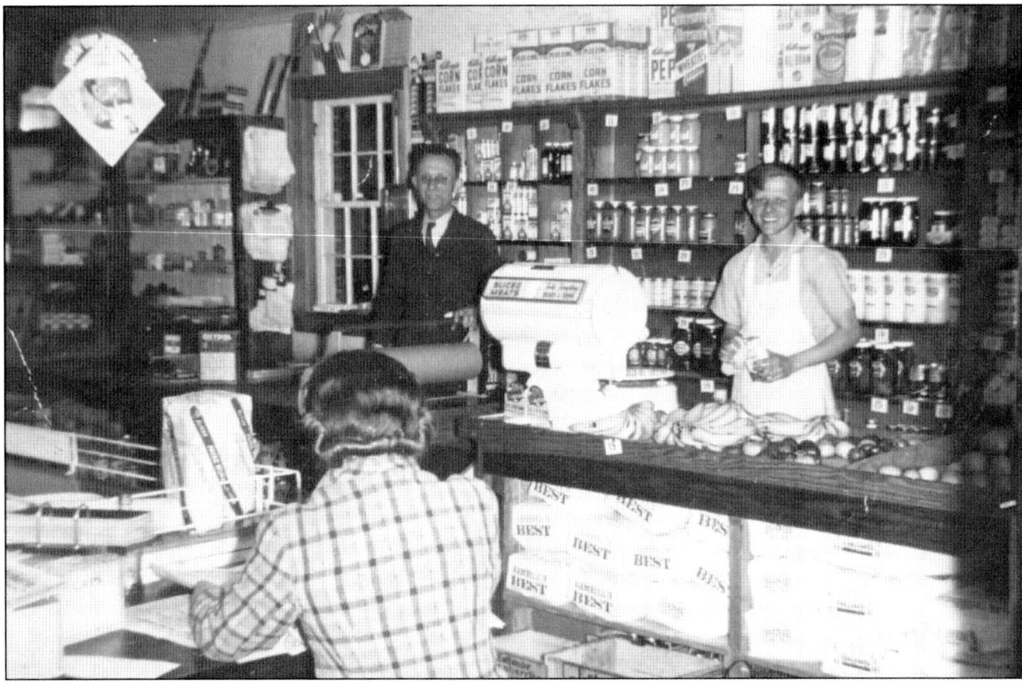

In 1935, Bland A. Painter (left) established his grocery store in Fincastle, where his son Bland Jr. (right) began his grocery career. Painter's wife, Martha, sits with her back to the camera. During World War II, Bland Jr. interrupted his commercial career to serve in the Navy. When he returned home from the war, he attended Richmond Professional Institute (now Virginia Commonwealth University) and married his high school sweetheart, Agnes Landers. (Courtesy of Betty Jeter Painter.)

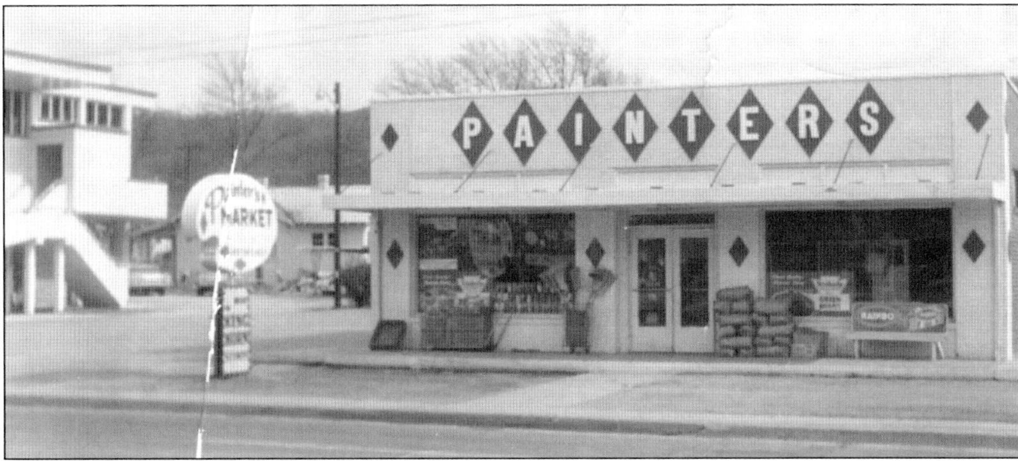

In 1941, the Painter store burned. The family built a new store, seen here around 1965, on the east side of Route 11 in Troutville. In 1950, Bland Painter Jr. became the owner. Later, with partners, he opened regional stores under the name Thriftway. For over 35 years, he operated the Troutville store with his daughter Page Weddle. Painter died in 2008, but the store remains open today. (Courtesy of Betty Jeter Painter.)

Lucille B. Lakes served as the postmaster in Cloverdale from April 30, 1957, to February 28, 1986. She had been a clerk when the previous postmaster, John Pat Guyer, died. She served as acting postmaster until June 27, 1960, when she received her official commission from President Eisenhower. Active in the National Postmasters Association, Lakes is seen here at a 1980s convention. She died in 2012. (Courtesy of Sibyl Lakes Young.)

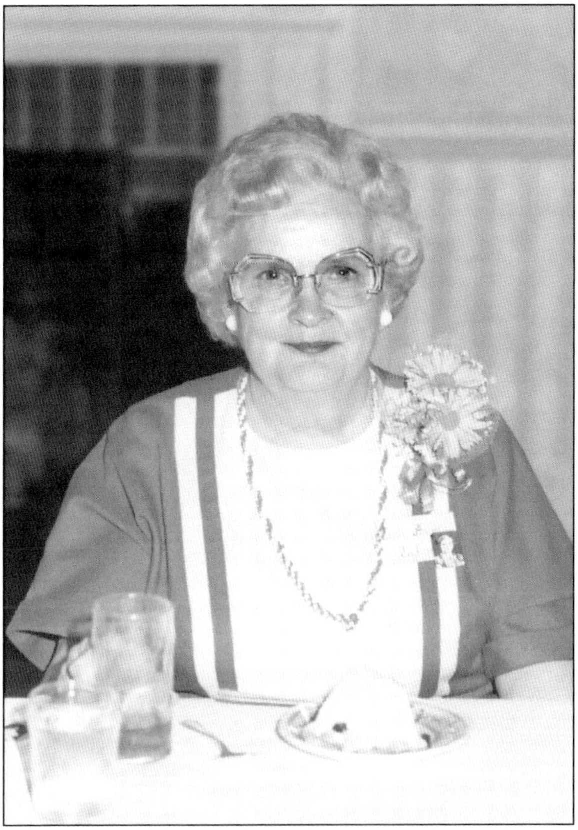

In 1988, *National Geographic* featured the Cloverdale post office in an article that described the experiences of hikers as they traversed the Appalachian Trail from Georgia to Maine. The photograph below shows hikers retrieving supplies at Cloverdale that they had mailed to themselves months earlier. Postmistress Lakes, who owned the property behind the post office, allowed hikers to pitch camp and stay overnight. (Courtesy of Sam Abell/*National Geographic* stock.)

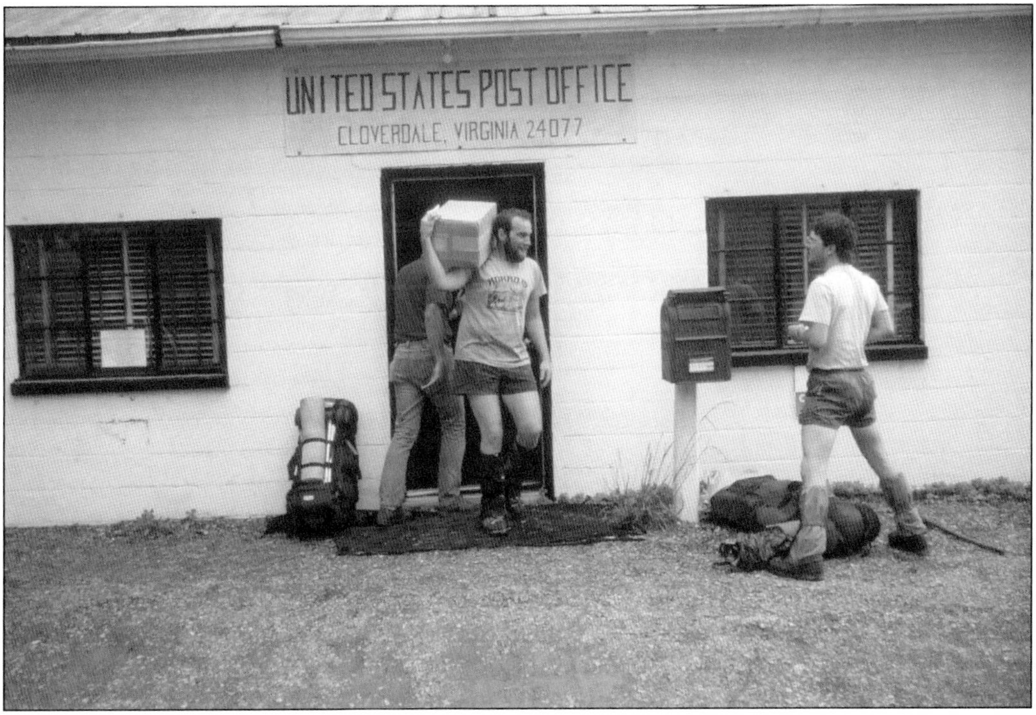

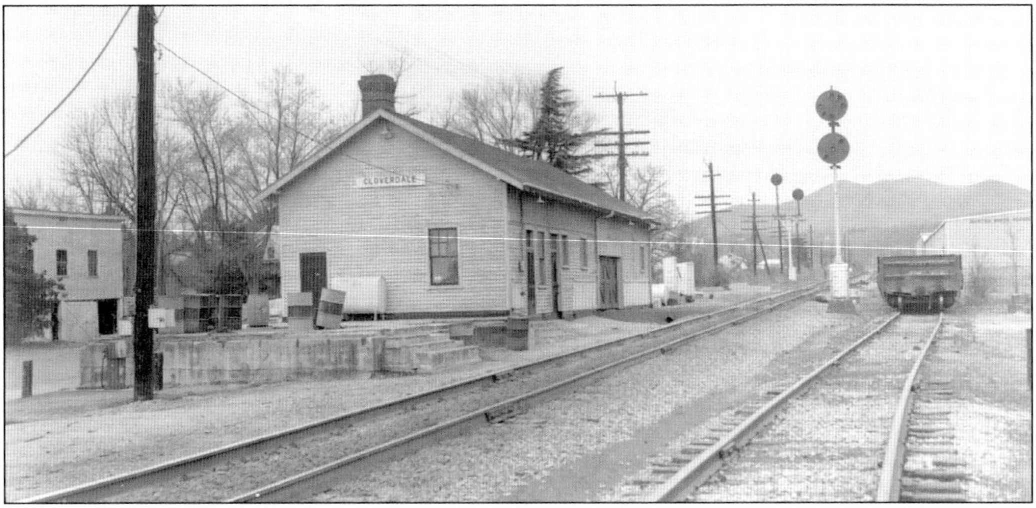

In 1915, the Norfolk & Western Railroad constructed a new combination passenger and freight station in Cloverdale. In 1917, a 10-mile spur line was planned to extend west to Catawba Furnace. Wartime shortages hampered the project, but, in 1922, another attempt, this one under the name Roanoke & Botetourt Railroad Company, planned to complete the line to mineral deposits to the west. The Great Depression later ended the endeavor. (Courtesy of NWHP, DLA, VT.)

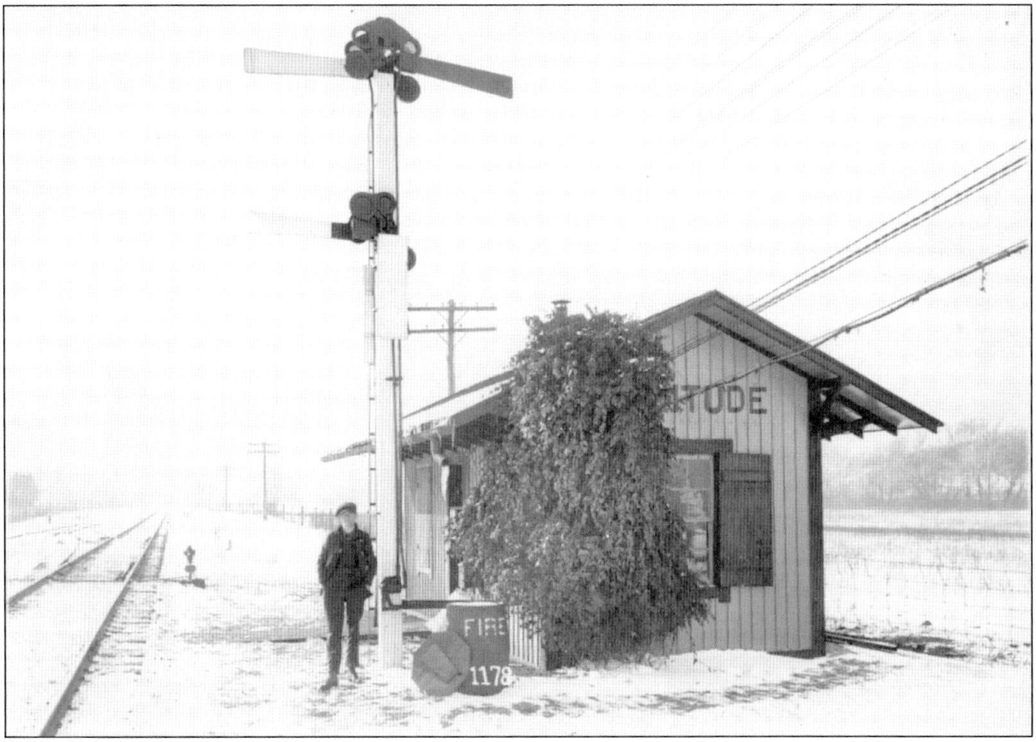

In 1882, the Shenandoah Valley Railroad acquired eight miles of the Richmond & Allegheny Railroad that included stops in Botetourt County. The order station known as Glenwood, located at mile post 207 on the east bank of the James River, was renamed Solitude, no doubt for its quiet surroundings. From Solitude, the line climbed a short grade to the flag stop near the Arcadia Iron Company. (Courtesy of NWHP, DLA, VT.)

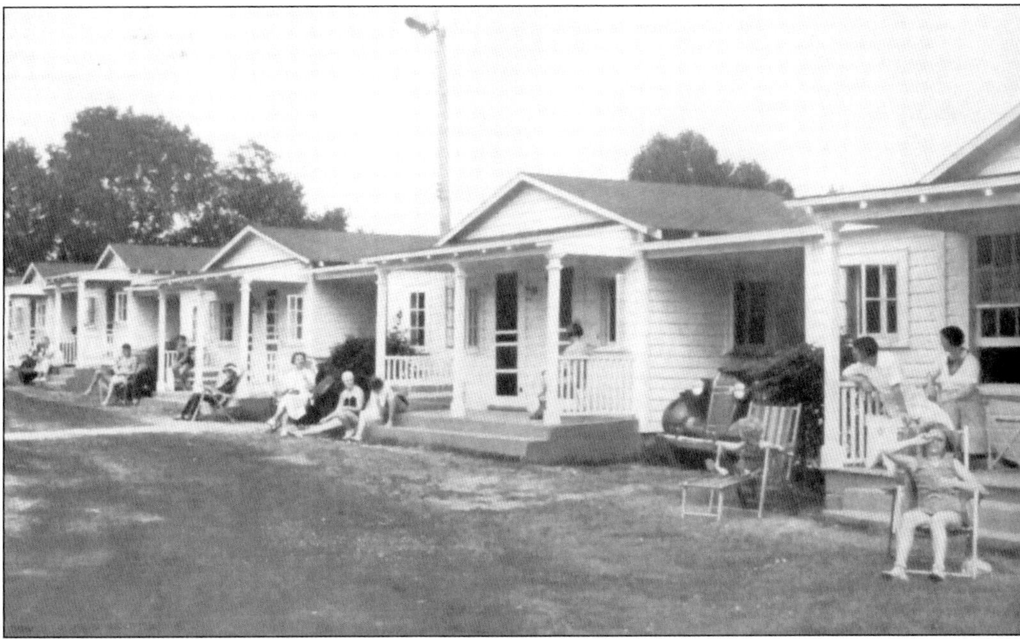

The 18 cottages above, owned and operated by Otis R. and Bertie Mae Buck, were the beginnings of the Traveltown Motor Court and amusement center. J.H. and Loulla Jarrett later owned the Cloverdale complex and developed the modern motel. The cottages were moved within Cloverdale as private homes. Traveltown offered a motor court wing, as well as a two-story hotel. The complex had a swimming pool, a miniature golf course, a restaurant, and a gift shop. Many travelers recall the "Big Chef" sign at the restaurant (bottom right). The 1985 flood closed the business, and the buildings were demolished around 2010. (Both courtesy of Mike Lee.)

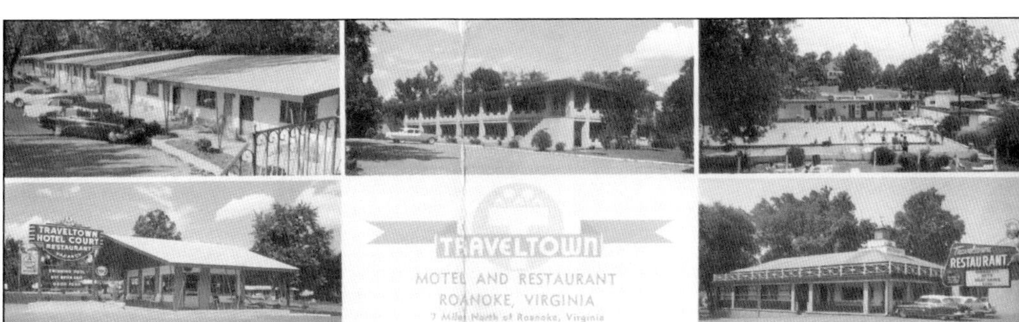

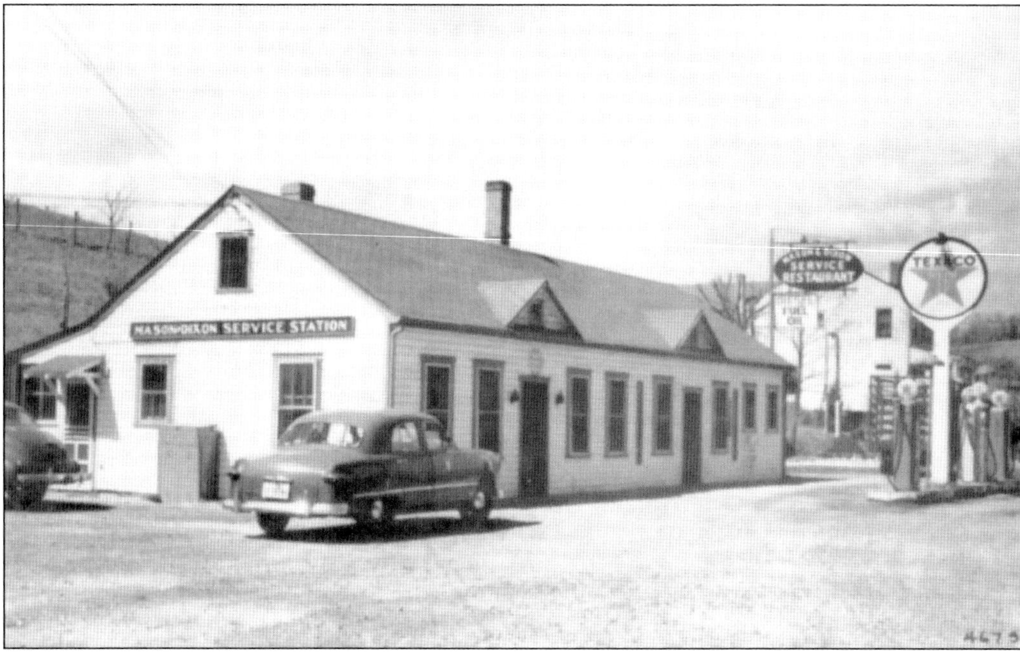

This 1940s view of the Mason & Dixon Service Station location on Route 11 north of Troutville shows the original frame building. At the time, Mrs. S.B. Moore operated the station and offered home-cooked meals at all hours. The building was enlarged in the 1960s and is now Scott's Thrift Store. (Courtesy of Mike Lee.)

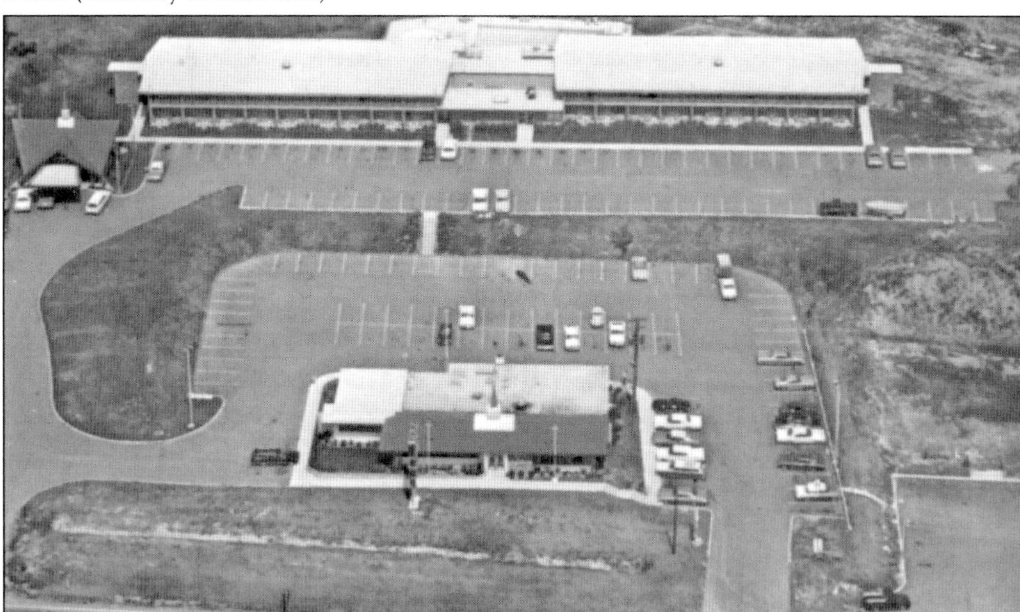

This aerial view shows the Howard Johnson's motel (rear) and restaurant (front) along Route 220. A Texaco station adjoined the property to the right. The national franchise was one of the first to open in Daleville when Interstate 81 was completed. Other motels, service stations, and restaurants soon followed, and Exit 150 (originally Exit 44) developed into a commercial hub. (Courtesy of Mike Lee.)

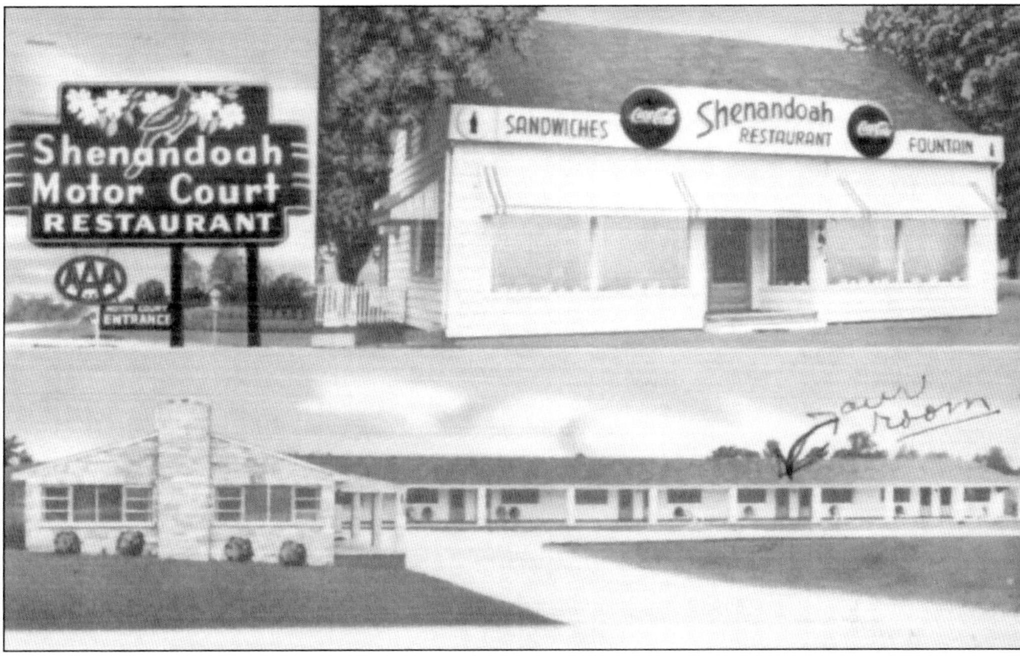

In the 1950s, Mike and Robert Buck operated the Shenandoah Motor Court and Restaurant, located on the west side of Route 11 north of Nace. The motor court was an L-shaped building with a covered porch along the front. On this postcard, the sender points out her room to the recipient, her college-aged son. (Courtesy of Mike Lee.)

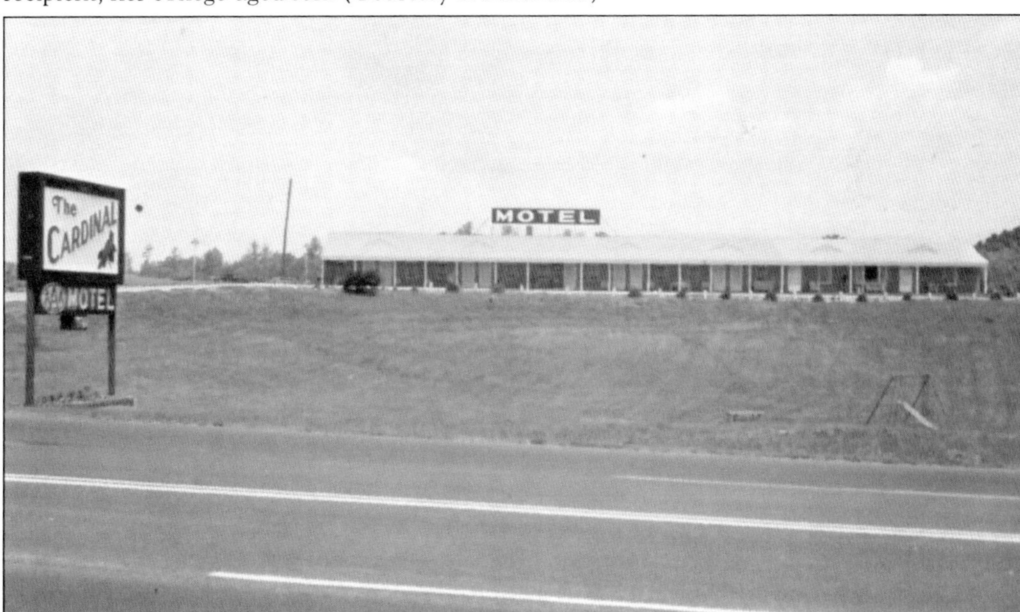

L.G. and Opal Wilkerson operated the Cardinal Motel on Route 11 near the Shenandoah. The motel was advertised as "Quiet—Well Back from the Highway—Modern." Today, the renovated Cardinal building is the Bethel Ridge Assisted Living facility. Many of the old motels went out of business as more traffic moved to the interstate and away from secondary routes. (Courtesy of Mike Lee.)

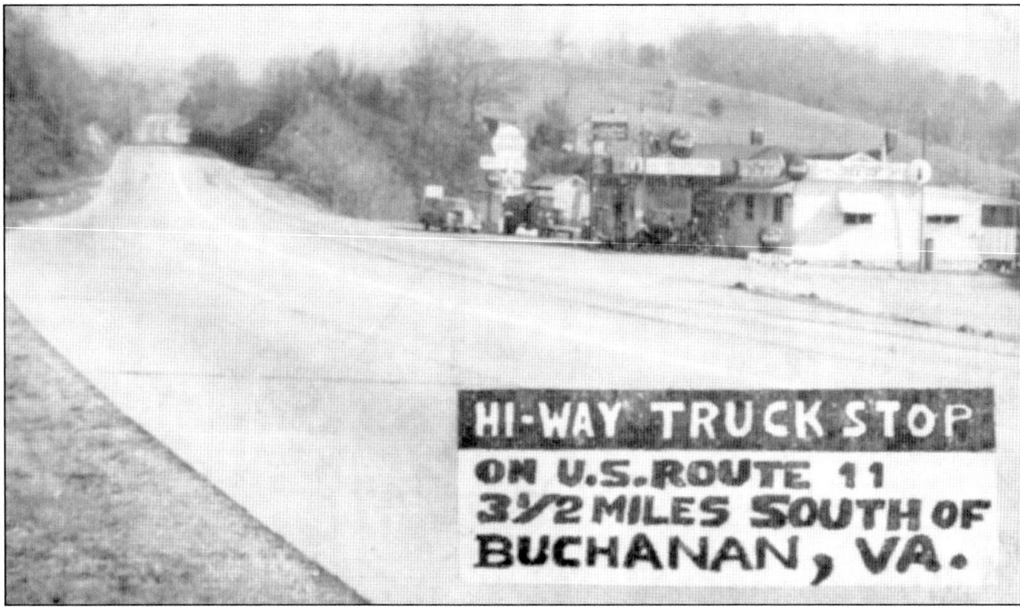

The Hi-Way Truck Stop and service station (above) was located on Route 11 south of Buchanan, across from Waskey's Mill. This view from around 1935 shows gas pumps out front of the small frame restaurant building. After a fire destroyed that building, Mr. and Mrs. F.M. Cooper built the Star Restaurant (below). In the 1950s, Russell and Virginia Maude "Tootsie" Hiner operated the restaurant. Now known as the Northstar Restaurant, it is operated by Debbie Painter, who began working at the restaurant when she was 17. House specialties include biscuits and gravy and homemade pies. (Above, courtesy of Debbie Painter; below, courtesy of Mike Lee.)

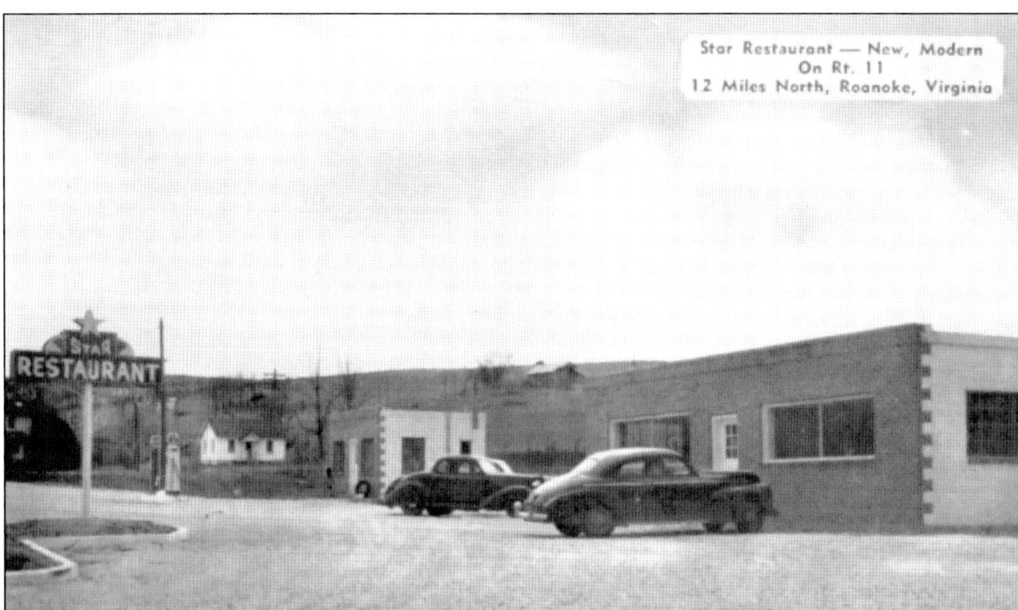

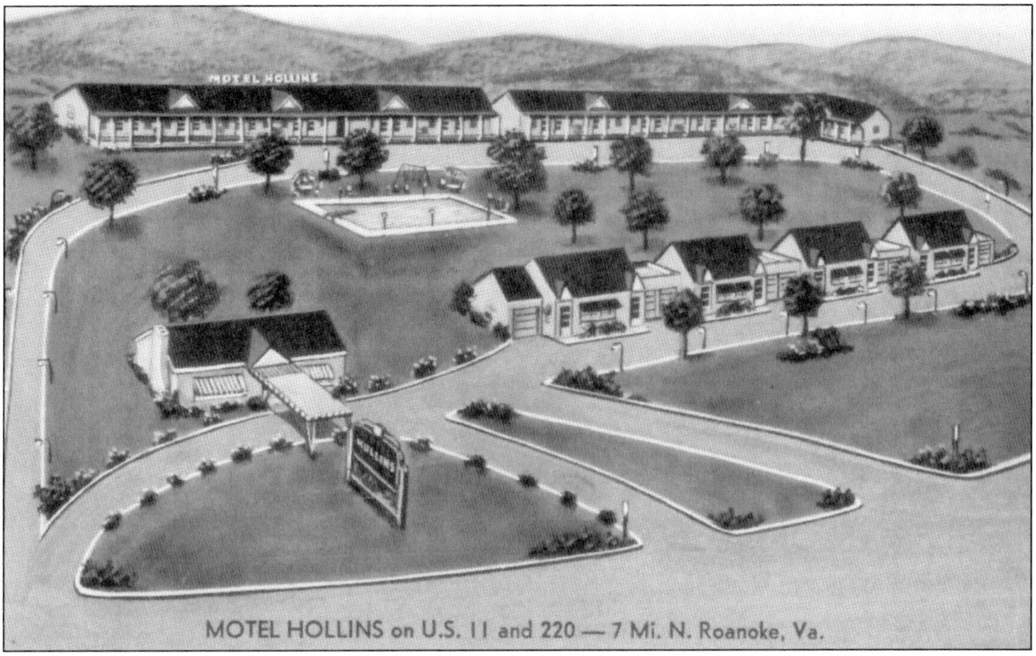

The Motel Hollins is located on Route 11 in Cloverdale, across from the McFarland store. B.D. and F.A. Oyler started the motel, which consisted of an office building, cottages with private garages, and a traditional motel at the top of the hill. Like others, the motel struggled after the construction of Interstate 81, which routed traffic off of Route 11. The motel buildings still stand. (Courtesy of Mike Lee.)

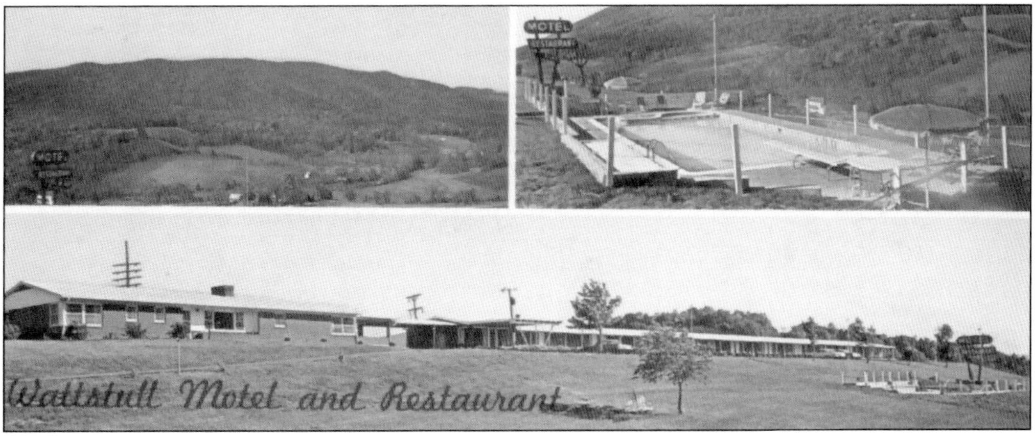

Located north of Buchanan in Arcadia, the Wattstull Inn has a commanding view over Interstate 81 toward Purgatory Mountain. In 1959, Edward N. Watts Sr. and Mary Sue Stull established the 20-room motel with amenities that included a pool, a playground, and a restaurant, making it an ideal stop for families traveling along the nearby Blue Ridge Parkway. The Wattstull, now with 26 rooms, is still family owned and operated. (Courtesy of Mike Lee.)

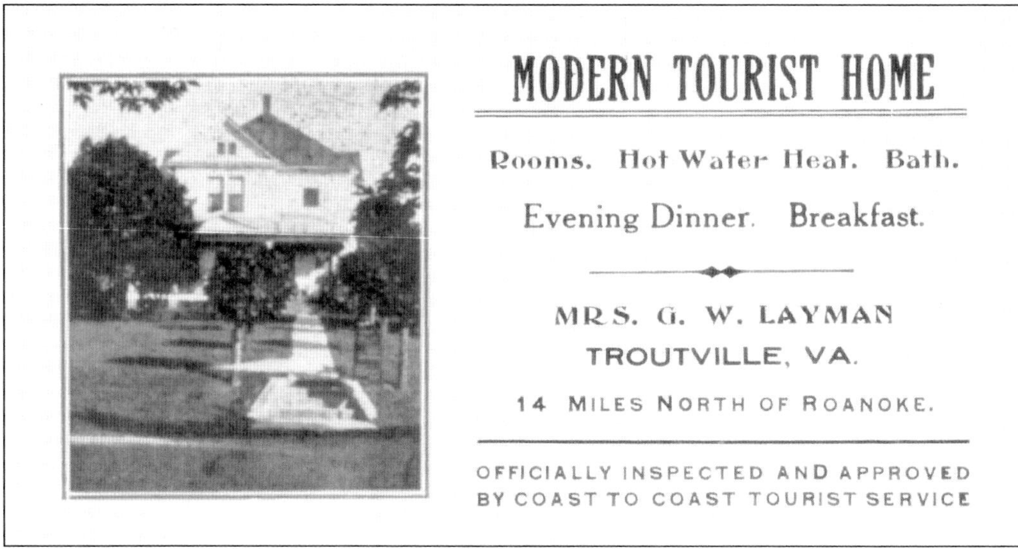

In the late 1920s, as automobile traffic began to increase, the cottage industry of "tourist homes" developed. Akin to today's bed-and-breakfasts, they offered travelers rooms for rent in private homes, meals, and often garage facilities. George and Lillie Layman operated the Layman tourist home on Route 11. Mrs. Layman and her daughter Pauline continued the business until 1943. (Courtesy of Mike Lee.)

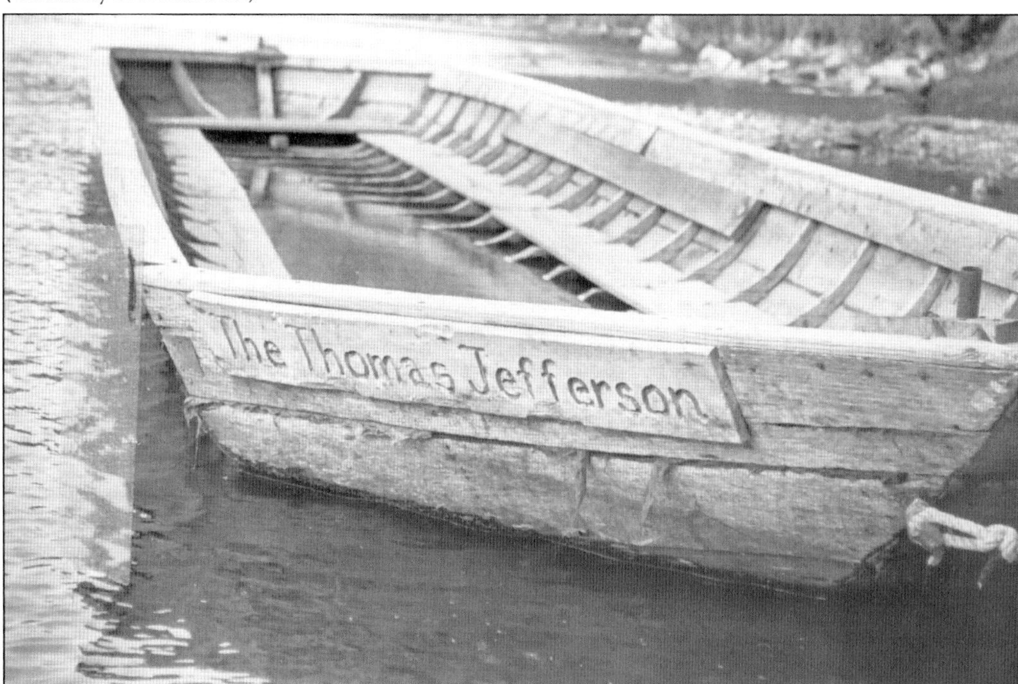

In the 1770s, the James River bateaux developed as a uniquely Virginian river vessel. The shallow-drafted boat, which was akin to a dugout canoe, was steered with a long oar called a sweep. While primarily used to transport hogsheads of tobacco, the boats also provided passenger service. Replicas like this one run in bateaux festivals and demonstrations held on the James River. (Courtesy of the *Fincastle Herald*.)

Five

Sesquicentennial of the Civil War

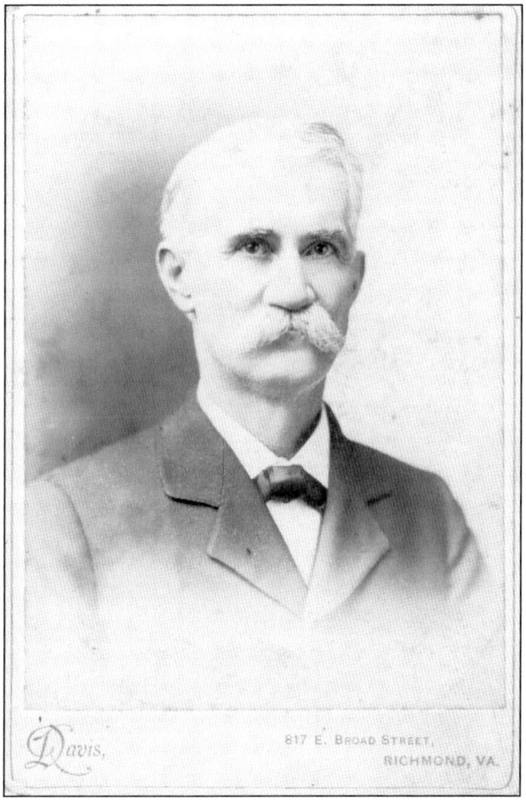

During the Civil War, Botetourt native John Metheny served in the Confederate army. In the 1862 Battle of Winchester, he was wounded in the left arm, which was later amputated. Metheny's life, however, was spared by a spoon he found on the battlefield, which he stuck in his breast pocket. The spoon deflected a bullet aimed at Metheny's chest. In 2007, Metheny's family donated a portrait, the spoon, and war-related mementos to the Botetourt County Historical Museum. (Courtesy of BCHM.)

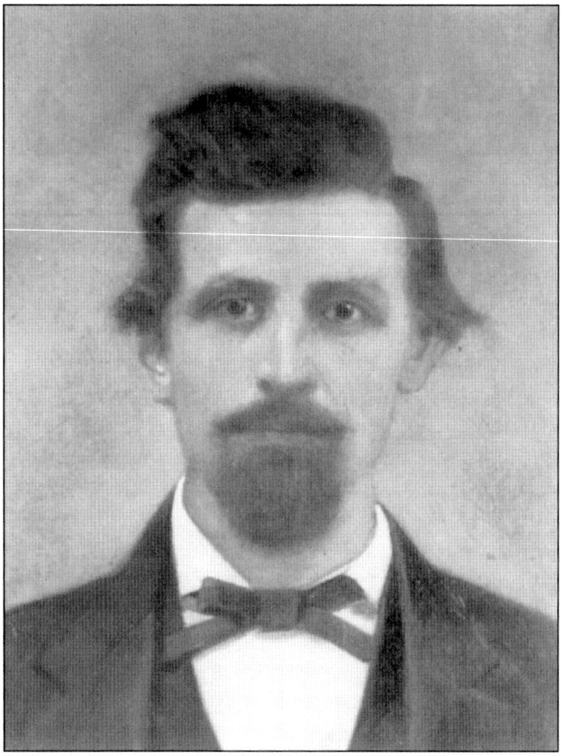

Robert James Thrasher (left), born in Botetourt County in 1832, married Martha Amanda Hammond in 1856. When the Civil War broke out, Thrasher enlisted in the 22nd Regiment, Virginia Infantry. Wounded and captured at Lewisburg, West Virginia, Thrasher was taken to the Union prisoner of war hospital in Gallipolis, Ohio. On July 3, 1862, the *Gallipolis Journal* listed Thrasher and Adam S. Rader (below), another Botetourt native in the 22nd Infantry, among the "Secesh prisoners." Rader was hit in the thigh with a minie ball, which remained there during his hospitalization. Both men died at the prison and were buried at the Pine Street Cemetery in Gallipolis. Rader's tombstone was incorrectly engraved with the name *Baden*. In 2012, John W. Rader discovered the mistake and placed a corrected stone over his cousin's grave. (Left, courtesy of Howard Revercomb Hammond; below, courtesy of John W. Rader.)

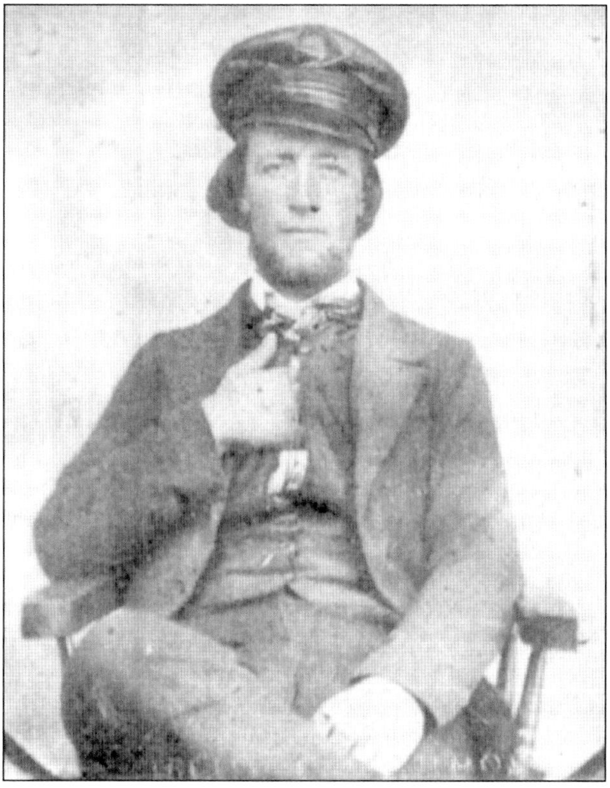

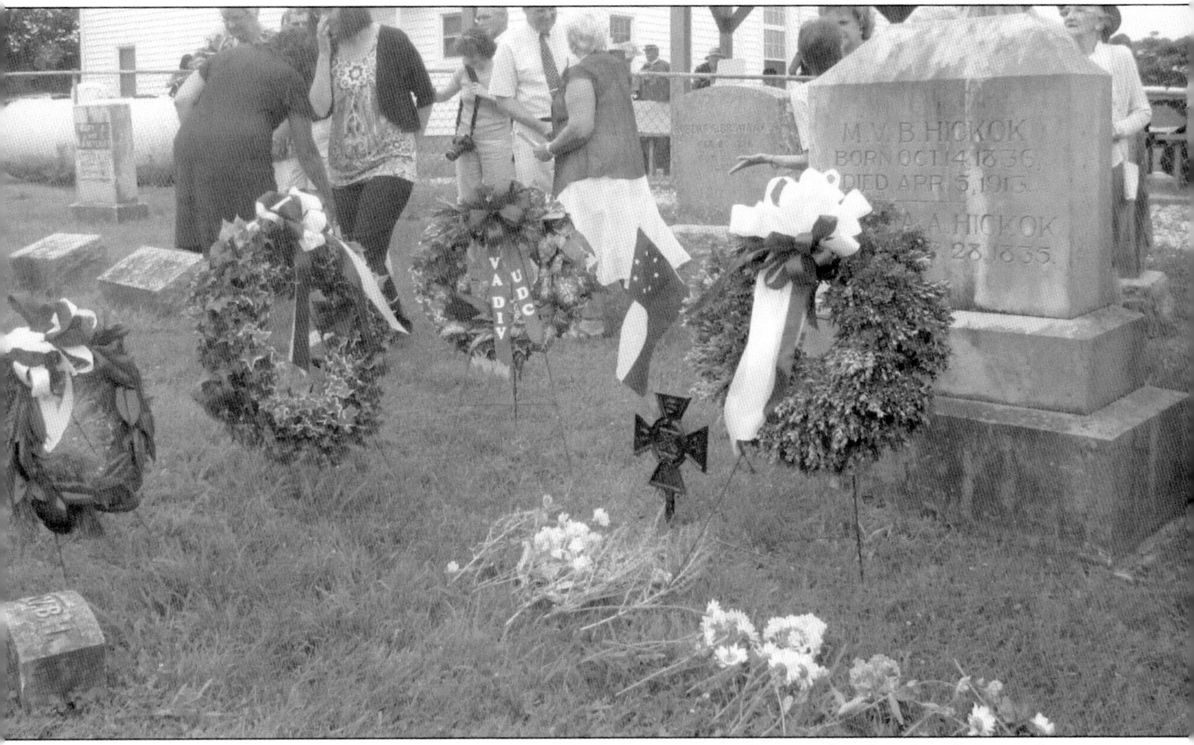

Martin Van Buren "M.V.B." Hickok was wounded three times during the Battle of Gettysburg, reportedly losing a leg, and was wounded again in both thighs at the Battle of Five Forks, only eight days before the surrender at Appomattox. In 1913, Hickok finally succumbed to complications from his war wounds. He and his wife, Martha Hammond, are buried at the Andrew United Methodist Memorial Chapel in Springwood. In July 2013, the Fincastle chapter of the United Daughters of the Confederacy dedicated a Southern Cross at Hickok's grave, 150 years after the Battle of Gettysburg. This photograph shows Hammond family members at the graveside during the ceremony. (Photograph by and courtesy of Patrick W. McClane.)

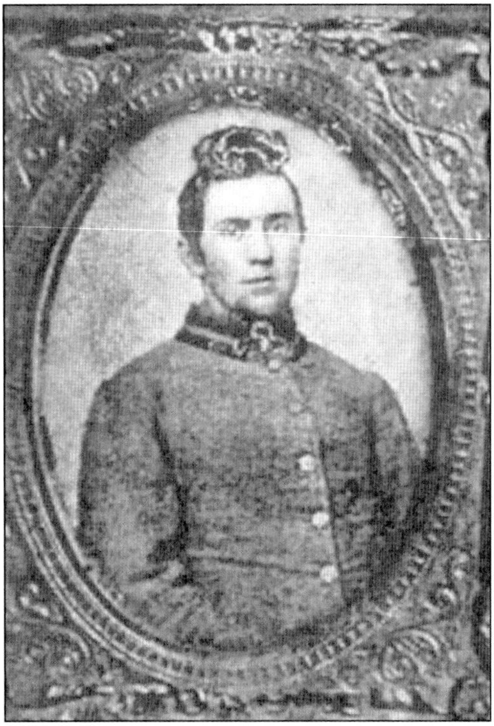

In 1859, Rufus H. Peck of Fincastle enlisted with the local militia, known as the Botetourt Dragoons. In May 1861, this group marched to Lynchburg, where they became Company C of the 2nd Virginia Cavalry. The unit fought in over 50 battles, including major engagements at Bull Run, Chancellorsville, and Cold Harbor. In his memoirs, published 50 years after the war, Peck recounted that the ladies of Botetourt presented the unit with a flag (below), which they carried during the first two years of the war. After the war, Peck safeguarded the flag until 1907, when he donated it to the Museum of the Confederacy in Richmond. The Fincastle chapter of the United Daughters of the Confederacy has undertaken fundraising efforts to restore the flag. (Left, from *Reminiscences of a Confederate Soldier*; below, courtesy of Katherine Wetzel, Museum of the Confederacy, Richmond, Virginia.)

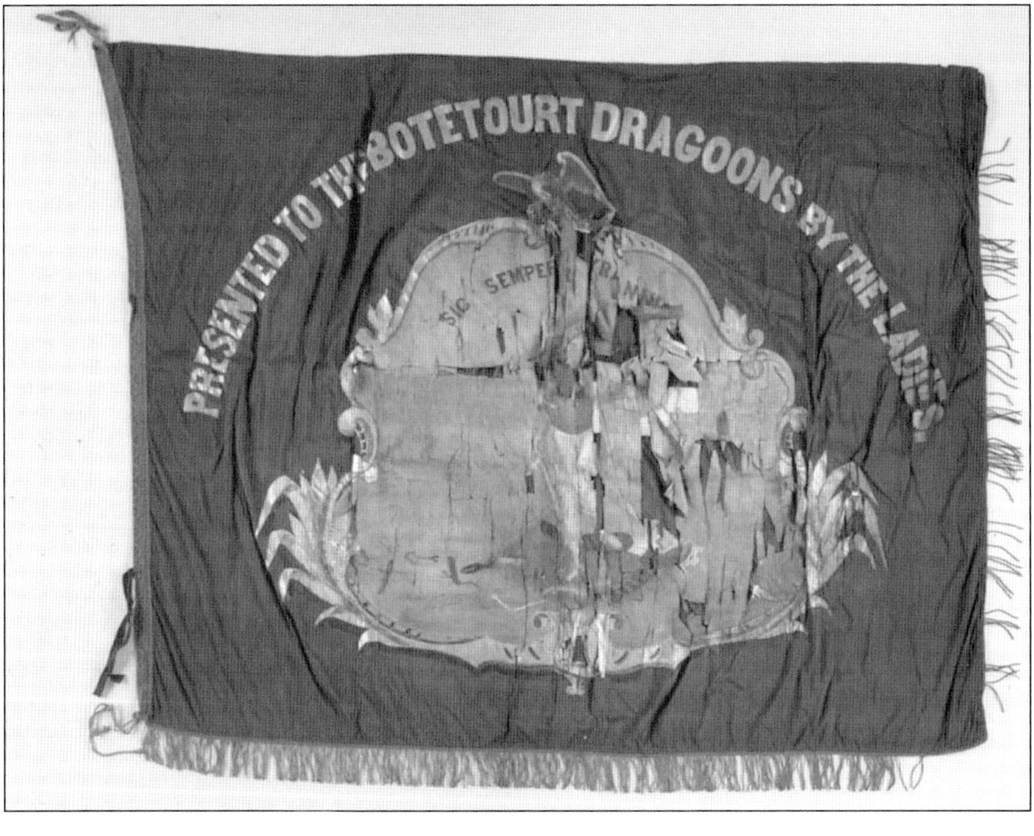

On May 26, 1864, Union general David Hunter (right) left Winchester en route to Lynchburg to sever the Southside Railway. The raid was part of a simultaneous attack on Confederate forces throughout Virginia intended to cut off the last lifelines of supply to Confederate general Robert E. Lee's army. Marching south through the Shenandoah Valley, Hunter entered Buchanan, the terminus of the James River and Kanawha Canal. The ensuing battle resulted in the destruction of the James River Bridge, several buildings in town, and Mount Joy, the home of Confederate colonel John T. Anderson. Virginia's Civil War Trails program includes a driving tour that follows the route of Hunter's Raid (below). Roadside signs mark significant sites, detailing the wartime events that occurred there. (Right, courtesy of the Library of Congress; below, courtesy of Virginia Civil War Trails, Inc.)

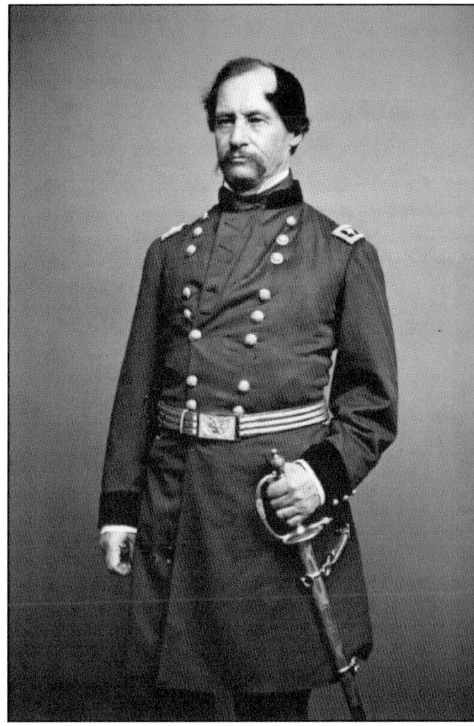

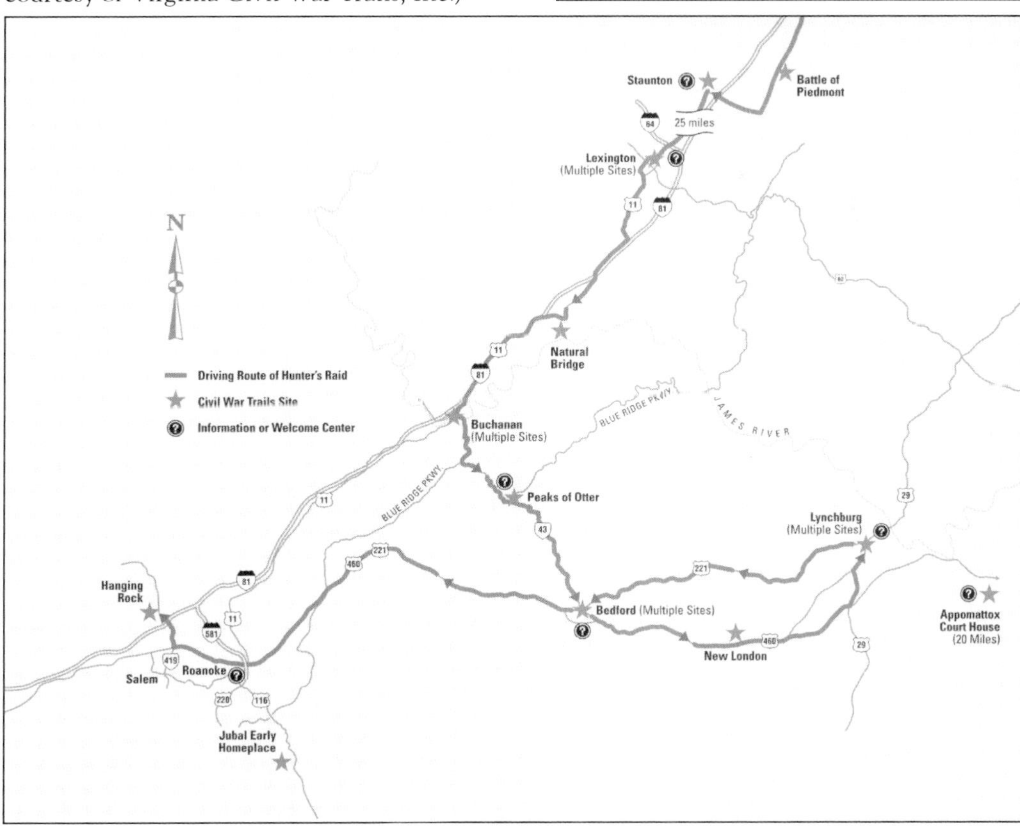

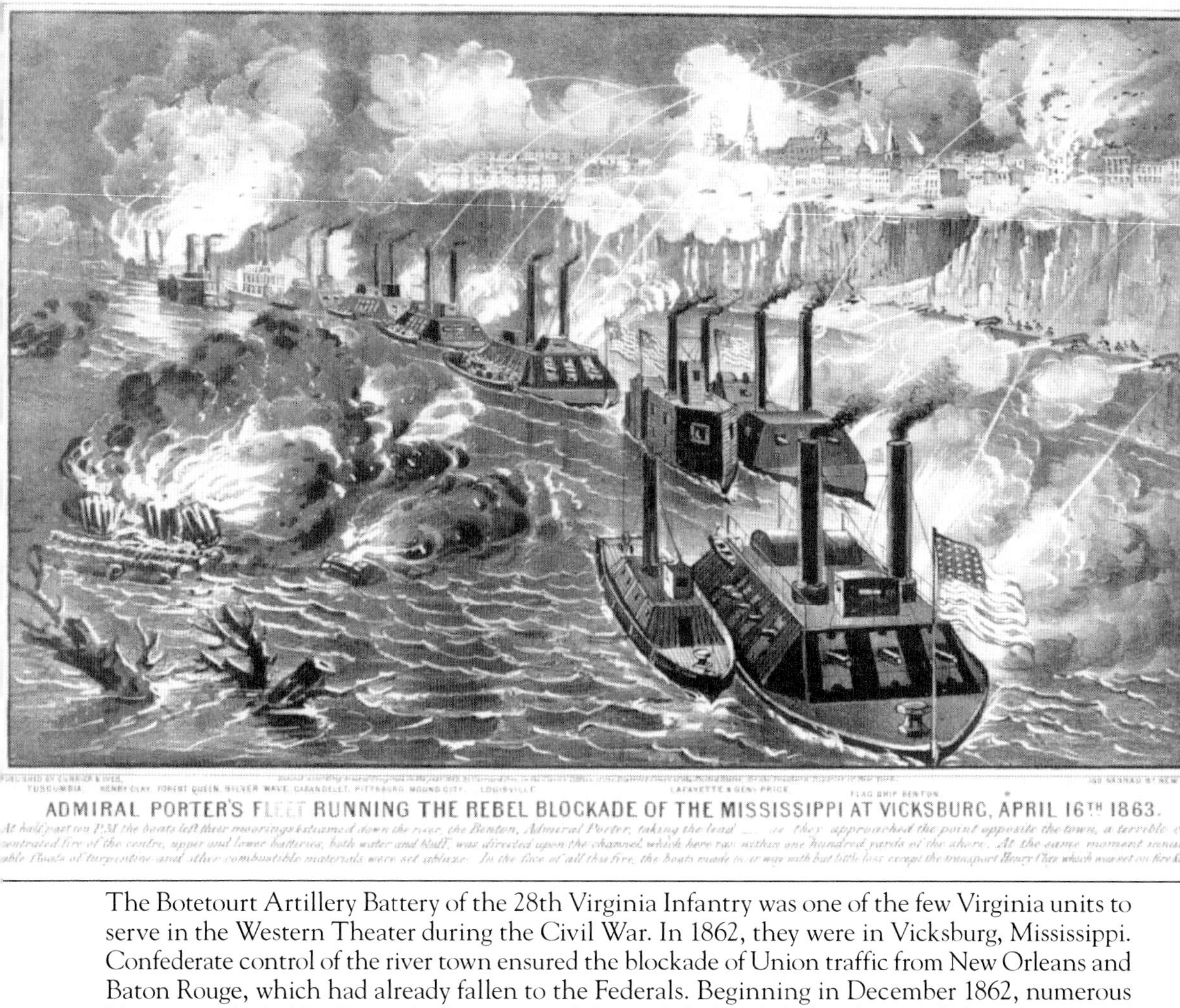

The Botetourt Artillery Battery of the 28th Virginia Infantry was one of the few Virginia units to serve in the Western Theater during the Civil War. In 1862, they were in Vicksburg, Mississippi. Confederate control of the river town ensured the blockade of Union traffic from New Orleans and Baton Rouge, which had already fallen to the Federals. Beginning in December 1862, numerous Union attacks led by Generals Sherman and Grant failed to dislodge the Confederates. In April 1863, the Federal fleet finally broke through the Rebel batteries, but they did not dislodge the troops. For 47 days, the Confederates, including those of the Botetourt Artillery, settled into a siege. Reinforcements from Gen. John Johnston, who had been forced to withdraw and was blocked by Union forces, did not arrive, and, suffering from illness, wounds, malnutrition, and short supplies, Gen. John C. Pemberton was forced to surrender on July 4, 1863. The day before, General Lee's forces had been repelled at Gettysburg. Although it continued for nearly two more years, these two events marked a turning point in the war. (Courtesy of the Library of Congress.)

In 1859, the unit organized as the Mountain Rifles Home Guard became Company H of the 28th Virginia Infantry. The battery participated in the Siege of Vicksburg, as well as in the defense of Buchanan in 1864. On July 20, 1902, the Botetourt Artillery Association erected a monument to its comrades near the Buchanan Presbyterian Church (right). Eloise Johnston, Gen. John Johnston's daughter, unveiled the obelisk. On November 22, 1907, another monument dedicated to the Botetourt Artillery Battery was unveiled at the Vicksburg National Military Park (below). The *Richmond Times-Dispatch* reported that many of the unit's 16 surviving members were present. Mary Johnston, a novelist and the oldest daughter of General Johnston, wrote a history of the unit for the occasion. (Right, courtesy of VDHR; below, courtesy of the author's collection.)

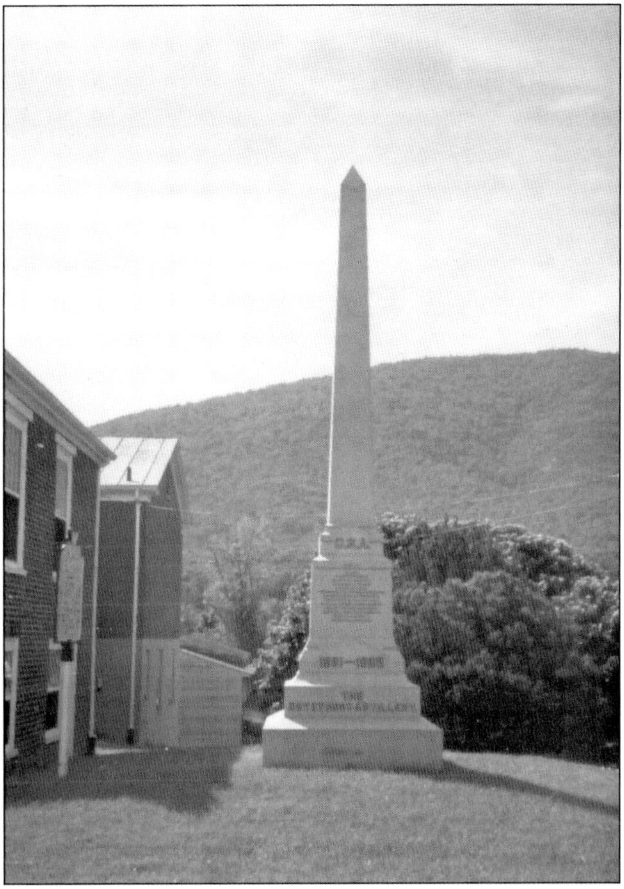

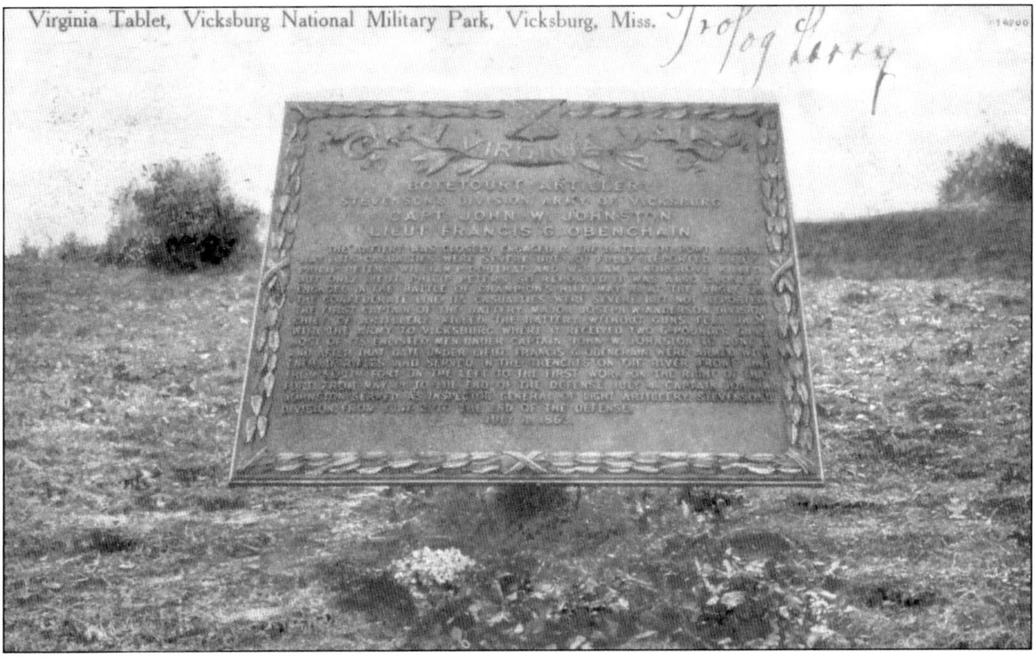

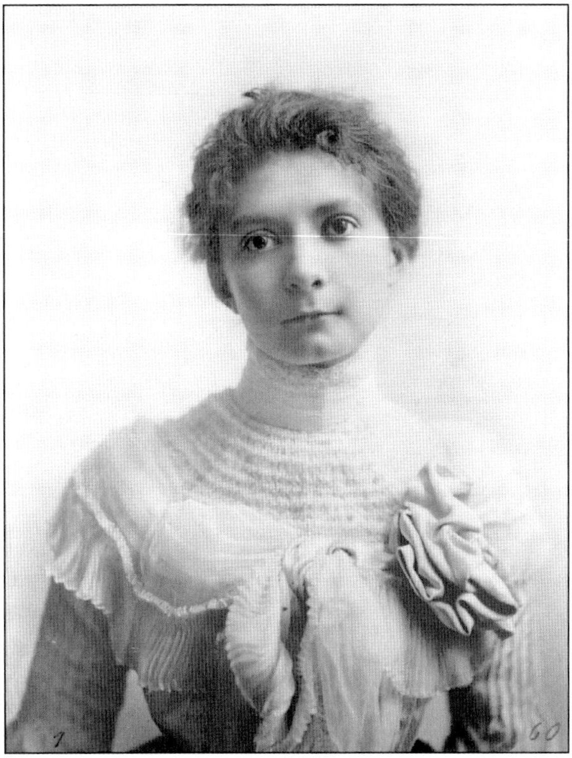

Mary Johnston was the daughter of Confederate general John W. Johnston. Until she was 15, Mary and her family lived in Buchanan. Mary became one of the country's most popular writers and was well regarded for her two historical novels about the Civil War, *The Long Roll* and *Cease Firing*, which she dedicated to the memory of her father and her cousin Gen. Joseph E. Johnston. She eventually published 23 novels, as well as plays and short stories. In 2011, Yale history professor David W. Blight listed *Cease Firing*, which contains lavish illustrations by N.C. Wyeth, as one of the five best novels on the war. Critics often praised Johnston's vivid and historically accurate details. Mary is buried with her family in Richmond's Hollywood Cemetery, overlooking the James River. (Left, courtesy of the Library of Congress; below, courtesy of the author's collection.)

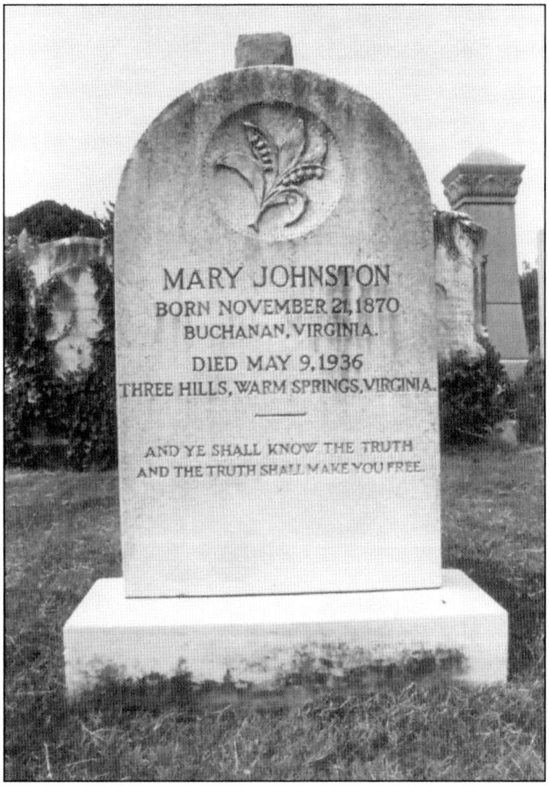

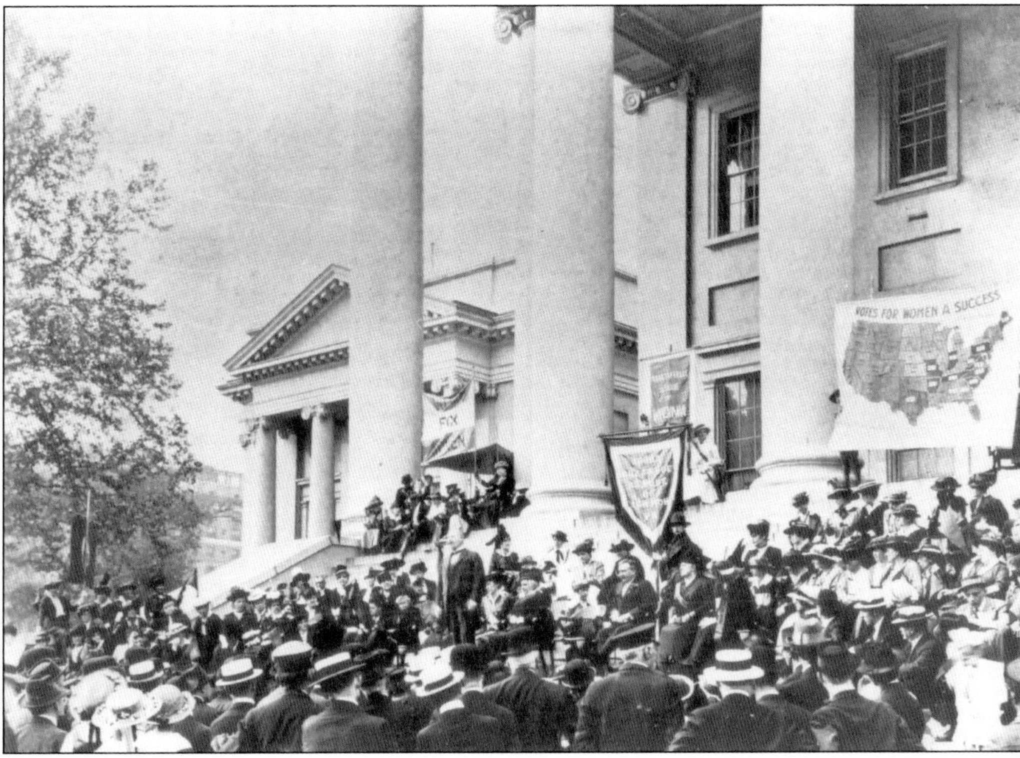

In 1900, Mary Johnston's *To Have and to Hold* topped fiction sales in the United States. She lent her popularity to several social causes, including woman's suffrage. In 1909, she joined the Equal Suffrage League of Virginia, in which she served as an honorary vice president. The group is seen above around 1915 at a rally on the steps of the state capitol. (Courtesy of Roanoke Public Library, Hollins Branch.)

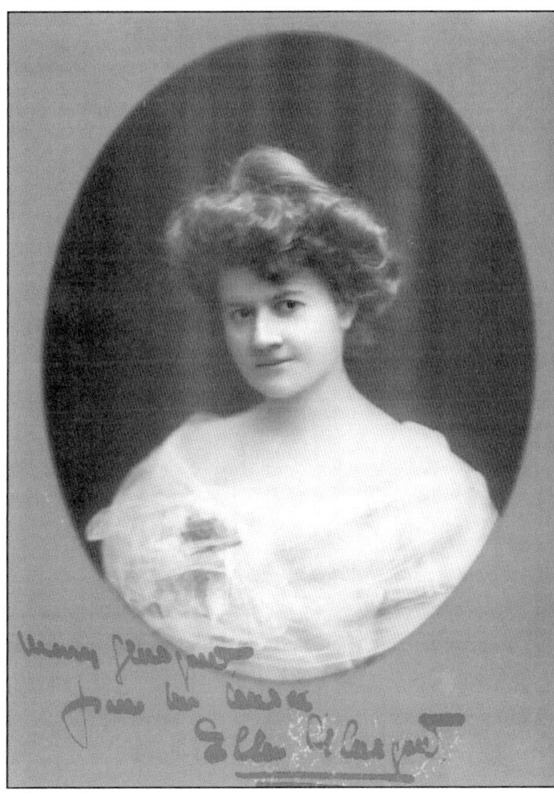

Mary Johnston and fellow Virginia author Ellen Glasgow (seen here) were close friends and shared much in common, including family ties to Botetourt County. Glasgow's father, Frank, was born in Fincastle and practiced law there from 1879 to 1885. Ellen, who won the Pulitzer Prize for literature, fondly recalled summers spent in Botetourt at her maternal grandparents' farm, Walnut Grove. (Courtesy of the Library of Congress.)

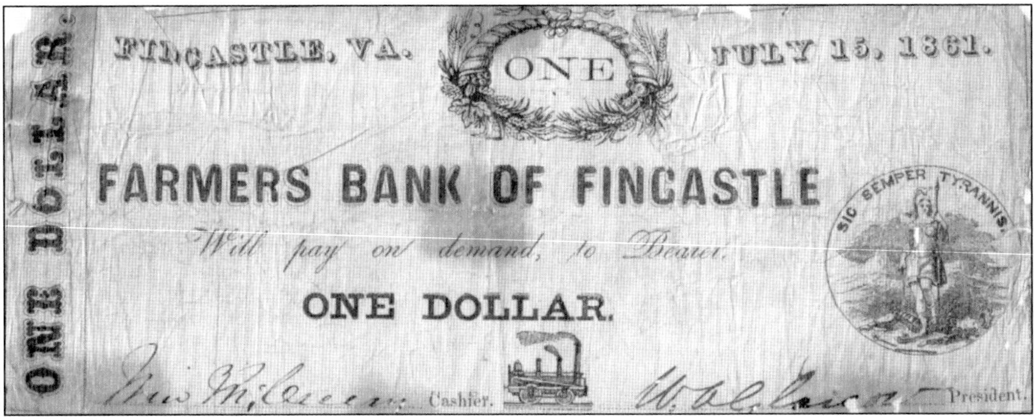

In 1856, the Farmers Bank of Fincastle opened to serve the rural-area citizens. During the Civil War, without a centralized Confederate treasury, banks printed their own currency. This dollar bill from 1861 bears the seal of Virginia, and the currency was backed by Confederate securities. As with other banks, the Farmers Bank of Fincastle collapsed after the war. The money proved worthless, but it has found new value as a collector's item. In 1875, a new bank formed, the Bank of Fincastle, which has been serving county residents ever since. In 1908, the bank built its handsome Fincastle branch building. After the *Fincastle Herald*, which began publication in 1866, the Bank of Fincastle is the second-oldest continually operating business in the area. (Above, courtesy of John E. Alderson Jr.; below, courtesy of the Bank of Fincastle.)

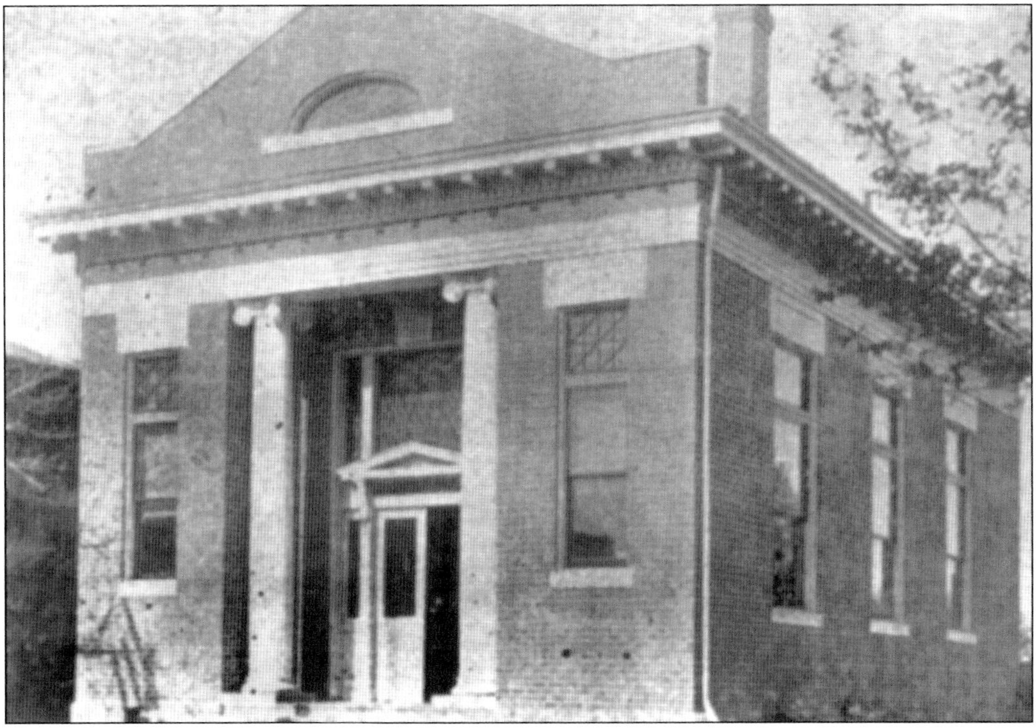

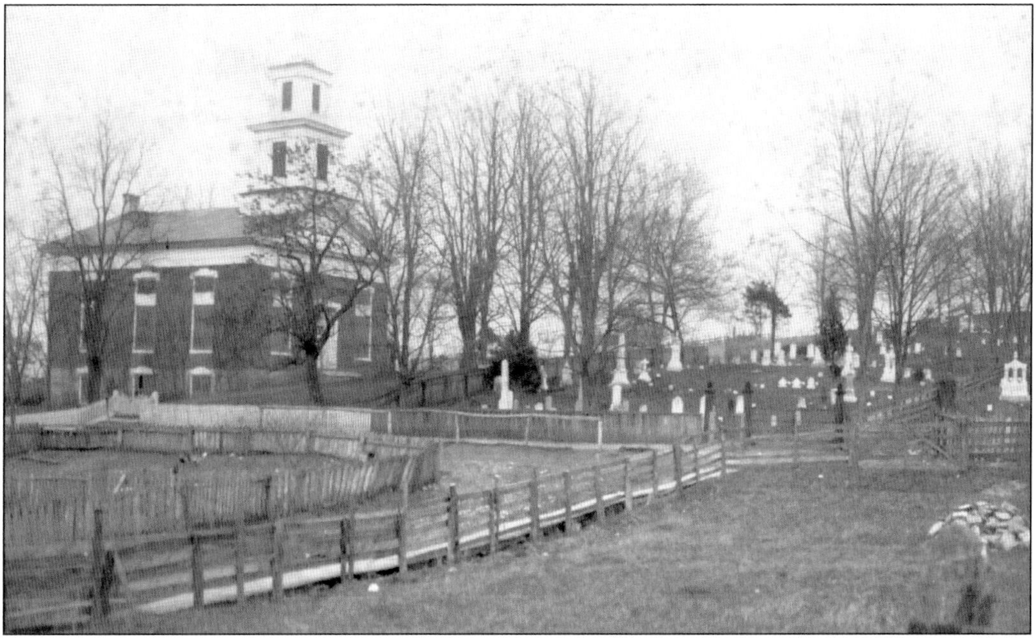

Prior to the Civil War, some local churches allowed free blacks and slaves to worship with white congregants, but required them to sit in upstairs galleries. The Fincastle Methodist Episcopal Church South (above) and Mill Creek Baptist Church followed this practice. In 1849, several free blacks and slaves organized the Fincastle African Baptist Church. In 1866, a frame building was erected on land purchased in Fincastle. When that building burned, a brick sanctuary was built with funding assistance from the Freedman Bureau of Philadelphia. The building's stone basement was used for a time as a school for African American students. Leaders from the church also helped form black churches in Amsterdam, Springwood, Lapsley's Run, Buchanan, and elsewhere in the county. (Above, courtesy of the *Fincastle Herald*; below, courtesy of Patrick McClane.)

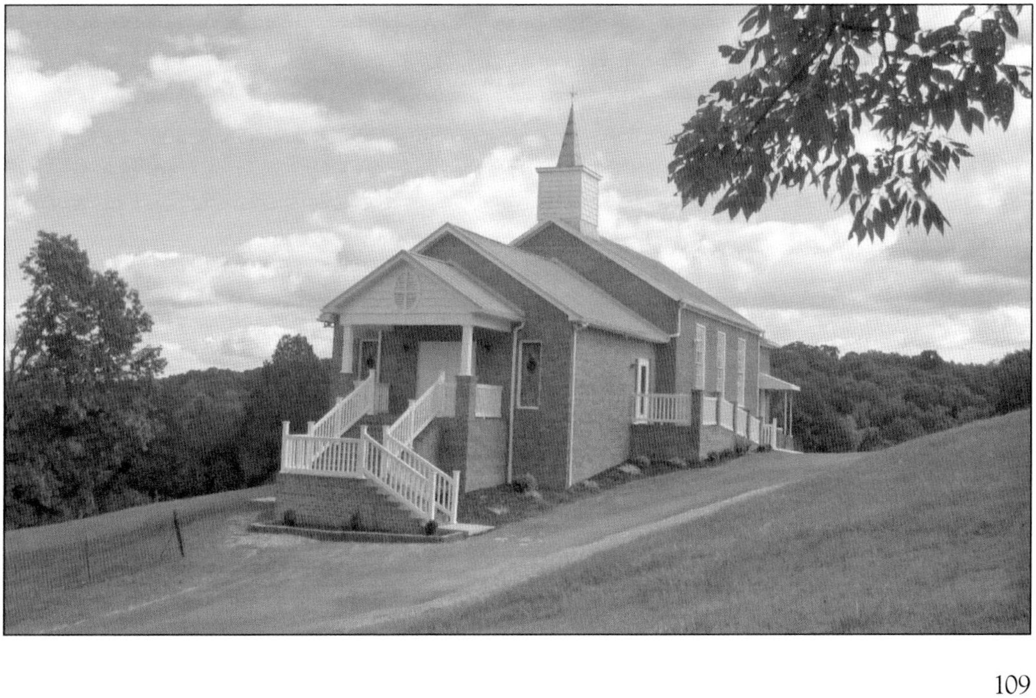

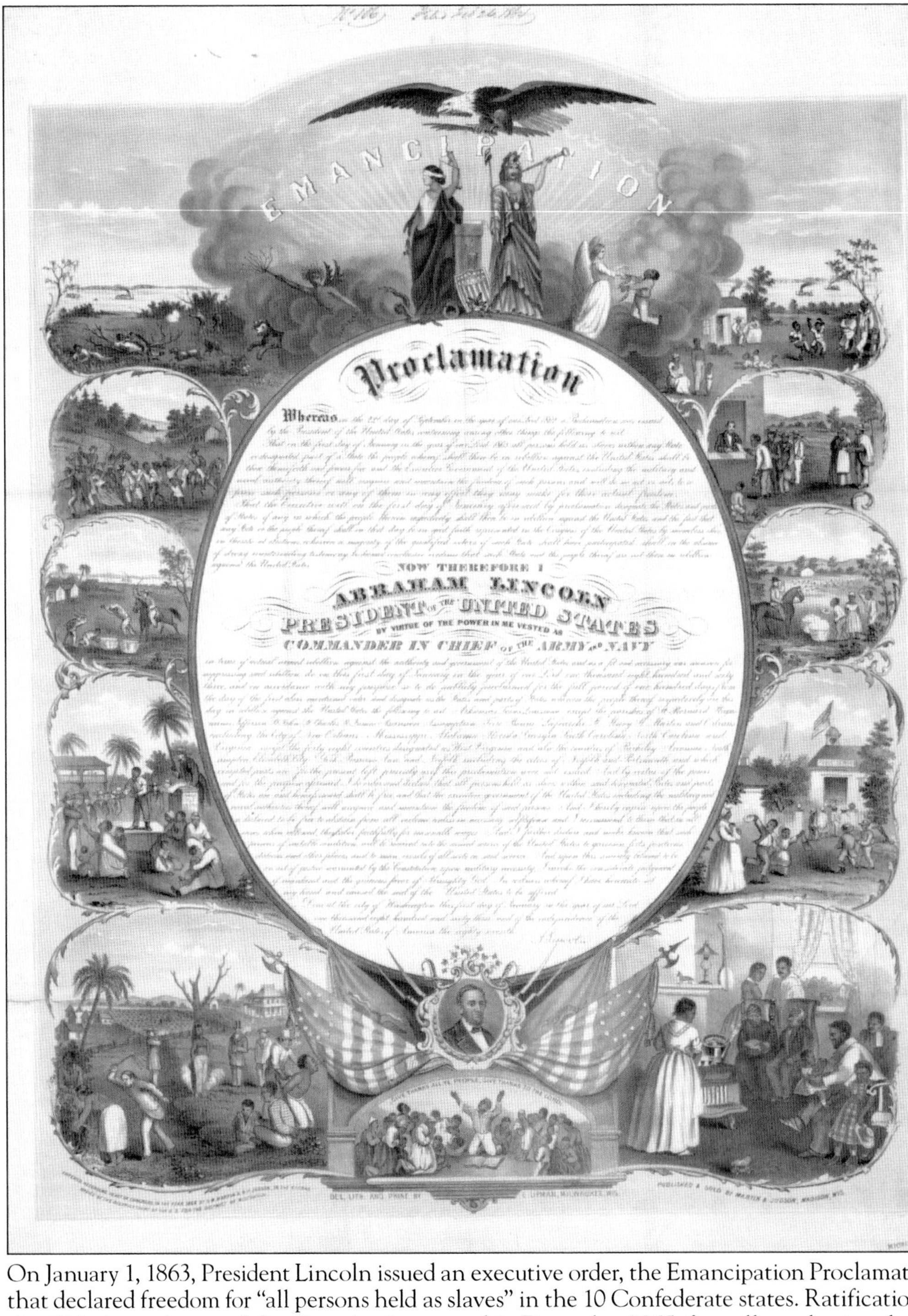

On January 1, 1863, President Lincoln issued an executive order, the Emancipation Proclamation, that declared freedom for "all persons held as slaves" in the 10 Confederate states. Ratification of the 13th Amendment of the Constitution passed in December 1865, formally outlawing slavery in the United States. This commemorative lithograph of the proclamation was illustrated with images of the tribulations and triumphs of the formerly enslaved people. (Courtesy of the Library of Congress.)

Six

TOURISM THEN AND NOW

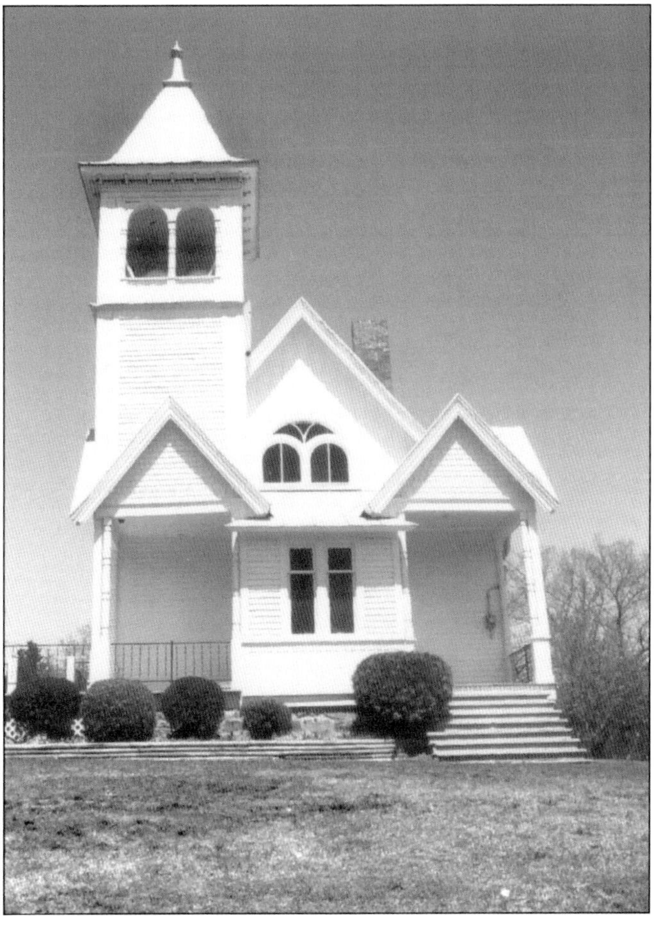

Oriskany's King's Memorial Community Church, formerly a Methodist Episcopal South church, was founded in 1904. The building, an exuberant example of Victorian-style architecture, features a tall corner tower with an open belfry and a bell-cast, pyramidal roof. The colored-glass windows provide a contrast to the church's white exterior. The nondenominational church is located in a peaceful setting along Craig's Creek, near the former mining town of Lignite. (Courtesy of VDHR.)

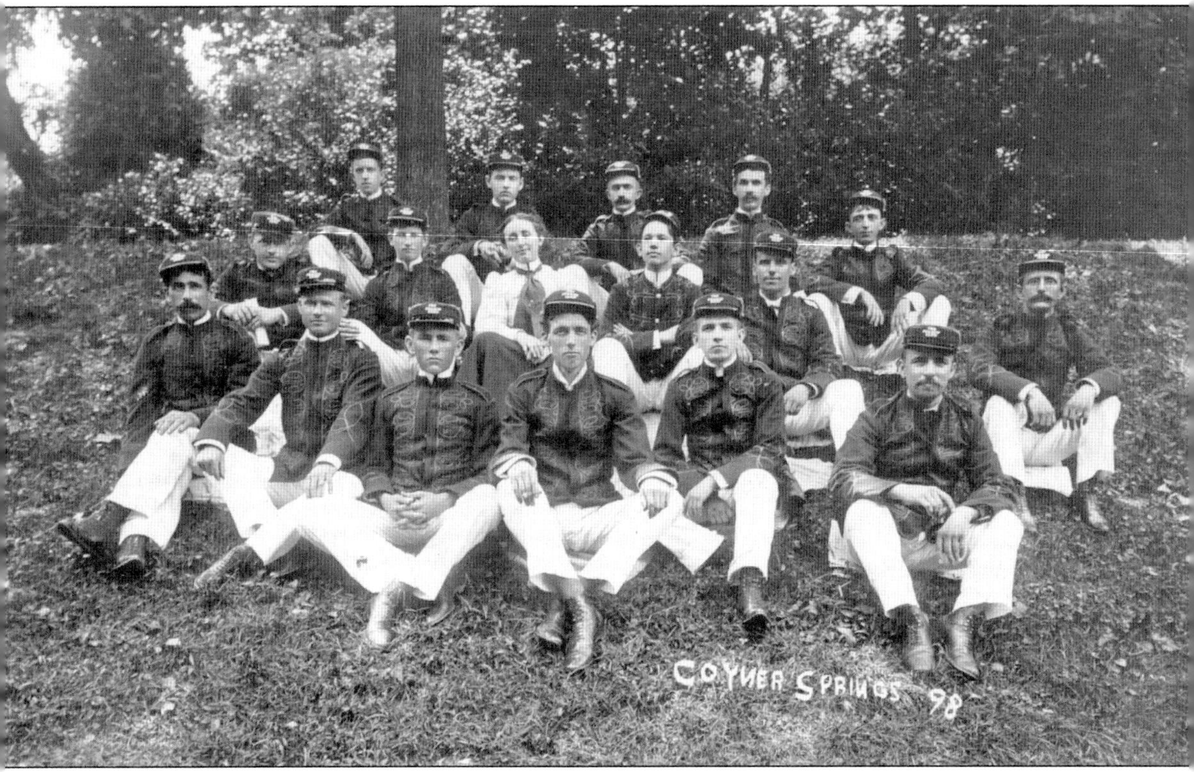

In the early 19th century, the site known as Coyner Springs, located northwest of Route 460, was the site of a gristmill operated by George Coyner. In 1850, Fleming James purchased the property and developed a hotel and resort there that highlighted the healthful benefits of the chalybeate mineral springs on the site. Guests arrived via the Virginia & Tennessee Railroad and by stagecoach. The resort thrived until the early 20th century, but, by 1918, the buildings were removed. This photograph shows the Coyner Springs Band around 1898. The band was part of the daily entertainment at the resort, which also included games and dancing. After another attempt to use the property as an entertainment site, the land was purchased by the City of Roanoke, and a tuberculosis sanitarium was built there in 1939. Later, the facilities were used as a nursing home. Today, the property is the site of a juvenile detention center. (Courtesy of the Virginia Room, Roanoke Public Libraries.)

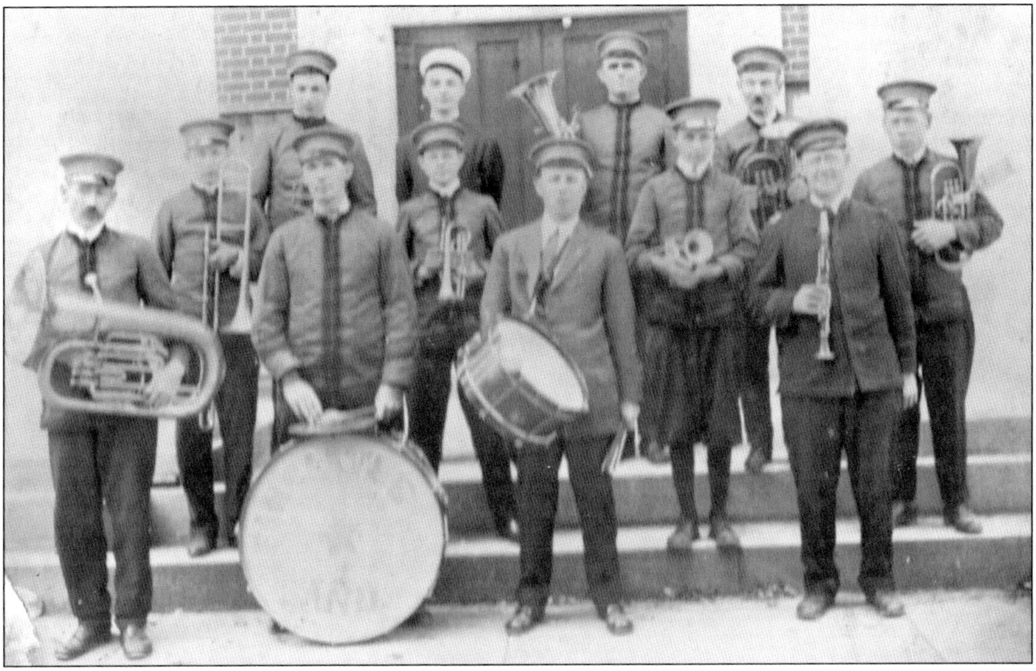

According to Historic Fincastle Inc.'s *Around Town*, the Fincastle Community Band organized at the end of the 19th century and was in existence until about 1940. The band played at Fourth of July and New Year's Eve celebrations, as well as at the county fair, and toured to regional events. The band, which included adults and children, is pictured here around 1905 on the courthouse steps. This image was donated by the J.D. Utt family. (Courtesy of BCHM.)

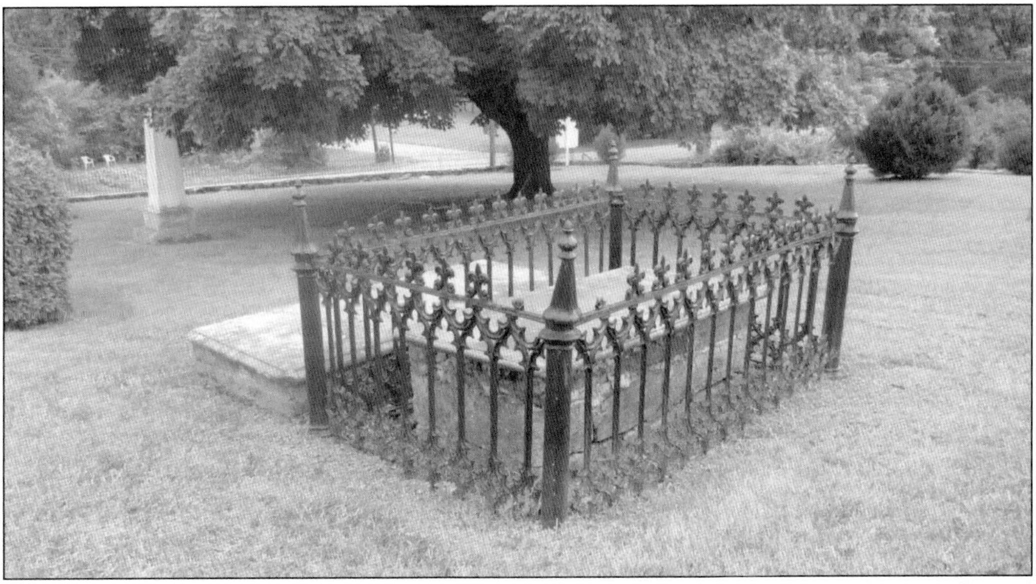

Although many traveled to the resort springs in the western part of Virginia for their proclaimed medicinal and curative effects, some visitors were not so lucky. One early-19th-century traveler, Maria Kollock of Savannah, Georgia, died in Fincastle on her way to Sweet Springs to seek treatment for "pulmonary consumption." She is buried in this ornate marble-topped grave in the Fincastle Presbyterian Church Cemetery. (Courtesy of the author's collection.)

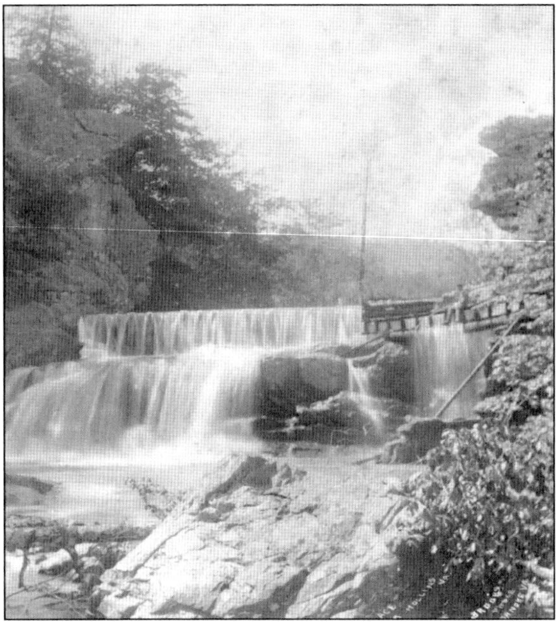

In 1746, King George II granted William Carvin a 900-acre grant in the Hollins area (then in Botetourt County). According to local legend, the rocky cliff seen in this late-19th-century photograph was the site where Carvin, pursued by Native Americans, plunged into the creek below to evade capture, or worse. The falls, also called cascades, were up creek from Joseph Riley's gristmill, which was built in the early 1800s and operated until about 1900. In 1899, Riley and his wife deeded the falls tract to Hollins Institute. The falls was a popular site for picnics and swimming. In the late 1920s, the Roanoke Water Company announced plans to dam the creek for a six-billion-gallon reservoir known as Carvin's Cove. (Courtesy of Hollins University, Wyndham Robertson Library Special Collections.)

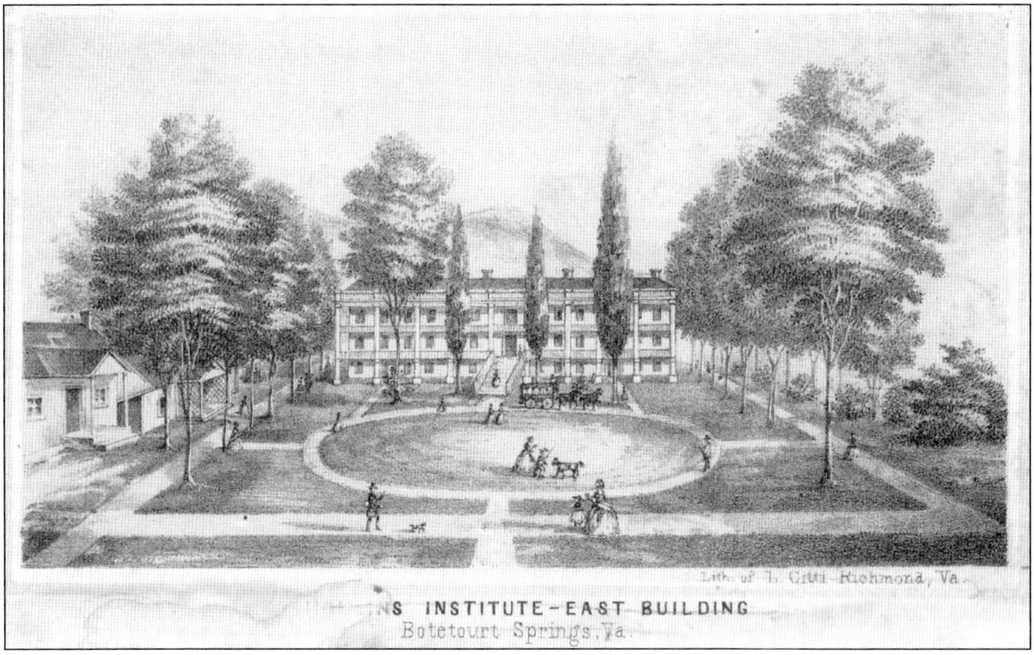

Charles Johnston, born in Lynchburg, led an exciting life prior to undertaking the operation of a resort spa in Hollins. In 1790, Johnston traveled to Kentucky, then still a wilderness, where he was captured by a Native American group. A French trader name Duchouquet ransomed him, and later visited Johnston's resort. In 1820, Johnston built a hotel he called Botetourt Springs at the site of a sulfur water spring on 475 acres at the foot of Tinker Mountain. Johnston operated the resort until his death in 1833. Hezekiah Daggs then became the manager. The spring's popularity waned, and it closed in 1839. The buildings, however, were given new life in the mid-19th century, when they became the core of the Hollins Institute. (Courtesy of Hollins University, Wyndham Robertson Library Special Collections.)

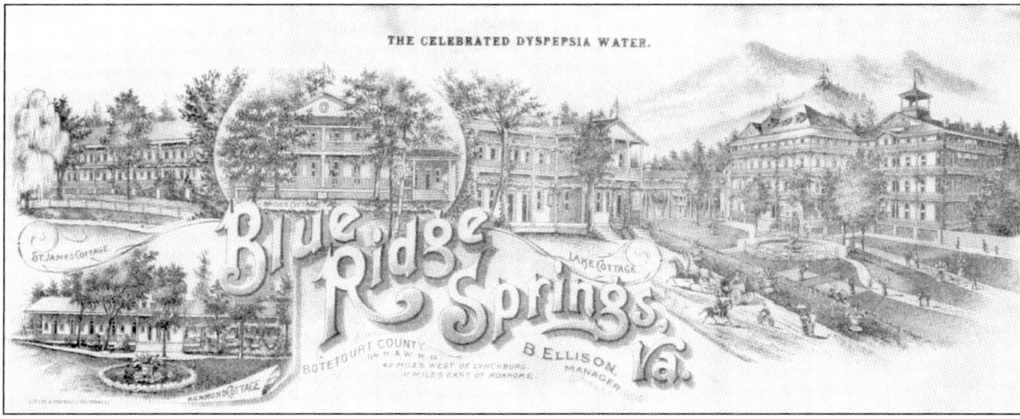

Mineral springs tourism in Botetourt began in the late 19th century with the establishment of Coyner Springs and the Blue Ridge Springs resorts. Even before the establishment of the resorts, these mineral waters were believed to have medicinal benefits and were often visited by Native Americans. The springs hotel at Blue Ridge was built in 1866 beside the Virginia & Tennessee Railroad and along the stage route from Lynchburg. By 1918, the original hotel had burned, and a larger one (above, right) was built, along with several cottages that held additional rooms and other amenities. Like other springs, Blue Ridge extended its commercial success by offering shipments of its bottled water by mail. In the 1920s, visitation to the resort declined, and, in 1936, all of the buildings burned. (Above, courtesy of Benton Bolton; below, courtesy of the *Fincastle Herald*.)

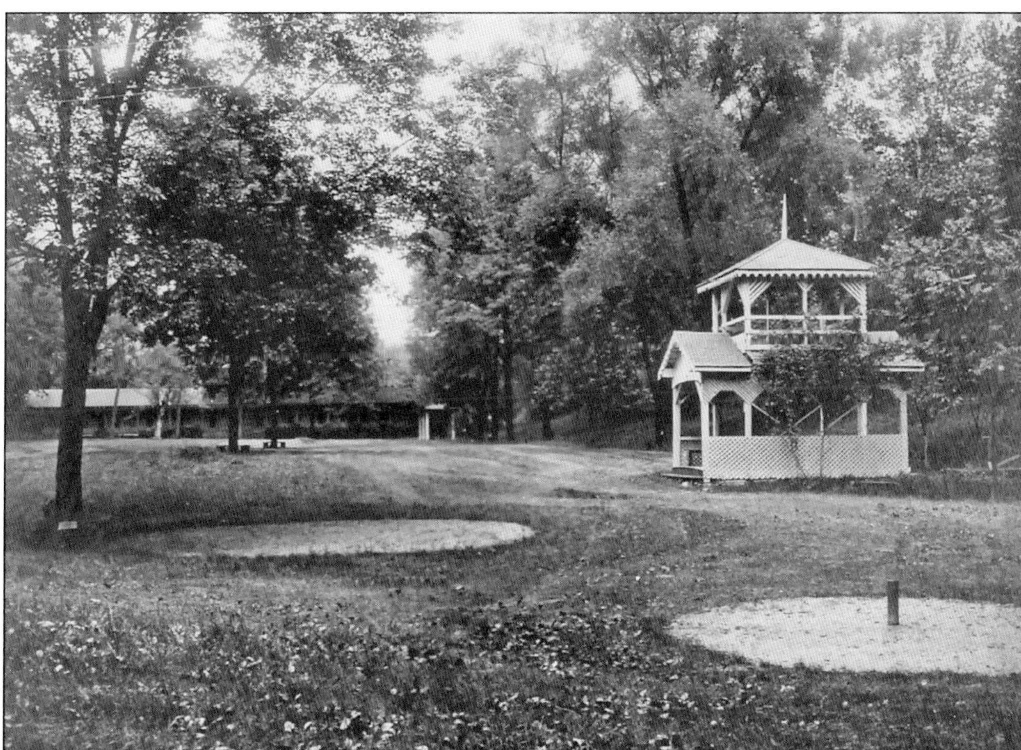

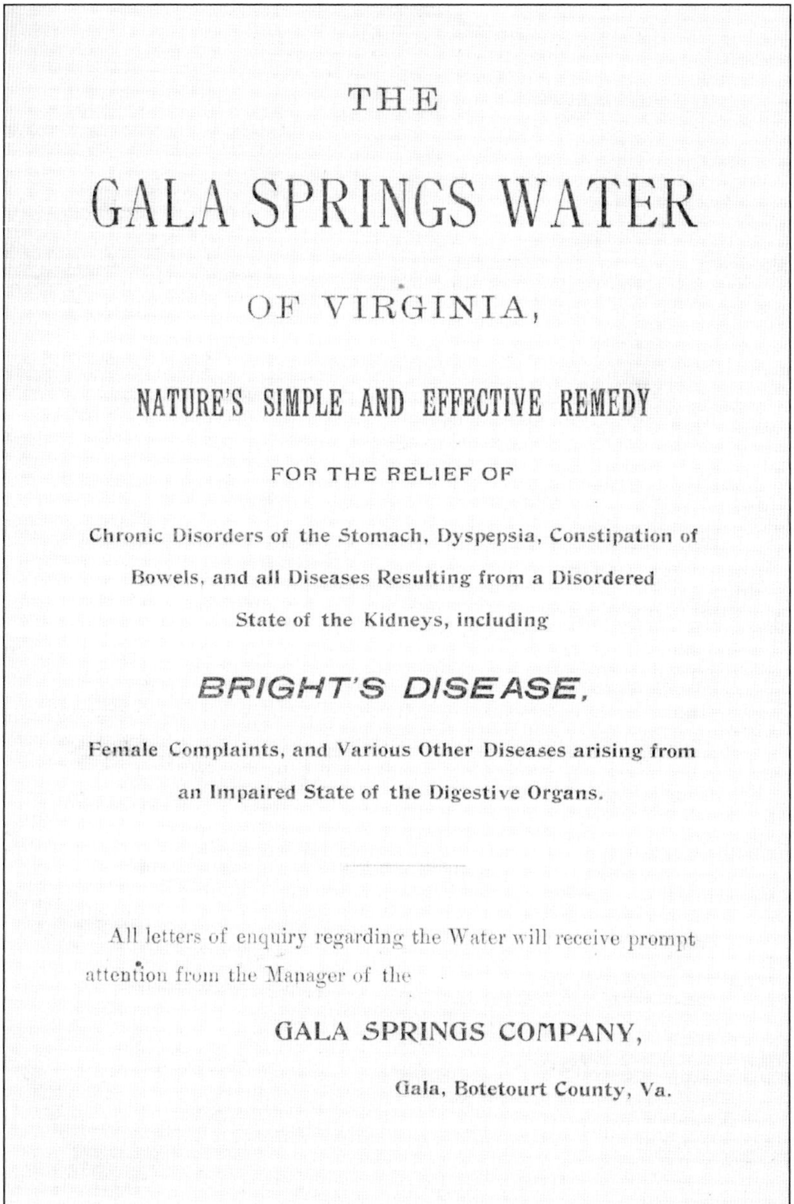

THE

GALA SPRINGS WATER

OF VIRGINIA,

NATURE'S SIMPLE AND EFFECTIVE REMEDY

FOR THE RELIEF OF

Chronic Disorders of the Stomach, Dyspepsia, Constipation of Bowels, and all Diseases Resulting from a Disordered State of the Kidneys, including

BRIGHT'S DISEASE,

Female Complaints, and Various Other Diseases arising from an Impaired State of the Digestive Organs.

All letters of enquiry regarding the Water will receive prompt attention from the Manager of the

GALA SPRINGS COMPANY,

Gala, Botetourt County, Va.

Around 1890, the owners of Gala Springs printed this informational brochure on the mineral content and curative powers of its water. E.T. Fristoe, a chemist; M.H. Farley, a businessman; and H. Worthington Paige, a doctor, purchased three springs at the foot of the Rich Patch Mountains, near the Chesapeake & Ohio's Gala station. An analysis of the spring water indicated that it was of an "alkaline saline nature . . . possessing tonic properties." Testimonials from users included one from a New York City gentleman whose mother had suffered from "an old abscess and neurosis of the stomach." He wrote that the water "has certainly worked wonders in my mother's case. She had not even tasted a morsel for more than ten years, subsisting entirely upon milk. After taking the first lot of Gala Water she has been eating steadily and we cannot help believing that the Gala is the cause." He then requested an additional shipment of "ten or twelve gallons." (Courtesy of Joseph B. Buhrman.)

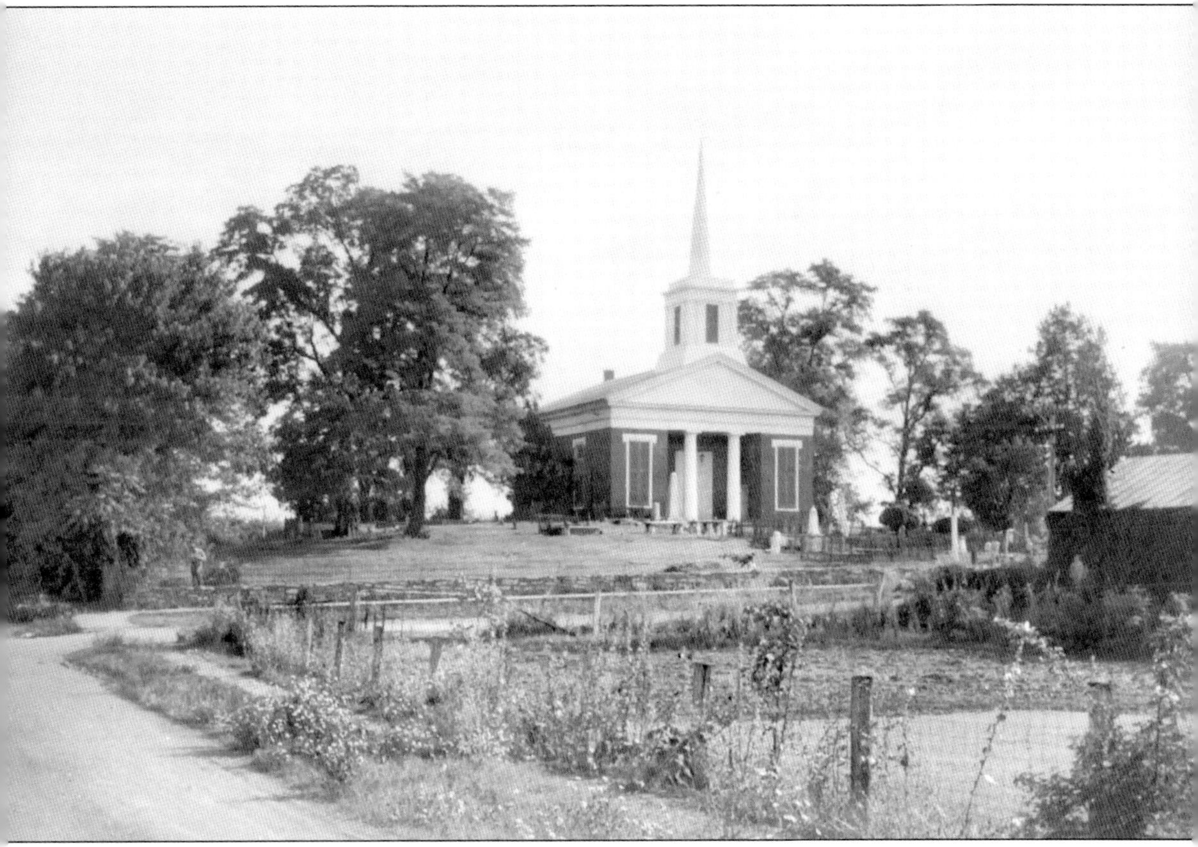

In 1940, Maude Hopkins, the chairman of restoration for the Roanoke Garden Club, garnered the support of the statewide organization to restore the Fincastle Presbyterian churchyard, which holds graves dating to the 18th century. The stone wall and brick terrace were built at the front of the church. Tombstones were repaired, and trees and shrubs were planted following recommendations by landscape architect Stanley Abbott. The church's history dates to the pre-Revolutionary period, when it served as an Anglican church. In 1813, after the disestablishment of the Church of England, local Presbyterians petitioned the Virginia General Assembly for use of the property. In 1958, the rear educational wing was constructed using bricks from the old 1842 Union Church, which was located along Trinity Road and was demolished for the construction of Interstate 81. In 2013, Fincastle Presbyterian celebrated its 250th anniversary. During recent projects, a Native American projectile point (arrowhead) was found on the grounds, attesting to the ancient history of this site, located above the Big Spring. (Courtesy of the Garden Club of Virginia, on deposit at the Virginia Historical Society.)

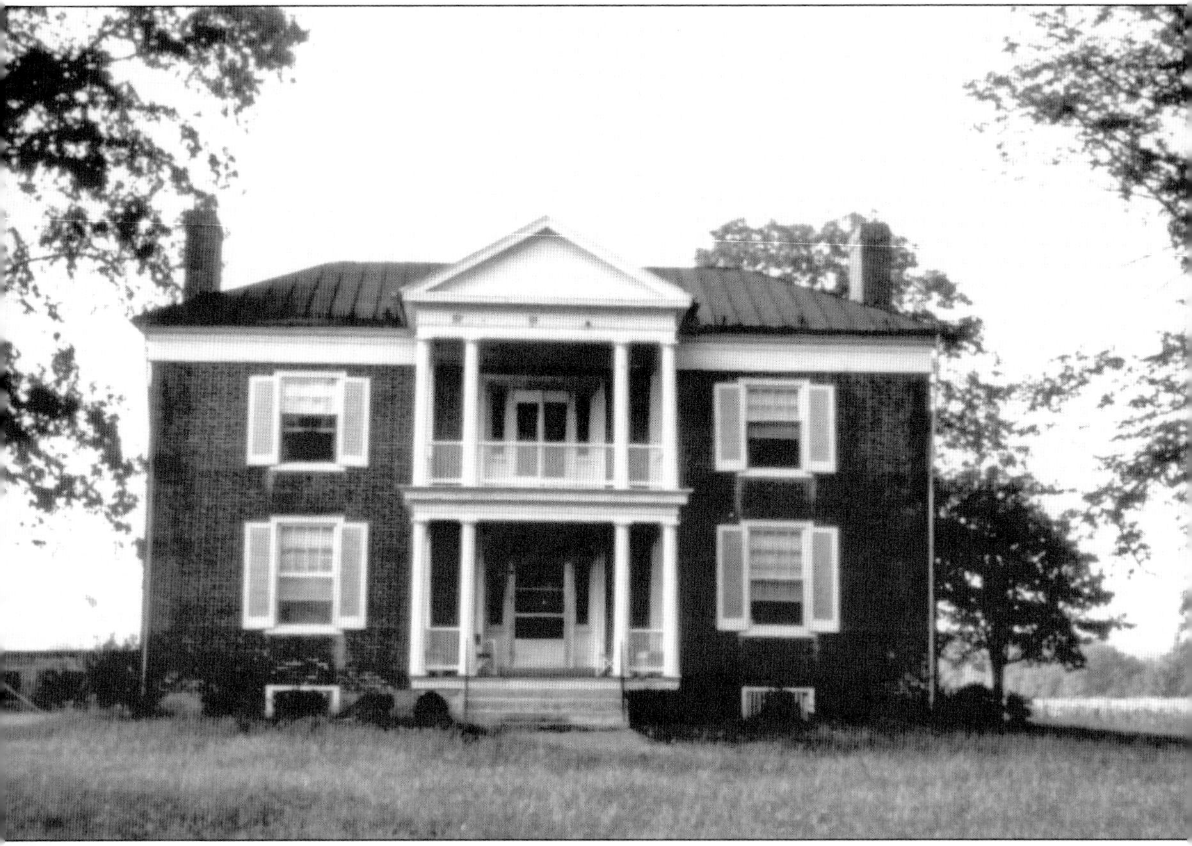

Botetourt's natural beauty is enhanced by the many historic homes and well-maintained farms that dot its countryside. The original section of Wiloma, located one mile north of Fincastle on Catawba Creek, was completed by 1848. The two-story, center-hall house (I-house) features two large rooms on each floor. The two-level front porch is an original feature. The interior features fine Greek Revival–style woodwork, some of which is derived from carpenter Asher Benjamin's pattern book *The Practical House Carpenter*, published in 1830. In 1888, the house was enlarged with the addition of a two-story wing with a two-level porch on the north. The house was erected for Morgan Utz, a prominent Fincastle merchant, on land originally granted to Benjamin Borden in 1739. Utz was born in Madison County but was living in Botetourt by 1830. He was a partner in the mercantile store Utz, Pettigrew & Carroll and, later, in the Utz & Hannah store. Utz deeded Wiloma to his daughter-in-law Anna Jane Hansborough and it remained in the family until 1944. (Courtesy of VDHR.)

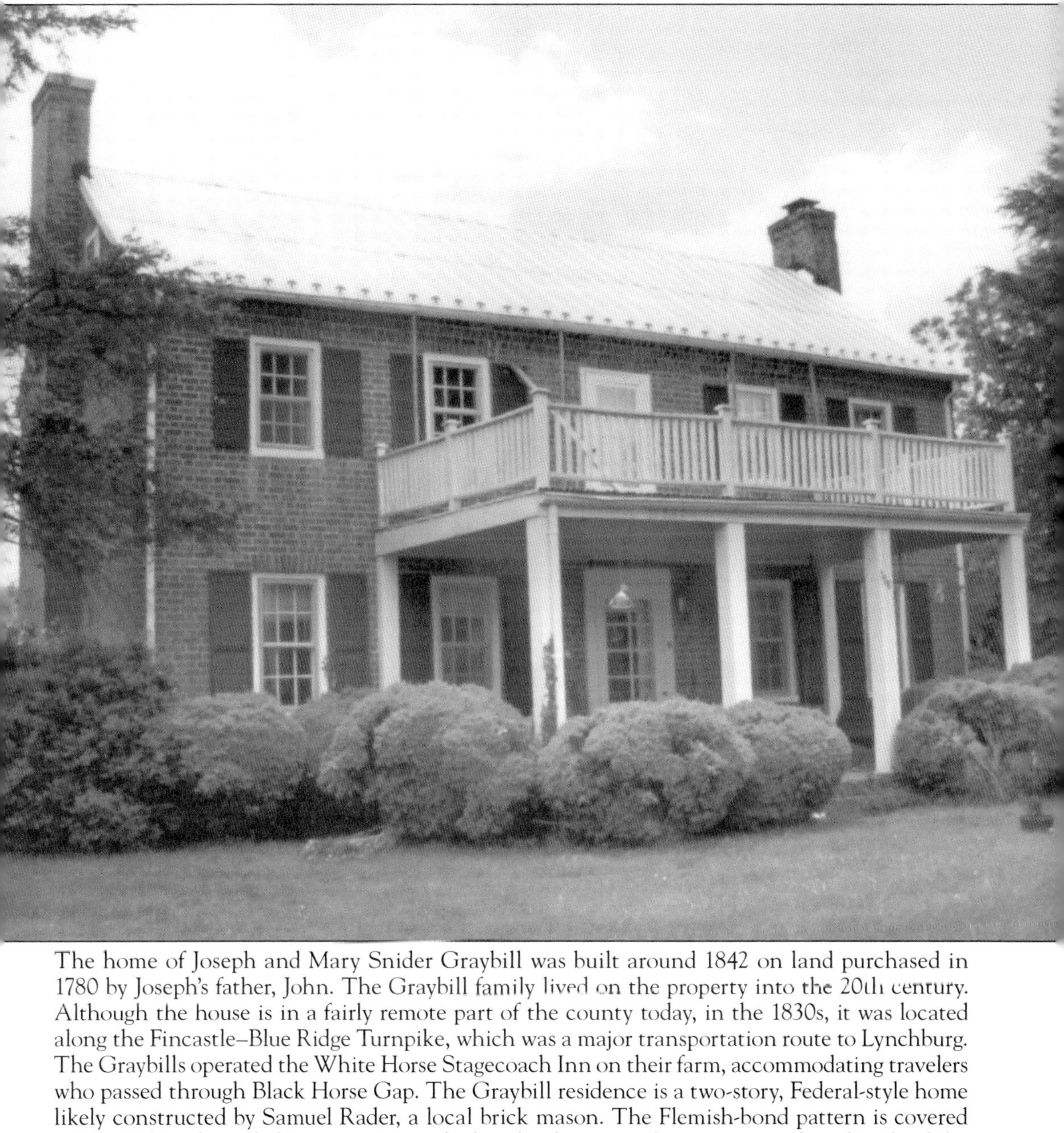

The home of Joseph and Mary Snider Graybill was built around 1842 on land purchased in 1780 by Joseph's father, John. The Graybill family lived on the property into the 20th century. Although the house is in a fairly remote part of the county today, in the 1830s, it was located along the Fincastle–Blue Ridge Turnpike, which was a major transportation route to Lynchburg. The Graybills operated the White Horse Stagecoach Inn on their farm, accommodating travelers who passed through Black Horse Gap. The Graybill residence is a two-story, Federal-style home likely constructed by Samuel Rader, a local brick mason. The Flemish-bond pattern is covered with a red wash, and the joints are marked with white penciling. In 1926, the Church of the Brethren purchased the home and land for its youth conference site, Camp Bethel. (Photograph by Michael Pulice; courtesy of VDHR.)

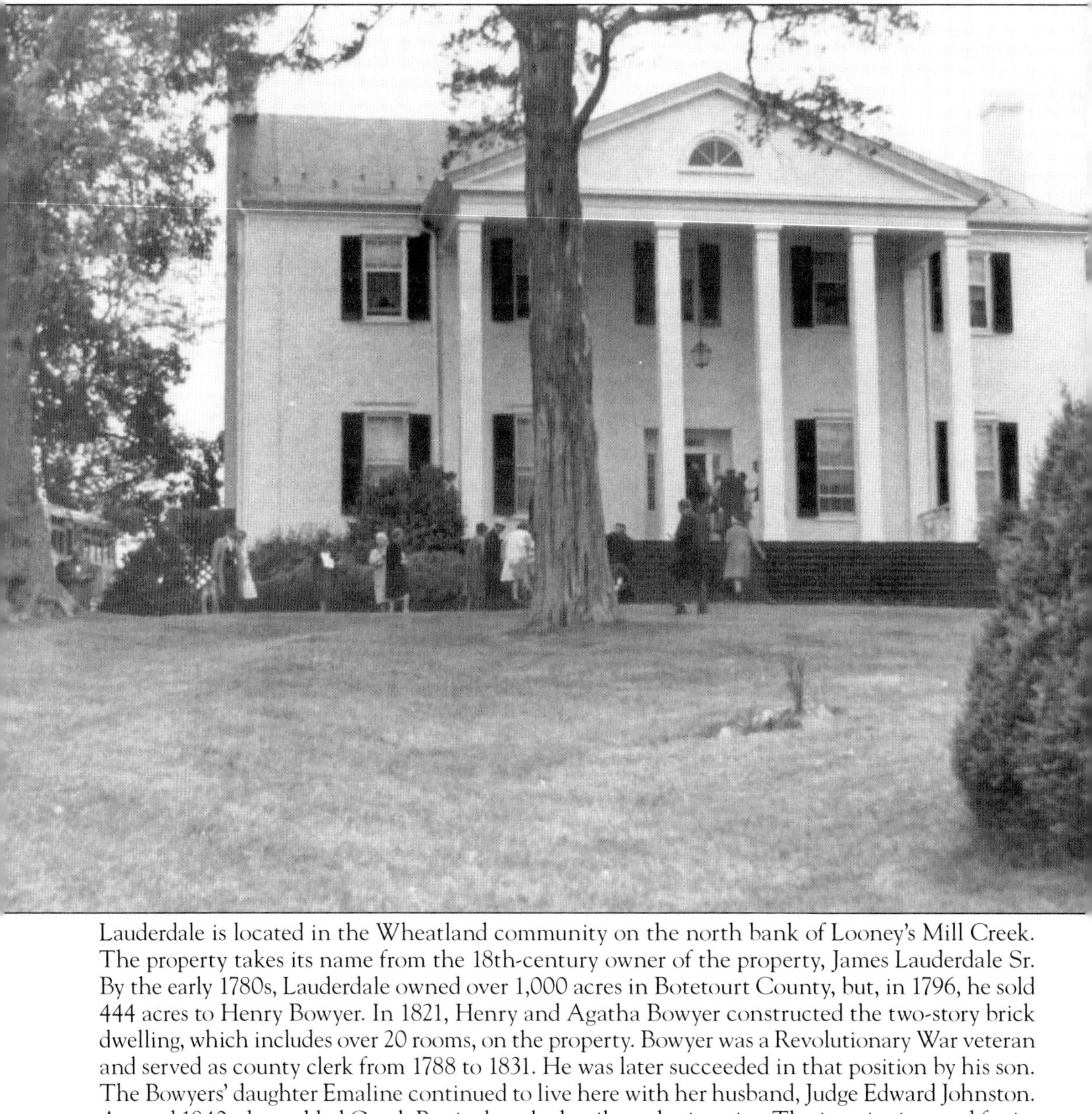

Lauderdale is located in the Wheatland community on the north bank of Looney's Mill Creek. The property takes its name from the 18th-century owner of the property, James Lauderdale Sr. By the early 1780s, Lauderdale owned over 1,000 acres in Botetourt County, but, in 1796, he sold 444 acres to Henry Bowyer. In 1821, Henry and Agatha Bowyer constructed the two-story brick dwelling, which includes over 20 rooms, on the property. Bowyer was a Revolutionary War veteran and served as county clerk from 1788 to 1831. He was later succeeded in that position by his son. The Bowyers' daughter Emaline continued to live here with her husband, Judge Edward Johnston. Around 1840, they added Greek Revival–style details to the interior. The interior is noted for its decorative 19th-century paint scheme of stenciling and faux finishes. A later owner added the monumental front portico in 1926. (Photograph by J. Daniel Pezzoni; courtesy of VDHR.)

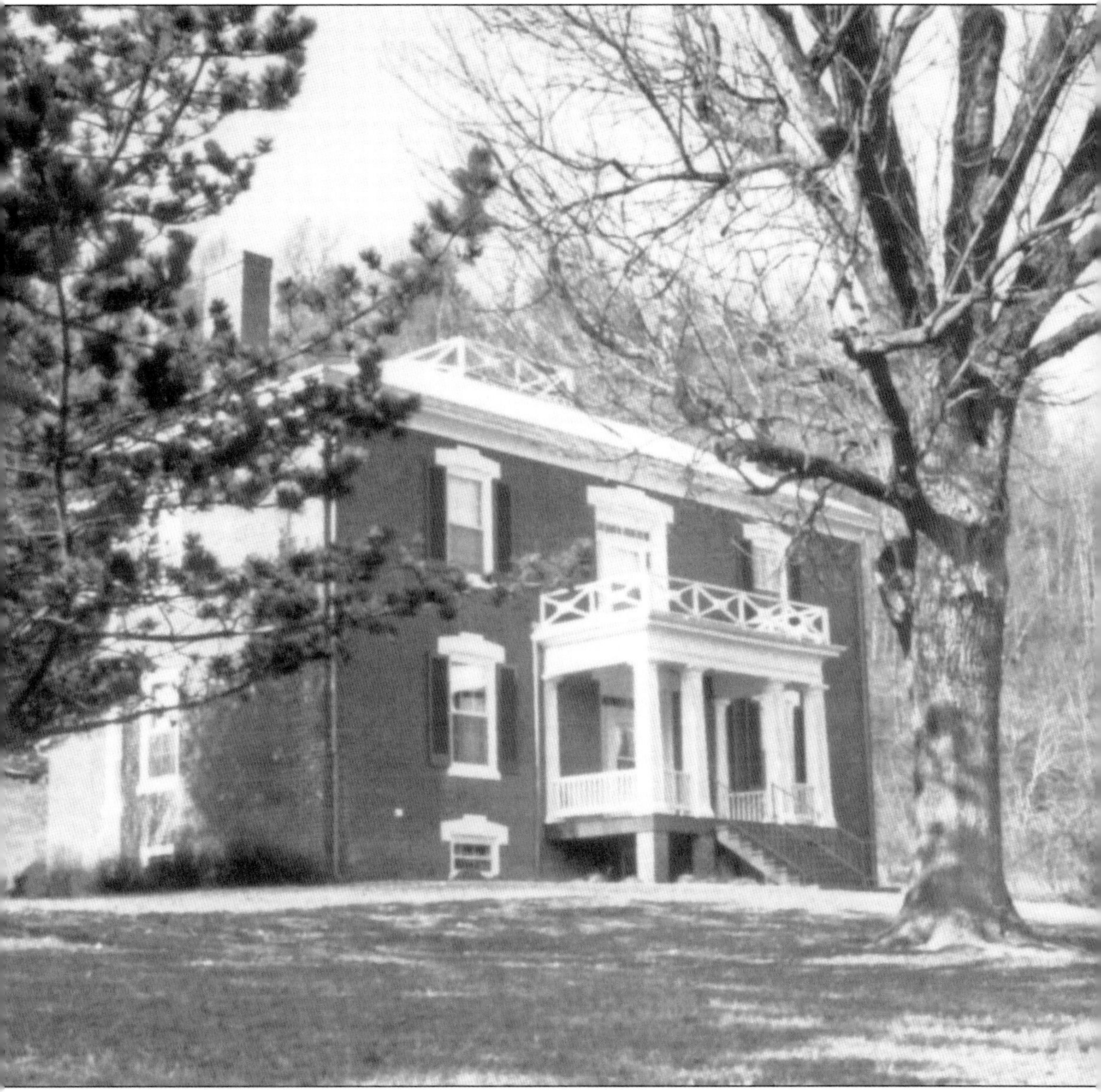

Located on the Botetourt-Rockbridge County line, Annandale was built in 1835 by Richard H. Burks, who purchased the land in Sassafras Bottom from the Campbell family. Burks's antebellum farm, which he operated with 64 slaves, produced substantial amounts of tobacco and wheat. During Burks's ownership of Annandale, the second division of the James River and Kanawha Canal was completed. This extension brought the canal to Buchanan, with one of the stone locks and a dam located on Burks's property. With the canal completed, Burks could easily ship his tobacco and other farm products downriver to market. When Burks died in 1857, the property passed from his heirs to several owners until 1875, when Frederick Johnston purchased it. Johnston had served as clerk of the court in Roanoke County. His son continued the farming operations at Annandale until the late 1880s. According to Robert Douthat Stoner, Johnston named the house Annandale after his family's ancestral home in Scotland. (Photograph by Diane Pierce; courtesy of VDHR.)

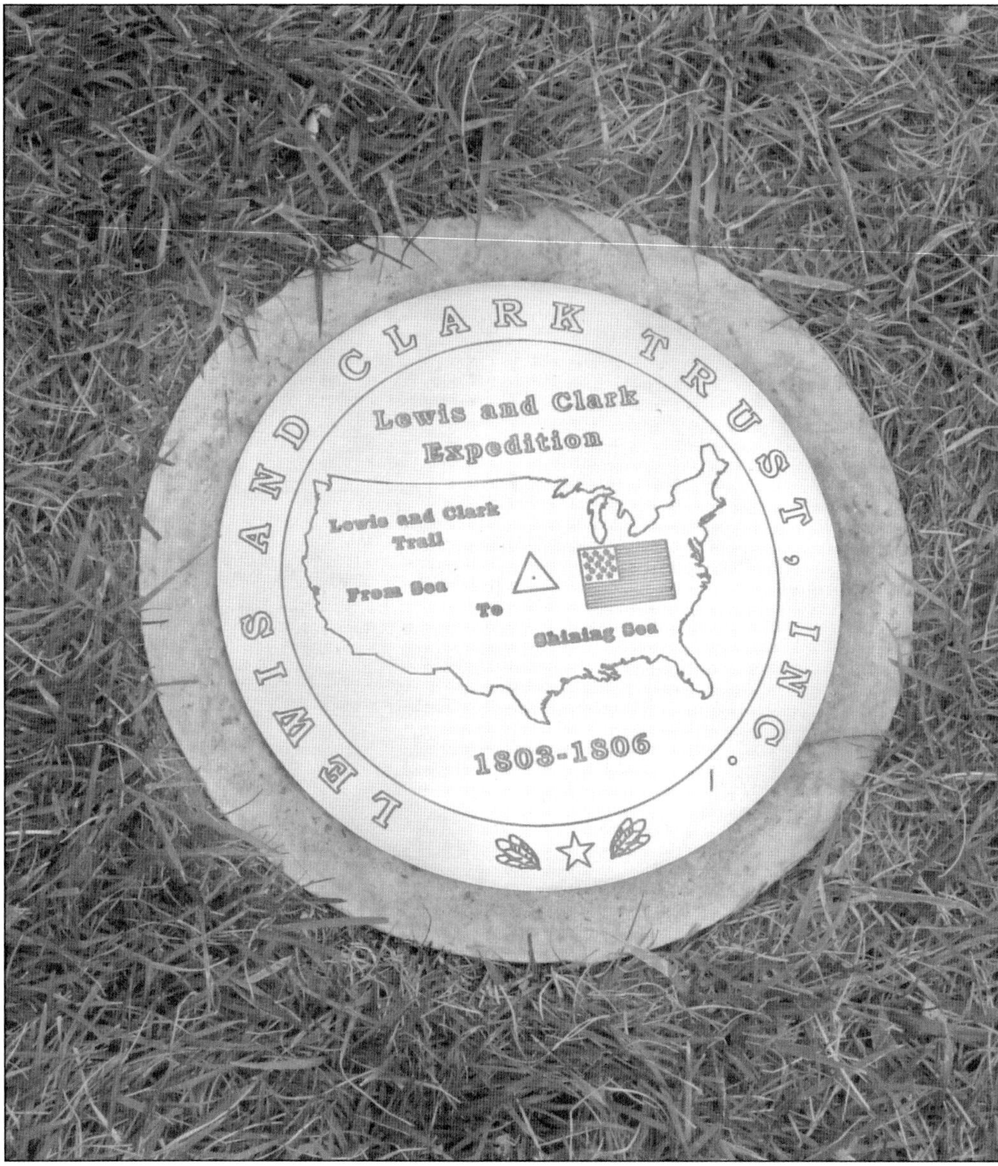

In 2012, the Virginia Tourism Corporation estimated that tourism generated over $51 million in county revenues. Tourism is tied to Botetourt's waterways (the Upper James River Water Trail), its agriculture (the Wine Trail), and its transportation routes (Wilderness Road). The anticipated establishment of the Lewis and Clark Eastern Legacy Trail will confirm Botetourt's role in the lives of the two Corps of Discovery explorers, Meriwether Lewis and William Clark, who often visited the area prior to and following their expedition. Of the trail's Virginia sites, three are in Botetourt. Greenfield Plantation, in Amsterdam, was the home of William Preston, an Army friend of the two explorers. The Fincastle Historic District was the scene of a grand celebration held in Clark's honor. Santillane was the home of Judith Hancock, Clark's wife. Clark returned to the Hancock home several times following the expedition. It was there that he and Nicholas Biddle compiled the journal from the Corps of Discovery expedition. In November 2012, this commemorative marker was placed at the courthouse signifying its inclusion on the trail. (Courtesy of the author's collection.)

The Appalachian Trail, the country's premiere hiking trail, enters southwestern Botetourt on Tinker Mountain, then crosses through Daleville before heading into the Blue Ridge Mountains to the northeast. Recently, the nonprofit group Together for Troutville, Inc., has organized Trail Days as a celebration of the community's ties with the trail and its hikers. Here, a day hiker enjoys the trail on Tinker Mountain. (Courtesy of the author's collection.)

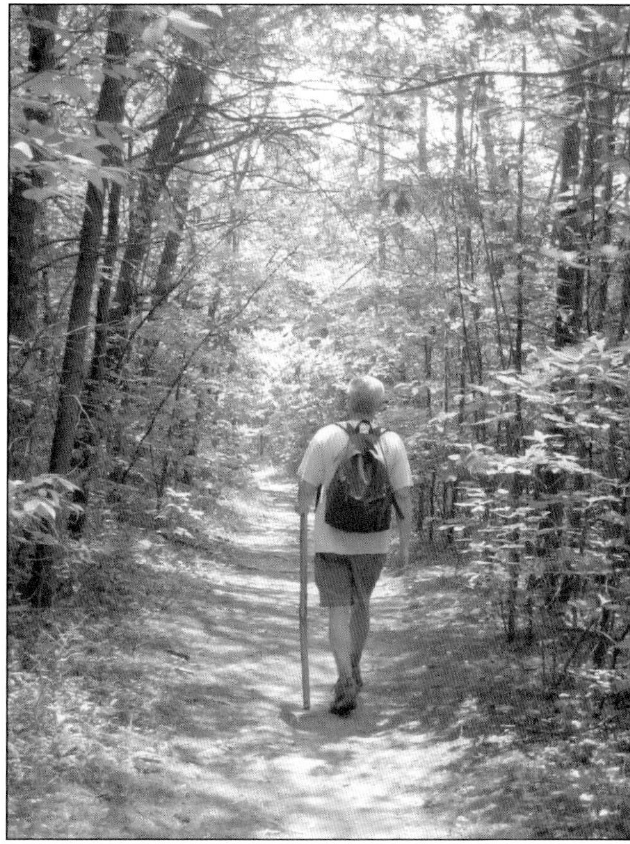

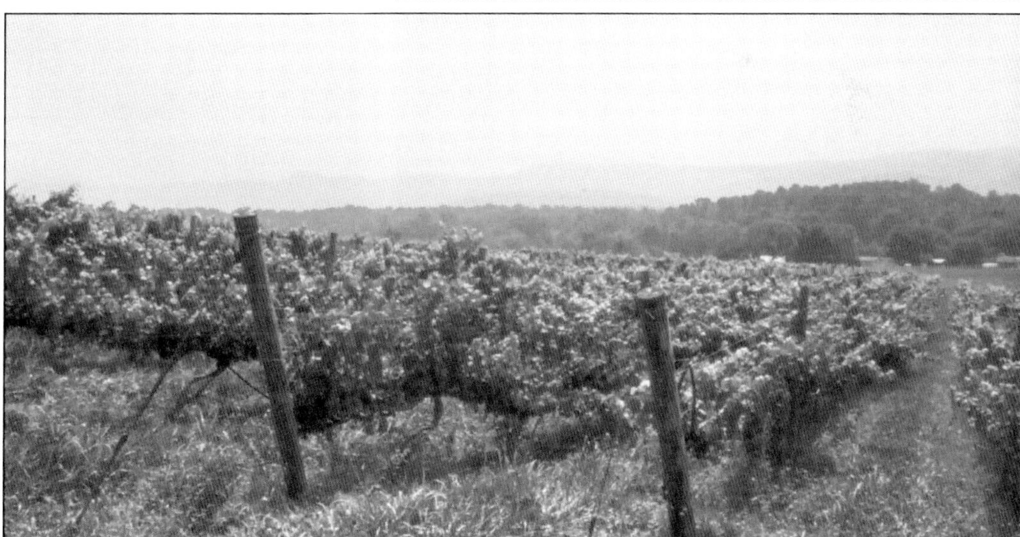

There are seven American Viticultural Areas (AVA) in Virginia. An AVA is a distinct grape-growing region that is defined by its geographic features, which influence the type and style of wine produced. Botetourt is located in the Shenandoah Valley AVA and currently has three commercial wineries: Fincastle Vineyard and Winery, in Nace (pictured), Blue Ridge Vineyard, in Eagle Rock, and Virginia Mountain Vineyards, in Fincastle. (Courtesy of the author's collection.)

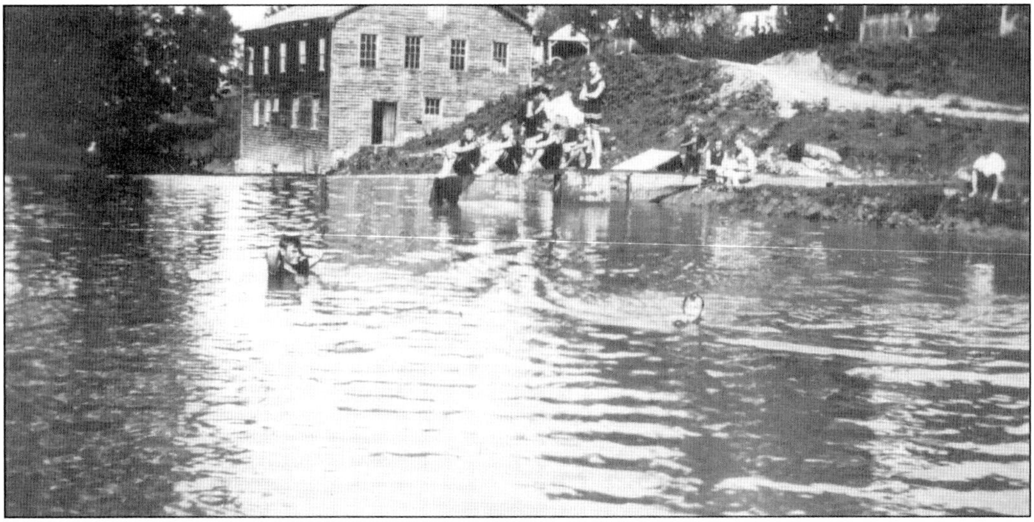

This postcard is a companion to the photograph on this book's cover. It is a more expansive view of the early-20th-century "beach" along Town Branch. The mill in this photograph was only one of several industries located along the branch. These Fincastle youngsters found enjoyment in the large swimming hole created by the milldam. (Courtesy of BCHM.)

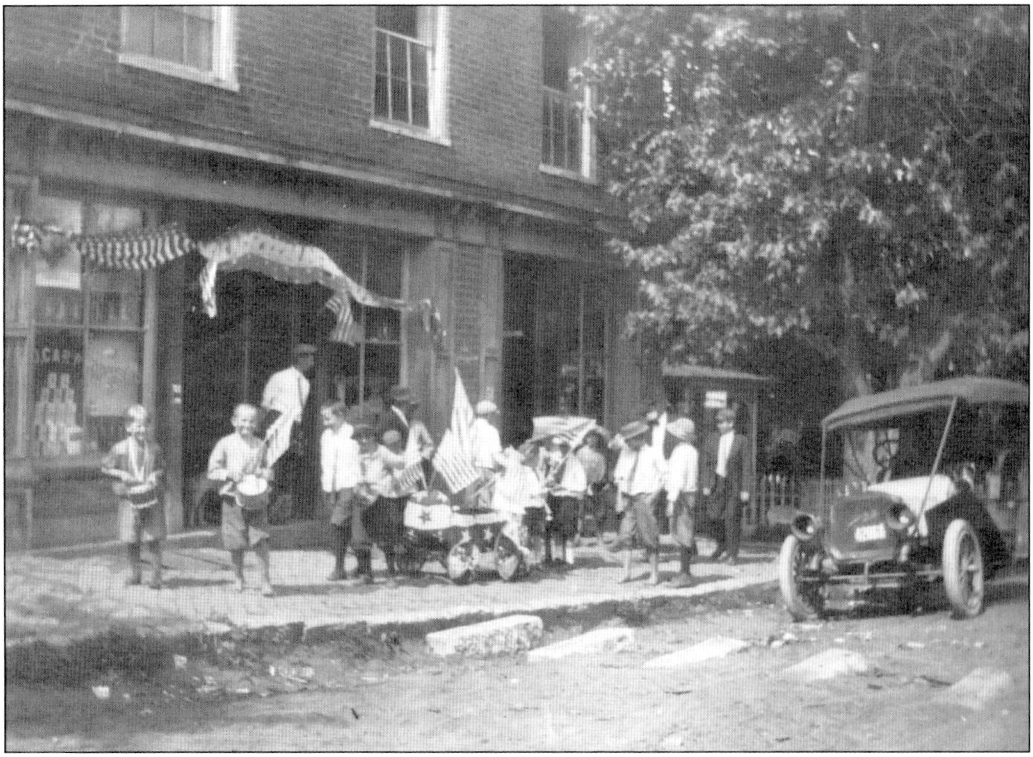

Both Fincastle and Buchanan are the sites of numerous parades and festivals. Christmas and Fourth of July parades bring out school groups, churches, fraternal organizations, and others in a show of community pride. This small but patriotic group marches through Fincastle, celebrating the Fourth of July around 1918. The stepping-stones are noticeable across the still-unpaved street. (Courtesy of BCHM.)

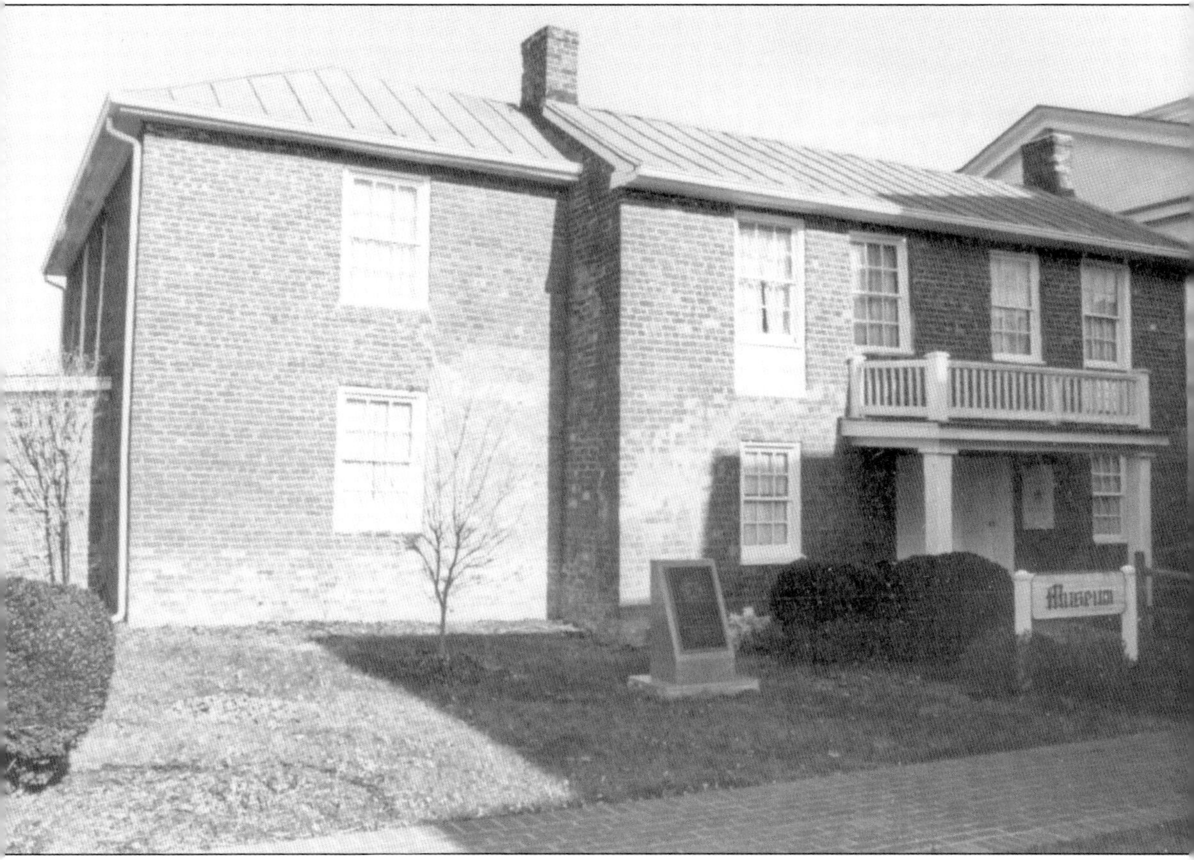

Many of the images in this book and in Images of America: *Botetourt County* were provided by the Botetourt County Historical Society, which maintains the Botetourt County Historical Museum. The museum, which opened in 1966, contains a fascinating collection of artifacts, archival documents, and photographs. The historical society works with other county groups, such as Historic Fincastle, Inc., the Botetourt County Wide League, and the Buchanan Town Improvement Society, to preserve county history. The museum building started out in the 18th century as a one-room law office that later became part of the Western Hotel. It is located in Fincastle behind the county courthouse. (Courtesy of the *Fincastle Herald*.)

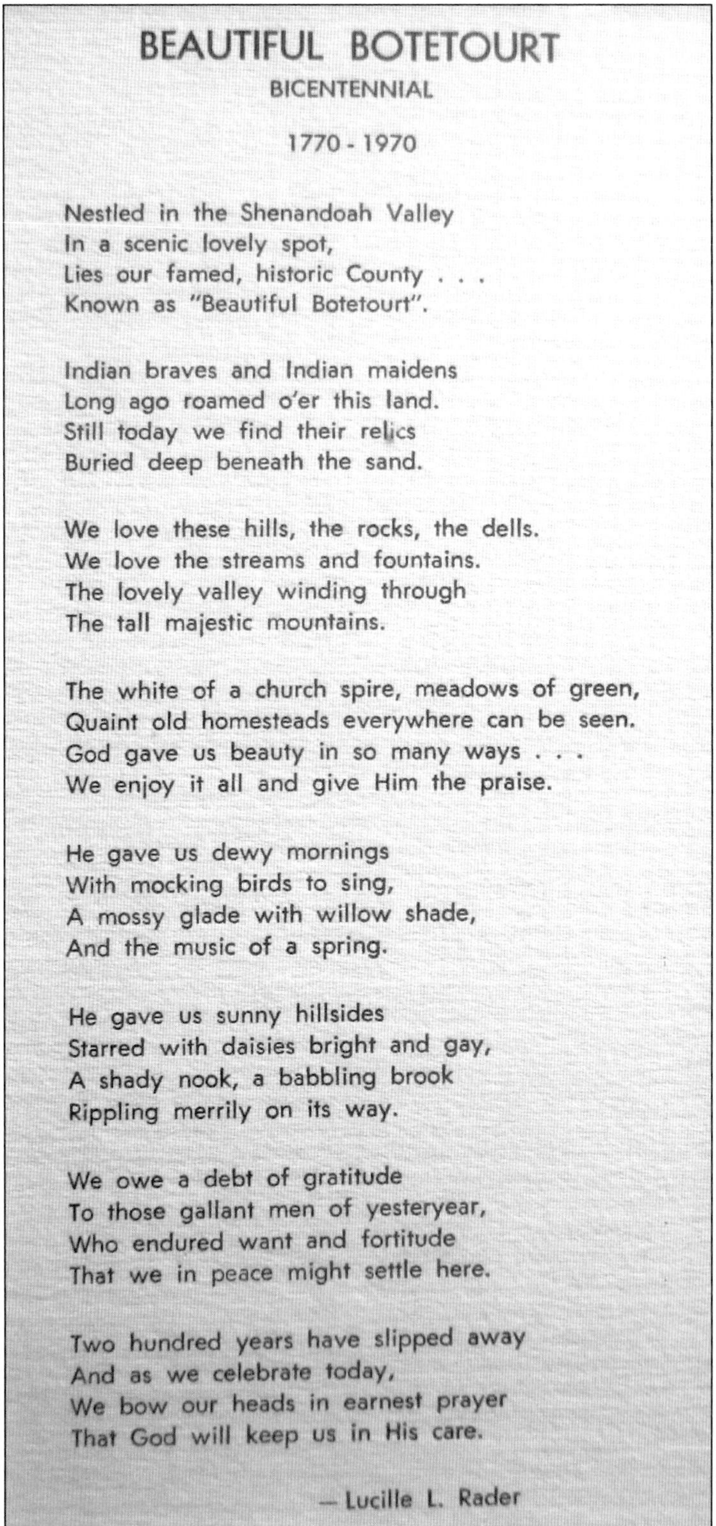

BEAUTIFUL BOTETOURT

BICENTENNIAL

1770 - 1970

Nestled in the Shenandoah Valley
In a scenic lovely spot,
Lies our famed, historic County . . .
Known as "Beautiful Botetourt".

Indian braves and Indian maidens
Long ago roamed o'er this land.
Still today we find their relics
Buried deep beneath the sand.

We love these hills, the rocks, the dells.
We love the streams and fountains.
The lovely valley winding through
The tall majestic mountains.

The white of a church spire, meadows of green,
Quaint old homesteads everywhere can be seen.
God gave us beauty in so many ways . . .
We enjoy it all and give Him the praise.

He gave us dewy mornings
With mocking birds to sing,
A mossy glade with willow shade,
And the music of a spring.

He gave us sunny hillsides
Starred with daisies bright and gay,
A shady nook, a babbling brook
Rippling merrily on its way.

We owe a debt of gratitude
To those gallant men of yesteryear,
Who endured want and fortitude
That we in peace might settle here.

Two hundred years have slipped away
And as we celebrate today,
We bow our heads in earnest prayer
That God will keep us in His care.

— Lucille L. Rader

In 1970, Botetourt County celebrated its bicentennial with music, plays, and homecoming gatherings. Each day was given a theme, such as patriotism, religious heritage, home and garden, arts and antiques, and agricultural and industry. As part of the program, Lucille Rader composed the poem "Beautiful Botetourt," which was included in the program. Her poem captures how many residents feel about their county and the many special things found there. (Courtesy of John W. Rader.)

Bibliography

Around Town: A Pictorial Review of Old Fincastle, Virginia. Fincastle, VA: Historic Fincastle, Inc., 1990.

Botetourt Heritage Book Committee. *Botetourt County, Virginia, Heritage Book, 1770–2000.* Summersville, WV: Walsworth Publishing Company, Inc., 2001.

Cooper, Mason Y. *Norfolk & Western's Shenandoah Valley Line.* Forest, VA: Norfolk and Western Historical Society, Inc., 1998.

Fulwiler, Harry Jr. *Buchanan, Virginia: Gateway to the Southwest.* Radford, VA: Commonwealth Press, 1980.

Garber, Mary. *The History of the Cloverdale Church of the Brethren.* Cloverdale, VA: Cloverdale Church of the Brethren, 1978.

Garber, Paul and Rebecca Wilson. *The History of the Cloverdale Church of the Brethren, Volume II.* Cloverdale, VA: Cloverdale Church of the Brethren, 2013.

Harnish-Kopco, Mary. "A Rich Furrow: The Old John Barger Farm." Thesis, James Madison University, 1987.

Kagey, Deedie Dent. *When Past is Prologue: A History of Roanoke County.* Roanoke, VA: Roanoke County Sesquicentennial Committee, 1988.

Niederer, Francis J. "Fincastle's Revival Architecture." *Arts in Virginia*, Vol. 6, No. 2 (Winter 1966), pp. 12–19.

———. *Hollins College: An Illustrated History.* Charlottesville, VA: University of Virginia Press, 1985.

Obenshain, Mary Anne Rader and Rosalie Hamilton Goad. *Town of Troutville, Virginia.* Troutville, VA: Privately published by the authors, 2002.

Prillaman, Helen R. *Places Near the Mountains: From the Community of Amsterdam, Virginia, up the Road to Catawba, on Waters of the Catawba and Tinker Creeks, along the Carolina Road as It Approached Big Lick and Other Areas, Primarily North Roanoke.* Roanoke, VA: Privately published by the author, 1985.

Russ, Kurt C. "Fincastle Pottery Kiln (44BO304): Salvage Excavations at a Nineteenth-Century Earthenware Kiln Located in Botetourt County, Virginia." Technical Report Series No. 3. Prepared by the Laboratory of Anthropology, Washington & Lee University, Lexington, Virginia. Prepared for the Commonwealth of Virginia, Department of Historic Resources, 1990.

Stoner, Robert Douthat. *A Seed-Bed of the Republic: A Study of the Pioneers in the Upper (Southern) Valley of Virginia.* Roanoke, VA: Roanoke Historical Society, 1962.

Vassar, Stephen D. Sr. *Life Along Back Creek and Looney's Mill Creek: the Lithia and Mill Creek Sections of Botetourt County, Virginia.* Roanoke, VA: Privately published by the author, 2001.